RISK MANAGEMENT ORGANISATION AND CONTEXT

by

Stephen Ward

OTHER BOOKS IN THE SERIES

Business Finance for Risk Management
Business Organisation and Finance
Corporate Risk Management
Insurance, Non Marine – An Introduction
Liability Exposures
Liability Risk and the Law
Local Government a Text for Risk Managers
Risk Analysis
Risk Control
Risk and the Business Environment
Risk Financing
Risk Management in Healthcare
Treasury Risk Management

British Library Cataloguing in Publication Data
Ward, Stephen
Risk Management Organisation and Context – 1st Ed.
1 Title
ISBN 1 85609 298 4

Notice of Terms of Use

While the advice given in this document ("document") has been developed using the best information currently available, it is intended purely as guidance to be used at the user's own risk. No responsibility is accepted by the Institute of Risk Management, the membership of IRM, or by any person, firm, corporation or organisation [who or which has been in any way concerned with the furnishing of information or data, the compilation or any translation, publishing, supply or sale of the document] for the accuracy of any information or advice given in the document or any omission from the document or for any consequence whatsoever resulting directly or indirectly from compliance with or adoption of guidance contained in the document even if caused by a failure to exercise reasonable care.

The Institute of Risk Management
6, Lloyd's Avenue
London EC3N 3AX
www.theirm.org
Tel No: 020 7709 9808

RISK MANAGEMENT ORGANISATION AND CONTEXT

First Edition

by

Stephen Ward

1st Edition 2005

WITHERBYS
PUBLISHING

© The Institute of Risk Management
and Stephen Ward

2005

ISBN 1 85609 298 4

Printed and Published by
WITHERBY & CO. LTD
32-36 Aylesbury Street
London EC1R 0ET
Tel No: 020 7251 5341   Fax No: 020 7251 1296
International Tel No: +44 20 7251 5341
International Fax No: +44 20 7251 1296
E-mail: books@witherbys.co.uk
www: witherbys.com

PREFACE

The principal *raison d'etre* for this book is to provide a core text for the Institute of Risk Management Diploma subject 'Risk Management: organisation and context' (RMOC). However, this book should be of interest not only to readers studying for the IRM Diploma, but to practitioners formally designated as 'risk managers', and all managers, particularly senior managers.

While the topics covered in this book are necessarily constrained by the syllabus for the Diploma subject RMOC, the scope is wide. Specifically, this book is not confined to describing current practice and the nature of common guidance on risk management, although this is useful basic information. This book also reflects on the limitations of common current practice and considers ways in which risk management should be developed.

This is consistent with the IRM's general aim to promote and develop the contribution that risk management makes to improving organisation performance. It is also consistent with the depth of study expected in IRM Diploma subjects. In particular, candidates for the IRM Diploma subjects are expected to have an appreciation of the key conceptual issues that should inform best risk management practice and continuous efforts to improve existing risk management practice. This calls for a willingness to reflect critically on concepts, tools, techniques, frameworks, processes and assumptions used in current practice, and discussed or advocated in the substantial literature on risk management. For other readers who are students of risk management in a wider sense, this willingness for critical reflection is also important. Without it risk management cannot develop effectively, and the quality of existing risk management, which is in general rather limited, will never improve.

THE NATURE OF RISK MANAGEMENT

Most people have some idea of what risk management is about, because 'risk' is a commonly used term and widely experienced in most aspects of our everyday lives. We do not need to be inside an organisation to appreciate the desirability of some degree of risk management.

The dictionary typically defines 'risk' as *hazard, chance of bad consequences, loss, exposure to chance of injury or loss.* This definition, or at least parts of it, are what most people have in mind when they think of 'risk'. Risk management is therefore something we do if we want to avoid risk or try to stop things going wrong. In this sense, pessimists are more likely to be risk managers than optimists. If we are trying to achieve particular things, whether it be taking a holiday, making a significant purchase of some kind, or simply trying to lead a quiet life, one needs to adopt a healthy balance between a neurotic obsession with the possibilities for disaster, and blithe, inordinate optimism that 'everything will be just fine'. This healthy balance in respect of attitude to uncertainty and risk management is also important in decisions about how we try to run our lives. Too much concern with things that might go wrong might mean we never 'go anywhere', and miss out on a wide variety of positive life experiences and opportunities. On the other hand, too little concern with what can go wrong, or how our plans might be thwarted, can lead, unless we are very lucky, to frequent inconvenience at best, and to major personal disasters at worst. Some degree of foresight and precaution is generally a prerequisite for survival.

Fundamentally, the situation is not much different when it comes to running organisations. However, much more complexity is involved, not least because organisations require co-operative activity, sometimes between very many people and other organisations. This complexity considerably increases uncertainty about possible opportunities and the scope for things to go wrong. Therefore, the scope for risk management is substantial, and the desirability of developing risk management in organisations is clear. Recent large company failures, uncertainties in global markets, and concerns about the effectiveness of corporate governance, merely serve to underline the central importance of risk management. Uncertainty and risk is inherent in all organisational activity. Every member of an organisation needs to make decisions, plan, and manage uncertainty to a greater or lesser extent, so risk management should find natural application in all organisation activity. Indeed, much existing good management practice in respect of effective planning, setting objectives, coordination, and control procedures could be regarded as risk management. This is an important point because it underlines the fact that risk management is already integrated or embedded in management practice.

However, the extent and quality of risk management carried out in an organisation can be very variable, ranging from sophisticated, formal processes in some areas, to a reluctance to contemplate uncertainty in any form. A common intermediate approach involves informal processes, often involving little more than an intuitive perception of risk, followed by *ad hoc* approaches to the management of risk. In the absence of formal processes, risk management is often implicit within existing business processes, so that risk management is not as effective as it could be. The challenge is how to develop risk management practice in ways that increase the extent and effectiveness of risk management in an organisation.

RISK MANAGEMENT DEVELOPMENT

Taking a strategic management approach to risk management development involves three main elements:

- understanding the strategic position;
- understanding strategic choices;
- turning strategy into action.   (Johnson and Scholes, 2002)

Each of these three elements is important and potentially non-trivial, even if the focus is development of risk management within a single organisation unit.

In risk management terms, 'understanding the strategic position' would be concerned with understanding the nature and extent of current risk management practice, in relation to the external environment, internal resources and competences, and the expectations and influences of stakeholders. This includes understanding and questioning assumptions or constraints which might have a fundamental influence on the selection of risk management development strategies. A key driver here is the extent of management's appreciation of the risks and associated uncertainties requiring management.

'Understanding strategic choices' involves understanding the options for developing risk management in terms of both the directions in which development might proceed and the methods of development. Selection of approaches involves evaluation of the suitability, feasibility, and acceptability of possible strategy choices (*Johnson and Scholes, 2002*).

'Turning strategy into action' is concerned with successfully implementing the chosen risk management strategy via appropriate administrative structures, resourcing, exploiting existing competences and effective management of change.

All of this development requires a systematic, formal approach. Part of this formality involves being clear about:

- what risk-management is for and what benefits risk management brings;
- what form risk management processes should take;
- how risk management is to be carried out in the organisation;
- what resources should be deployed;
- where risk management should be used;
- who should be involved in risk management.

Such issues are addressed in this book.

THE STRUCTURE OF THIS BOOK

Chapter 1 begins by considering what is meant by risk management. This is followed by a six dimension framework which identifies the possibilities for developing risk management.

Chapter 2 outlines the basic requirements and features of the infrastructure needed to support formal risk management activities.

Chapter 3 argues for an uncertainty management focus for risk management. This recognises the importance of managing not only uncertain events, but important sources of ambiguity and uncertainty associated with objectives.

Chapter 4 considers the broad scope and nature of sources of uncertainty facing the organisation. The approach taken is to consider sources of uncertainty from five basic perspectives:

- a corporate strategy perspective,
- an asset management perspective,
- a people perspective,
- a project perspective,
- a systems perspective.

Each of these perspectives is useful in it's own right, but taken together they facilitate a deeper insight into sources of uncertainty that warrant management attention.

Chapter 5 discusses the quality of decision making processes and the scope for embedding risk management in decisions. This chapter also provides an overview of ever-present threats to high quality decision making due to the way individuals and groups engage in decision making and think about uncertainty.

Chapter 6 argues that the benefits of risk management need to be identified at an early stage and proactively sought out by designing risk management processes accordingly. A multi-level structure of possible objectives for risk management is described related to: the quality of a risk management process, purposes for a given application, possible performance criteria, and the development of strategic capability.

Chapters 7 and **8** consider the content of formal risk management process frameworks. Chapter 7 compares a number of well-known process frameworks including the AIRMIC/ALARM/ IRM risk management standard. This identifies common features and important differences between frameworks that should inform future development of risk management process definition. Chapter 8 considers the scope of the tasks that comprise the risk management process, and identifies issues that should be addressed to achieve effective risk management.

Chapter 9 discusses the potential scope of the corporate risk manager's role beginning with a strategic perspective that draws on experience of similar issues with the role of corporate planners. This chapter also considers the factors that influence the roles adopted by individual risk managers.

Chapter 10 discusses the nature of an organisation's risk management capability and briefly considers the scope of benchmarking and attempts to assess an organisation's risk management 'maturity'. Consideration of risk management capability and its development incorporates the six dimensions discussed in Chapter 1, infrastructure, organisation culture, and the ability of individuals to undertake risk management. Developing risk management capability implies risk management of the associated change processes.

ACKNOWLEDGEMENTS

I would like to acknowledge the contributions of a large number of colleagues, risk management practitioners and students who have assisted and influenced my thinking on risk management. In particular, I would like to thank the management team at the Institute of Risk Management for giving me the opportunity to write this book.

However, most of all, I would like to thank my close colleague for many years, Professor Chris Chapman. His expertise, guidance, and confidence in our work together have been a continuous source of inspiration and encouragement to me. Thanks Chris.

Stephen Ward

PUBLISHER'S ACKNOWLEDGEMENTS

I am grateful to the following for permission to reproduce copyright material:

Chapters 1 and 10, Table 1.1, Table 6.4, and Table 10.1 use material reprinted from *Risk Management an International Journal*, Volume 5 Number 4, S. C. Ward 'Approaches to integrated risk management: a multi-dimensional framework', pages 7-23. Copyright 2003 reproduced by permission of Perpetuity Press, 50 Queens Road, Leicester, LE2 1TU.

Chapters 1,3,4 and 5 use material reprinted from the *International Journal of Project Management* Volume 21, Ward, S. and Chapman, C. 'Transforming project risk management into project uncertainty management', pages 97-105. Copyright 2003, with kind permission from Elsevier, PO Box 800, Oxford OX5 1GB.

Some elements of the text, Table 4.6, Table 7.4, and most of Chapter 8 are extracted from Chapman, Chris and Ward, Stephen, *Project Risk Management: processes, techniques and insights*, second edition, copyright 2003, with kind permission of the publishers John Wiley & Sons Ltd., The Atrium, Southern Gate, Chichester, West Sussex PO19 8SQ.

Chapter 4 includes extracts from *The British Journal of Management*, Volume 5 Number 3, Turner, B. A. 'Causes of disaster: sloppy management', pages 215 - 219. Copyright 1994 the British Academy of Management. Used with permission.

Some elements of the text, and Table 5.2, are extracted from Chapman, Chris and Ward, Stephen, *Managing Project Risk and Uncertainty: a constructively simple approach to decision making,* copyright 2002, with kind permission of the publishers John Wiley & Sons Ltd., The Atrium, Southern Gate, Chichester, West Sussex PO19 8SQ

Table 6.2 is reprinted under licence from *Management of Risk: guidance for practitioners,* Annex A. Crown copyright 2002, The Stationery Office, London.

Chapter 9 including Tables 9.1, 9.2, and 9.3 use material reprinted from *Risk Management an International Journal,* Volume 3 Number 1, S. C. Ward 'Exploring the role of the corporate risk manager', pages 7-25. Copyright 2001, reproduced by permission of Perpetuity Press, 50 Queens Road, Leicester, LE2 1TU.

Contents

1

DIRECTIONS FOR RISK MANAGEMENT DEVELOPMENT

1.1   INTRODUCTION

This chapter is concerned with identifying the nature of risk management (RM) development choices available to provide a basis for RM development strategy. The rationale for this is that unless the possibilities for developing RM are clarified it is not possible to make the most effective choices about how to develop RM practice and organisational capability for RM.

This chapter outlines six separable directions or dimensions in which an organisation's RM practice could be developed. These dimensions provide a framework that can be used by either corporate or unit management to identify options for RM development, and to analyse an organisation's 'strategic position' in respect of RM practice.

1.2   ENTERPRISE RISK MANAGEMENT AND ALL THAT

In order to consider how RM can be developed in an organisation, it is first necessary to clarify what we mean by RM. An immediate problem for RM developers is that commonly held views of what constitutes RM can be unduly limited. To address this problem the temptation is to introduce supplementary terminology to broaden perspectives. In particular, the desirability for corporate wide use of RM has motivated the introduction of terms such as 'integrated RM', 'enterprise RM', 'enterprise wide RM', 'holistic RM', 'total RM', and 'organisation RM'. Such terms attempt to encapsulate key features of the envisaged RM activity, but can mean different things to different people. For example, the term 'integrated RM' is frequently used by corporate risk managers to refer to the joint management of all RM functions in the organisation. However, the term is also well established in the financial RM literature where integration relates to the combined treatment of the various sources of financial risk, recognising inter-dependencies between both sources of risk and management responses. Integrated RM in the financial sense is concerned with employing insurance, debt, equity, and financial derivatives in a co-ordinated manner to manage the organisation's overall financial position (see for example, Doherty, 2000). The term 'integrated' has also been used to describe the combined treatment of two or more areas of management concern. For example, CFO Research Services (2002) introduce the term 'strategic RM' in discussing the integration of RM and strategic planning. Similarly, Miller and Waller (2003: p 99) use the term integrated RM in discussing *'how scenario planning and real option analysis contribute to an integrated approach to managing risk'*. A somewhat different definition of integrated RM uses the word integrated to mean the embedding of RM processes into all aspects of decision-making. For example, AIRMIC's integrated RM special interest group define the achievement of integrated RM as *'when RM is integrated (or embedded) into all of the functions and processes within the organisation'* (AIRMIC, 1999: p4).

'Enterprise RM' is defined by COSO (PricewaterhouseCoopers 2004) as follows:

'Enterprise risk management is a process, effected by an entity's board of directors, management and other personnel, applied in strategy setting and across the enterprise, designed to identify potential events that may affect the entity, and manage risk to be within its risk appetite, to provide reasonable assurance regarding achievement of entity objectives.'

For COSO, enterprise RM is *'not one event or circumstance, but a series of actions that permeate an entity's activities'*. Enterprise RM is most effective when built into the organisation's infrastructure and intertwined with operating activities as *'part of the essence of the enterprise'*.

'Enterprise wide RM' is described by Mottershead and Godfrey in terms of the extent of application as an approach *'that looks at risk across the whole organisation rather than through the traditional functions [and] aligns RM activities to shareholder value levers'* (Mottershead and Godfrey, 2001: p11). Hodgkinson gives a wider, more detailed definition of enterprise wide RM as *'a RM philosophy that is: positive and proactive; value based and broadly focused; embedded in processes; integrated into strategy and total operations; and continuous'*. (Hodgkinson, 2001: p27)

The term **'holistic RM'** is sometimes used in the simple sense of the management of all sources of risk (Hopkin, 2002). Miller and Waller (2003: p 99) clearly regard this an a necessary part of their view of integrated RM as they state: *'the essence of integrated risk management is consideration of the full range of uncertain contingencies affecting business performance'*. However, in its proper sense, 'holistic' implies a systemic perspective, which recognises system properties that are distinct from the properties of system components. In this sense, holistic RM would imply recognition and management of interactive effects between organisation activities and associated risks. Waring and Glendon (1998: p56) argue that *'holism does not imply consideration of every possible aspect of the particular whole, but a consideration of the essence of all the significant aspects. Holism is in contrast with reductionism whereby significant features may be lost deliberately (and often in ignorance of the adverse effects on understanding and outcomes) in the search for simplicity, elegance and convenience'*. From this perspective, many corporate risk identification exercises are more reductionist than holistic, in that little effort is directed at considering the interactions between identified areas of risk.

Linking the concepts of enterprise-wide, holistic and integrated approaches, DeLoach (2000: p5) defines enterprise-wide RM as meaning that: *'a truly holistic, integrated, forward looking and process orientated approach is taken to manage all key business risks and opportunities – not just financial ones – with the intent of maximising shareholders' value for the enterprise as a whole'*.

The forgoing definitions illustrate the potential for ambiguity, and even confusion, between the terms 'integrated', 'enterprise wide', and 'holistic' RM. Terms such as 'total RM' and 'organisation RM', are even more ambiguous. At best these terms and associated definitions may be useful in conveying a vision of corporate capability, but they offer little guidance about the directions in which appropriate RM practice might be developed.

A number of recent publications aimed at managers have attempted to set out the concepts of integrated RM, enterprise wide RM, and holistic RM (AIRMIC, 1999; PricewaterhouseCoopers, 2004; DeLoach, 2000; Hopkin, 2002; Hunt, 2001). Such publications tend to focus on describing basic process frameworks and some related organising principles. While this may be useful in explaining what a generic process of RM involves, such guidance offers limited advice on how organisations might deploy and develop RM. One consequence of this can be that organisations attempt to adopt particular RM processes as an 'add-on' to existing administrative processes, and in a simplified form to facilitate implementation. This can make it difficult to subsequently embed RM more closely into decision making, or increase its sophistication in useful directions. External pressures to implement measures by a certain date can exacerbate this tendency. For example, in the UK, an important development was the publication of the *Combined Code on Corporate Governance* (Committee on Corporate Governance, London Stock Exchange, 1998), and subsequent guidance to company directors on complying, published by an Internal Control Working Party of the Institute of Chartered Accountants in England and Wales (ICAEW), chaired by Nigel Turnbull. This 'Turnbull guidance' was based on the adoption by a company's board of *'a risk based approach to establishing a sound system of internal control and reviewing its effectiveness'* (ICAEW, 1999: para. 9). Understandably for a document addressed to board directors, the Turnbull guidance was confined to broad principles and provided little detailed guidance on the form that RM processes might take. The need for companies listed on the London Stock Exchange to become 'Turnbull compliant' by the end of 2001 obliged many to augment their existing control systems with risk-based review processes in a relatively short space of time. For many firms this has resulted in a new risk reporting structure that operates in parallel with, and somewhat separately from, other reporting and control systems (not to mention decision processes). While such arrangements may be considered to be compliant with requirements of the *Combined Code on Corporate Governance*, they fall well short of the possibilities for developing effective RM.

1.3 DIMENSIONS OF RISK MANAGEMENT DEVELOPMENT

Table 1.1 suggests six dimensions or directions in which RM might be developed. For easy reference these dimensions are given the labels: 'what', 'when', 'why', 'whichway', 'who', and 'wherewithal'. While these labels are somewhat contrived, these six Ws provide a convenient nomenclature, building on the six Ws employed for somewhat different purposes by Chapman and Ward (2003) in the context of project RM. In each dimension, a range of approaches is possible, depicted by the column entries. The columns in Table 1.1 represent levels of development and entries in each row illustrate the nature of possible progression in each dimension. The use of four levels for most of the dimensions is somewhat arbitrary, but sufficient to illustrate the possibilities for progression. The development choices indicated for each dimension are in some cases suggestive rather than definitive, and in several dimensions a much more detailed and complete set of choices could be articulated. The key idea is that for each dimension there is a spectrum of possible choices, moving from left to right with choices on the extreme right presenting the highest level of development, and choices to the left, the lowest. The approaches at the extreme right of Table 1.1 might be regarded as a clarification of what organisations aspire to when pursuing enterprise wide, holistic, and/or integrated RM. For convenience and brevity, the term 'fully integrated' RM will be used to describe a RM approach characterised by the far right column of Table 1.1.

Table 1.1 Six dimensions of risk management development (Adapted from Ward, 2003. Copyright Perpetuity Press, used with permission.)

Dimension label	Nature of dimension	Range of choices			
		Level 1	Level 2	Level 3	Level 4
What	The focus of attention	Threat management	Opportunity and threat management	Uncertainty management	
When	Application contexts – the decisions to which RM is applied	Operations	Projects	Programmes	Strategies
Why	Objectives adopted for RM	Crisis management	Business continuity	Proactive control	Strategy formulation
Whichway	The nature and quality of RM processes employed in terms of: – degree of formality, – scope of the process, – tools and techniques employed, – extent of quantification.	Ad hoc informal processes, little documentation. Qualitative, superficial analysis.	Some specific formal processes. Analyses documented Some quantification.	Generic, formal processes. Quantitative analyses documented and collated.	Flexible, cost effective use of generic processes. Use of best practice techniques. Continuous improvement.
Who	Parties involved and the allocation of responsibilities for RM	Scattered, ad hoc, left to individuals.	Specific functions with limited roles.	All functions, all levels, effective RM facilitation.	Effective corporate wide involvement extended to customers, suppliers.
Wherewithal	Resources applied to RM.	Implicit, ad hoc allocation of resources.	Formal, but ad hoc allocation of resources.	Widespread, explicit, formal allocation of resources. Planned investment of resources to develop and maintain RM.	Explicit, formal, flexible allocation, more if cost effective.

The six dimensions in Table 1.1 are separable in the sense that choice of approach in one dimension need not dictate choice of approach in other dimensions. Thus in a given organisation, any combination of choices from each dimension might be possible. In practice certain combinations of choices would be unlikely to occur. For example, if few resources are formally allocated to RM, the operation of formal RM processes and significant use of sophisticated software tools would be very difficult, if not impossible, to sustain. Clearly, a version of Table 1.1 could form the basis of a framework for assessing the extent of RM currently operated by an organisation, or serve as a framework for bench-marking comparisons between organisations. This is not the prime purpose of presenting this six dimension framework, although the issue of assessing the extent of RM practice in an organisation will be discussed briefly later. The primary reason for presenting Table 1.1 is to indicate the variety of ways in which organisations might develop more effective RM, even if they do not aspire to 'fully integrated' RM represented by choices at the far right of Table 1.1.

Dimension 1: The Focus of Attention

The 'what' dimension of Table 1.1 concerns the focus of attention of RM activity, which is driven by the interpretation placed on the term 'risk'. It is the simplest dimension to characterise in terms of choices, but the choice made here has a fundamental impact on the nature of RM carried out and the benefits achievable. A limited definition of risk will limit the application of RM, while a broad definition of risk will encourage and facilitate a wider use of RM. Essentially the choice is whether to consider risk solely in threat terms, or in opportunity (and threat) terms, or as a wider concern about uncertainty.

A common approach is to view risk as a possible adverse effect on organisational performance, and a 'source of risk' as a threat to ongoing and planned activities. Then RM becomes primarily a threat focused activity concerned with protecting or preserving corporate assets. The existence of specialists who focus on the management of specific classes of threat (for example, health and safety, security, legal and treasury staff), serves to encourage separate treatment of particular classes of threat. In this way RM can appear to be a fragmented activity carried out in 'functional silos' and separated from line management decision making, rather than an activity that is fully integrated into all management decision processes. Indeed, a possible obstacle to developing more integrated RM may occur when RM is assumed to mean management of a particular class of threat.

A broader view of risk is that it relates to the possibility of either adverse or beneficial effects on performance, as in terms such as 'speculative risk' or 'commercial risk'. Effective management of both requires a proactive approach that seeks to reduce the size and possibility of threats, and increase the size and possibility of opportunities. Potentially, these are separable activities, but it is not usually efficient or effective to treat them as such. Opportunities and threats are seldom independent. Just as it is inadvisable to pursue opportunities without regard for the associated threats, so it is rarely advisable to concentrate on reducing threats without considering associated opportunities.

RM that considers opportunities and threats together is substantially more useful than RM focused purely on threats. However, greater benefits are available from RM that focuses not only on opportunities and threats, but on significant sources of uncertainty which can give rise to opportunities and threats. A weakness in most current RM processes is that they are not readily focused on all sources of uncertainty about performance of organisational activities. An 'uncertainty management' perspective facilitates such a focus and also draws attention to the need to understand and manage variability in organisational activities, not just specific events.

Opportunity management and uncertainty management represent a significant progression from the scope of threat orientated RM, and a necessary progression if fully integrated RM is to be achieved. Chapter 3 discusses this progression in more detail.

Dimension 2: Application Contexts

The 'when' dimension of Table 1.1 is concerned with the kinds of decision to which RM is applied. In this dimension, 'fully integrated' RM would imply, among other things, that RM was applied in all organisation decisions large and small, strategic or tactical, complex or simple. This corresponds to Hopkin's (2002) notion of 'aligned' and 'embedded' RM that supports strategic and project plans, and operational procedures. Table 1.1 characterises decision area choices for RM development as operations, projects, programmes (coherent groups of projects), and strategies (OGC, 2002). This is a rather simplistic characterisation of decision areas, but it serves as an indication of the range of decisions, moving from largely short-term, tactical decisions in operations on the left, to longer term, major investment decisions as strategy to the right of the 'when' row in Table 1.1. This dimension is separable from the 'who' dimension because operations, projects, programmes, and strategies are all relative concepts which can be applied to decisions made at any level of organisation unit. What is considered to be an operational issue at corporate level, may be regarded as a project issue at business unit level, and as a strategic issue for a functional unit within the business unit. From a given location in the organisation, distinguishing these types of decision is useful because the RM issues vary significantly between them. This dimension is discussed in more detail in Chapter 6.

Dimension 3: The Objectives Adopted for Risk Management

The 'why' dimension of Table 1.1 involves considering the fundamental question of what RM is trying to do. The essential purpose of RM in organisations is to improve organisational performance via the systematic identification, appraisal and management of risks to that performance. However, RM may be either reactive or proactive. This distinction is illustrated in Figure 1.1.

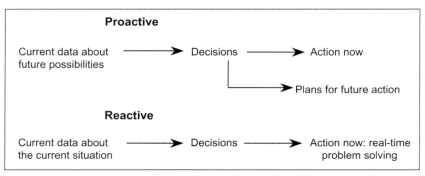

Figure 1.1 Proactive and Reactive Management of Uncertainty

Reactive RM is an after-the-event approach, usually concerned with mitigating the effects of threats that have occurred, as in managing crisis situations. Effective reactive RM requires the capability to rapidly identify and respond to a wide range of possible events that present as problems to be remedied.

Proactive RM is an *ex ante* approach to handling uncertainty. The focus is usually the identification of potential threats and planning for and influencing future events. Where uncertainty presents potential future threats, proactive RM seeks to modify the future incidence and quality of threats and their possible impact on performance goals. Proactive RM can also be concerned with managing the positive side of uncertainty. Thus, where uncertainty appears to offer potential opportunities to improve performance, then proactive RM involves manoeuvring to increase the future incidence and quality of opportunities and their possible effect on performance criteria.

In any given context, RM may occur in either a proactive mode, in a reactive mode, or in a combination of the two. A focus on reactive RM to the exclusion of proactive RM is always an option for management. A lack of proactive RM will usually increase the need for reactive RM subsequently. Unfortunately, reactive RM, in the form of fire-fighting or trouble-shooting capability, frequently receives more attention than proactive RM. Effective fire-fighting is usually more visible than proactive preventative activity, and often is more likely to be rewarded than a proactive, safe pair of hands in an organisational culture that fosters a macho, trouble-shooting style of management.

Practising proactive RM will not remove the need for reactive RM some time in the future, since uncertainty is ever-present. However, effective proactive RM can reduce the need for subsequent reactive RM.

Table 1.1 indicates a range of more specific objectives that might be held for RM activity, linked to the level of anticipation adopted. These objectives are characterised broadly as 'crisis management', 'business continuity', 'proactive control', and 'strategy formulation'. Crisis management represents the most limited objective, strategy formulation the most extensive. 'Fully integrated' RM would imply practice that employs RM for all four of these purposes.

In its most limited form, the crisis management objective involves purely reactive 'fire fighting', that is mitigating the effects of a serious and urgent problem. A focus on crisis management implies a concern for systems that can recognise crises quickly, and respond rapidly and decisively. More usefully, crisis management might involve contingency planning for significant and unanticipated events by setting aside contingent resources such as 'rapid response teams', or back-up operating facilities. The business continuity objective involves similar concerns, but implies a less passive role by attempting to change the probability of certain identified possibilities occurring, as well as attempting to mitigate potential adverse impacts (or exploit potential opportunities). The proactive control objective implies a wider set of concerns, subsuming crisis management and business continuity, but also the revision of performance targets where appropriate. 'Control' may resemble basic crisis management or a highly anticipatory approach which seeks to set appropriate performance targets, having put in place proactive measures to reduce the likely incidence of threats to performance (and increase the incidence of events which might improve performance). Beyond 'proactive control', the objective of RM might be to influence and inform strategy formulation. This extends concern beyond the evaluation and development of contingency plans in support of basic organisation strategies, to the formulation and evaluation of these strategies. 'Fully integrated' RM in the 'why' dimension will influence the basic shape of the organisational strategies. This might also include consideration of the appropriate parties to be involved in the strategy, their motives, the range of performance criteria adopted, and the formulation of appropriate organisational objectives.

A variety of more detailed objectives for RM can be pursued within this anticipatory characterisation of objectives. These are discussed in more detail in Chapter 6.

Dimension 4: The Nature Quality of Risk Management Processes Employed

The 'whichway' dimension of RM development describes the nature and quality of the RM processes employed, given choices made in the other five dimensions. In this dimension choices relate to the degree of formality and documentation in RM processes, the scope of processes, the sophistication of tools and techniques employed, and the nature of the issues addressed. Table 1.1 suggests one relatively simple way of characterising the range of choices in this dimension.

At the minimal end of the 'whichway' spectrum, RM processes are informal and ad hoc with little or no documentation. More integrated RM requires the introduction of formal, documented processes, developing a common, generic process, moving from purely qualitative analysis to increasingly sophisticated quantitative analyses, and using documentation to inform ongoing RM practice. 'Fully integrated' RM involves 'expert' use of formal processes which does not imply a rigid, 'paint by numbers' approach, but a flexible approach which varies in depth and complexity to suit the context. 'Fully integrated' RM also involves an emphasis on continuous improvement in RM processes, and a concern to use 'best practice' techniques (as distinct from common practice).

Formalisation implies the use of structured processes for RM which make explicit the tasks to be carried out in a given context, and help to clarify the relative importance and role of each component task. For example, a simple specification might describe the RM process in terms of phases such as: identifying, analysing, assessing, treating and monitoring risk. In addition to defining process phases, the quality of the RM process depends on the depth of analysis undertaken. For example, efficient and effective risk identification usually requires more than unstructured brainstorming. Structured approaches using particular frameworks to prompt identification of risk sources are usually much more appropriate (see Chapter 4).

A related design consideration is the range contexts that will be subject formal RM processes, and the extent to which RM will be mandated in such contexts or merely facilitated. Use of RM in all contexts and all significant decisions may be the ultimate target, but would imply different levels of RM for different types of context. For example, a cost-effective approach to RM in projects implies different levels of detail and effort for different sizes and types of project, and for RM applications at different stages in the project life cycle (Chapman and Ward, 2003).

The extent of quantitative analysis is another aspect of quality in the RM process. Issues here include the manner in which estimates are obtained, the form in which uncertainty is quantified, treatment of dependency between different sources of uncertainty, methods used to combine and evaluate risk, and the extent to which trade-offs between different risk/return options are considered (Chapman and Ward, 2002; 2003). Integrated RM would involve high quality processes which incorporate appropriate attention to quantification.

A high level of integrated RM is achieved in the 'whichway' dimension by adopting processes capable of handling the forgoing considerations, and by seeking continuous improvement in the quality of analyses undertaken. A more detailed discussion of the choices involved in this dimension is provided in Chapters 8 and 9.

Dimension 5: The Parties Involved and Allocation of Responsibilities for Risk Management

The 'who' dimension of Table 1.1 refers to the parties involved and the location of RM activity in the organisational structure. Widespread corporate application implies RM employed horizontally across all areas of the organisation's operations, and vertically throughout all levels in the organisation hierarchy, from corporate and business unit levels, down to the smallest operating units, teams and even individual operatives.

Development of RM requires recognition of where RM processes already occur in the organisation and then decisions about where further attempts to develop RM should be made, and who should be involved. Such decisions might adopt a 'logical incrementalist' approach (Quinn, 1989), first targeting areas of the organisation where the benefits from RM will be greatest, and then using this experience as a learning process before attempting more widespread deployment. For example, in a project based organisation, a natural starting place for RM is at project manager level, working down into project components and then teams. Further development of RM might be targeted at the function based units which provide support to projects. The Turnbull guidance encourages a top-down approach, but leaves organisations to decide how far down the hierarchy risk-based control should extend (and in what form). One issue for many organisations is how to develop RM more widely given pre-existing separate pockets of RM activity in so-called 'risk silos'. Should one attempt to build on this ad hoc specialist activity, or introduce alternative RM activity in entirely different parts of the organisation?

A particular issue is the design of the organisational RM infrastructure, what Hopkin (2002) calls the 'risk architecture', and the associated allocation of responsibilities for corporate wide systems and processes. From a corporate perspective, responsibility needs to be clearly allocated (Hopkin, 2002):

- for development of RM strategy and standards;

- for implementation of standards and procedures;

- for monitoring compliance with established standards.

A key aspect is the choice of roles allocated to corporate and business unit 'risk officers', line management, internal audit and other specific functional areas. Possible roles and responsibilities for these different groups are discussed in Chapter 2.

The parties involved in establishing an organisation's RM capability include those who might champion the initiative, the individual or project team responsible for making it happen, those who use the associated RM systems and procedures, and those who subsequently support and maintain RM activities. Outside parties may also be influential, such as banks, major customers, or regulators. The experience, seniority and role of the RM capability project manager is obviously of critical importance. That such a manager is appointed with these responsibilities is a basic tenet of effective project management.

Even if it is agreed to designate a particular individual as 'guardian of the organisation's RM architecture, strategy and protocols' (Hopkin, 2002: p136), or as corporate facilitator of RM development, the variety of roles that could be undertaken is large, and is dependent on a variety of situational factors under top management control. In addition, RM departments are not always best located or equipped to progress the general development of RM throughout the organisation. These issues are discussed in Chapter 9.

For a particular organisation, the establishment of fully integrated RM should also include the development of RM activity in other partner or agent organisations. For example, an organisation contracting with buyers or suppliers ought to be concerned with the potential for risk transfer between the contracting parties. The nature and extent of RM operated by buyers and suppliers should have some influence on the nature and extent of RM undertaken by their business partners. In particular, a client organisation might seek to manage risks by implicitly transferring them to contractors via a firm fixed-price contract, but this implicit transfer might be no guarantee that contractors will identify all relevant risks or accept responsibility for managing them. This is one reason why some client organisations, such as the UK Ministry of Defence, require offering contractors to demonstrate RM capability by requiring them to submit RM plans along with their fixed price tenders.

Dimension 6: The Resources Applied to Risk Management

The 'wherewithal' dimension concerns the extent of resources formally invested in developing and maintaining RM. Such resources include personnel in terms of both numbers and expertise, the time allocated to RM, the provision of supporting infrastructure, and funds applied to the management of identified risks. The greater the investment of such resources, the easier it will be to move towards more integrated RM in terms of the other five dimensions, and choices made in the other five dimensions may be influenced by the resources available.

In terms of personnel resourcing, choices include decisions about the number, expertise and location of dedicated RM personnel deployed, and the resources available to them, and the extent of training to develop the expertise of other employees. An obvious issue is the location and size of any corporate RM department. Such departments are often surprisingly lean and resource limited given the substantial potential for making improvements in RM activity in most organisations (see Chapter 9 and Ward, 2001). In project based organisations, resourcing of RM for projects might involve:

- no specific RM support for project managers, but limited training in RM techniques;

- the provision of a central risk analysis support unit which project managers can call on as necessary;

- project managers provided with RM support in the form of a full-time, dedicated risk analyst.

Formal allocation and resourcing of time dedicated to RM is another important aspect of 'wherewithal' choices. Clearly much time may be spent by line managers on RM matters inherent in their decision making. However, for Table 1.1 purposes, it is more useful to consider choices about the time that is explicitly set aside for formal RM deliberations, whether by individuals, committees, or working groups. For example, a directive that formal project review meetings should also consider RM issues may not result in much additional RM if it has to be squeezed into already busy one-day meetings. A directive accompanied by an expectation that RM deliberations should involve an additional full day's consideration is a rather more substantial resource commitment. Similar observations apply to the establishment and maintenance of information systems to support RM.

Approaches taken to risk financing arrangements are also part of choices in the 'wherewithal' dimension, and are not confined to insurance arrangements (Doherty, 2000). A key issue is the arrangements made for self-insurance via contingency funds, the size of such funds, and which level in the organisational hierarchy is responsible for holding them. The location and motivational effects of contingency funds are a very important aspect of effective, integrated RM (Chapman and Ward, 2002). In addition to contingency funds, specific expenditure could be allocated to manage particular sources of risk, be they threats, opportunities, or sources of uncertainty such as variability in specific areas of performance. 'Fully integrated' RM would recognise that decisions have to be made about investment expenditure of this nature.

1.4   PATHWAYS FOR RISK MANAGEMENT DEVELOPMENT

The aim of this opening chapter has been to describe a six dimensional framework for identifying the nature of RM development choices where the choices in each dimension form a progressive sequence. Clearly, if management is to make informed choices about developing RM practices, it is desirable to identify the nature of current practice. In the six dimensional framework, this implies assessing where current practice lies with respect to the levels in Table 1.1. The term fully integrated RM is a convenient term to denote the situation where RM is used to maximum effect in an organisation. Most organisations are a long way short of this. Working towards 'fully integrated' RM requires attention to each of the six dimensions, and ultimately choices to the extreme right of Table 1.1 in all dimensions. The plausible choices for further development in terms of strategic choice criteria of suitability, feasibility, and acceptability, are likely to be approaches in the next highest level in each dimension. However, development of practice towards integrated RM need not proceed evenly across all dimensions simultaneously, and at any given time practices in each dimension may not correspond closest to the same nominal level in Table 1.1. For example, an organisation's practice may be largely threat orientated, level 1 in the 'what' dimension, confined to specific functions as in level 2 of the 'who' dimension, and correspond to level 3 development in all other dimensions. Plausible and preferred pathways through the development levels could form a useful subject for research. For example, a survey by CFO Research Services (2002) outlines three preferred implementation methods for RM development (in order of popularity): focus on building RM into one organisation unit or process; launch a company wide initiative; and pursue an expanded audit exercise which concentrates on risk identification. What exactly these approaches involve could be usefully explored and elaborated on using the six dimension framework of Table 1.1.

A common approach to RM development is to begin with a simplified RM process, perhaps limited to probability impact diagrams and checklists, introduced fairly rapidly with a minimum of piloting. Following rapid introduction, the intention is to continue operating the simplified process in a well-defined administrative framework, without major changes in format. The problem with this approach is that it does not facilitate further development of RM practice. Chapman and Ward (2003) advocate a pilot study approach, applying a comprehensive RM process in a selected context to learn on, before developing practice in a methodical fashion on a more widespread basis.

2

RISK MANAGEMENT INFRASTRUCTURE

2.1   INTRODUCTION

As noted in Chapter 1, risk management (RM) activity can take many forms, take place in different parts of the organisation, and may be formal or informal activity. Whatever the choices made about the directions in which to develop RM activity, such activity requires a supporting infrastructure. This RM infrastructure is in turn influenced, facilitated and supported by the organisation's administrative infrastructure which includes: physical deployment of resources; processes for co-ordination and control; and associated documentation of policies and procedures. All RM activity takes place within the organisation's administrative infrastructure. However, not all RM activity, particularly informal RM carried out by individuals, will be carried out within the RM infrastructure. This dependence structure is illustrated in Figure 2.1.

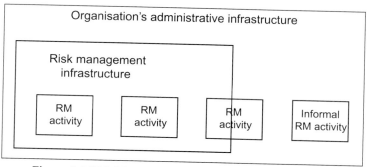

Figure 2.1 Risk Management Infrastructure Dependence

In principle, the RM infrastructure facilitates and supports all formal RM activities. In some organisations the extent of RM that is treated formally can be quite limited, for example confined to operating a Turnbull compliant RM process in respect of corporate governance. In such situations the RM infrastructure can be regarded as synonymous with the Turnbull compliance RM process. However, in general, the RM infrastructure should be distinct from the individual RM activities that it facilitates and supports. This distinction is important. It recognises that any RM infrastructure should be driven top-down by a strategic perspective on the possibilities for RM development as described in Chapter 1. The development of RM infrastructure should not be led by the nature of one particular RM process. If it is, then the opportunity to consider the possibilities for RM development (towards fully integrated RM for example) may well be missed or obstructed.

To the extent that RM activities are formalised, then the supporting infrastructure needs to include:

- individuals and groups responsible, accountable, and with authority for carrying out and supporting RM activity;

- guiding principles for RM activity;

- a strategy for RM development;

- policies (operating rules) for RM;

- guidelines for undertaking RM;

- information systems and decision support.

This chapter provides an overview of these aspects of RM infrastructure. Following chapters expand on this material.

2.2   ROLES AND RESPONSIBILITIES

In terms of developing RM throughout the organisation there is a need for top-down systematic development, co-ordination, and support of RM activities. A key part of such an initiative is being clear what the relevant roles and responsibilities of different parties in the organisation should be. Relevant parties in this respect include: the chief executive officer (CEO) and the board of directors, the audit committee and internal audit, line management, specialist RM functions, and the corporate risk manager.

Board of Directors Responsibilities

Generally the board of directors provides guidance and direction to the organisation's management. Typically this involves setting strategy, formulating higher level objectives, broad base resource allocation, and responsibility for shaping key infrastructures of the organisation, including organisation structures and information systems. In particular, the board has ultimate responsibility for managing risk in the organisation, and for creating the infrastructure for RM to operate efficiently and effectively. This infrastructure may include: an executive group, a non-executive committee, an internal audit function, a risk management function, business unit committees, or such other functions that suit the organisation's way of operating and are capable of facilitating, monitoring and developing risk management activity.

The board of directors should:

- understand the most significant risks facing the organisation;
- consider the risk implications of board decisions;
- know the possible effects on shareholder value of deviations from expected performance;
- ensure that an appropriate risk management infrastructure is established and maintained;
- know how the organisation will manage in a crisis;
- be assured that risk management processes are working effectively;
- publish a clear risk management policy covering risk management philosophy, responsibilities and procedures.

(Adapted from AIRMIC, ALARM, IRM Standard, 2002)

In evaluating the effectiveness of RM processes, particular attention needs to be paid to corporate governance requirements which include the review of all controls, including financial, operational, and compliance controls, and risk-management (Committee on Corporate governance, 1998: provision D.2.1). Good corporate governance requires that companies adopt a methodical approach to risk management which:

- protects the interests of their stakeholders;
- ensures that the board of directors discharges its duties to direct strategy, build value, and monitor performance of the organisation;

- ensures that management controls are in place and are performing adequately.

In evaluating systems of internal control, the board should consider as a minimum:

- the nature and extent of downside risks acceptable for the company to bear within its particular business;
- the likelihood of such risks becoming a reality;
- the organisation's ability to manage such risks;
- how unacceptable risks should be managed;
- the cost and benefits of control activity undertaken.

Roles for a Risk Management Committee

Given the complexity and scale of RM activity, the board may decide to delegate most of the above tasks to a sub-committee. Such a committee may have three basic responsibilities which need to be clearly distinguished: supporting and facilitating RM; carrying out RM at a corporate level; and reviewing the effectiveness of RM activity.

1.   *Supporting and Facilitating Risk Management*

A key responsibility of the board is to facilitate and support ongoing development of effective RM throughout the organisation. This implies the following responsibilities for:

- maintaining an organisational commitment to the effective operation of RM, and ongoing development of RM capability;
- defining and maintaining policy, methodology, and standards for RM including clarifying responsibilities for managing and bearing risk;
- assisting management to implement necessary measures across the organisation, including resourcing of a corporate RM department;
- monitoring developments in RM techniques generally and considering their relevance to the organisation's RM capability;
- providing guidance for management on conducting risk assessments, improving risk control, and monitoring risk on an ongoing basis.

2.   Carrying out RM at Corporate Level

Whatever RM activity is undertaken at lower levels in the organisation, the board needs to undertake RM associated with a corporate portfolio perspective of the organisation's activities. The board should also carry out RM in respect of all major investment decisions, including mergers and acquisitions, and changes in strategy. Thus the RM committee should:

- provide a forum for considering how RM can support strategic initiatives;

- monitor developments in the organisation's policy, strategy, operations, and environment that may have a significant effect on the uncertainties faced by the organisation.

This includes reviewing periodic status reports on major initiatives and significant risk issues, and ad hoc reports on significant incidents.

3.   Reviewing the Effectiveness of RM Activity

As with all other management systems, top management has a responsibility for ensuring that any formalised RM systems are operating appropriately and effectively. This implies the need for frequent monitoring and review of these formal systems, including the RM committee's activities. Responsibilities in this respect should certainly include reviewing the impact of significant incidents, including near-misses, recent major strategic decisions, and the appropriateness of subsequent management responses. The organisation's audit committee via internal investigations, should provide separate review and evaluation of RM systems. Consideration of these evaluations and any associated recommendation should also form part of the RM committee's review work.

Some organisations make use of Risk Forums which meet quarterly or biannually to discuss major sources of risk, develop RM strategies and monitor RM activities. The number attending such events might be fairly large and include risk officers from business units or other senior representatives of business units, plus directors representing Finance, IT, Legal Services, Human Resources, Operations, together with heads of Health and Safety, audit, insurance and security. Such events lend themselves to formal presentations, discussion of common issues, and increasing awareness of RM activities across the organisation. Where the organisation contains a small number of business units, a single

Risk Committee may suffice and be attended by corporate managers together with representatives from each business unit. Larger organisations with many business units may operate a hierarchy of Risk Committees, a Group level committee and sub-committees in each business unit. In this case the Group Risk Committee might focus on Group risks together with oversight of the operation of business unit risk committees.

Roles of Business Units

Managers in charge of business units in the organisation hierarchy have a cascading responsibility for operationalising RM within units in a manner which is consistent with high-level requirements. The business units also have primary responsibility for managing risks on a day-to-day basis, and for promoting risk awareness within their operations. In particular, business units should:

- introduce RM objectives into their business;

- understand the risks which fall into their area of responsibility, the possible implications of these on other areas, and the consequences other areas may have on them;

- formulate performance indicators which allow them to monitor the key business and financial activities, progress towards objectives, and identify developments which require intervention;

- have systems which communicate variances in budgets and forecasts appropriate frequency to allow action to be taken; ensure that RM is a regular management meeting item to allow consideration of exposures and to re-prioritise work in the light of effective risk analysis;

- report systematically and promptly to senior management any perceived new risks or failures of existing control measures.

(Adapted from AIRMIC, ALARM, IRM Standard, 2002)

The Role of Internal Audit

The role of internal audit is likely to differ from one organisation to another, but in general terms the internal audit function is closely concerned with RM. In determining the most appropriate role for internal audit in a particular organisation, the internal auditors' professional requirements for independence and objectivity must be preserved. Consequently, internal audit may use risk assessment to identify organisation systems that warrant appraisal, and it may audit the organisation's RM processes, but it should not be responsible for operating these processes. The scope of the internal auditor's work is summarised by the UK Institute of Internal Auditors (IIA) as providing *'an independent appraisal of the adequacy, application and effectiveness of the arrangements put in place by management'.* More specifically internal auditors should (IIA, 1998a):

- review the reliability and integrity of financial and operating information, and the means used to identify, measure and classify, and report such information (specific standard 310);

- review the systems established to ensure compliance with those policies, plans, procedures, laws, regulations, and contracts which could have a significant impact on operations and reports, and determine whether the organisation is in compliance (specific standard 320);

- review the means of safeguarding assets and, as appropriate, verify the existence of such assets (specific standard 330);

- appraise the economy and efficiency with which it resources are employed (specific standard 340);

- review operations or programmes to ascertain whether results are consistent with established objectives and goals and whether the operations are being carried out as planned (specific standard 350).

This scope of work definition clearly includes review of an organisation's RM systems.

Internal audit may make direct use of RM in two ways. First, by using risk assessment to identify organisation systems that warrant appraisal, internal audit effort can be deployed to maximum effect. Second, a risk orientated approach can be used to evaluate particular controls. This involves analysing the organisation activity to be reviewed and assessing the risks a control system is supposed to be addressing. This allows subsequent evaluation of existing systems and recommendations for improvements to be soundly based on requirements for managing the underlying risks.

A consequence of this approach is that internal audit can assist in the management of risk more widely by identifying risks and recommending appropriate controls as part of its work, even where management has no explicit RM process in place (IIA1998b: para. 5.33). However, it is generally recognised that this direct involvement in identifying risks, particularly when no explicit RM process exists, can create a moral hazard for internal audit because of a potential conflict of interest. Fundamentally, designing and installing operating systems (including RM processes addressing operations) are not audit functions. Performing such functions is presumed to impair audit objectivity (IIA 1998a: para. 120.03). Internal audit cannot offer an independent review of RM systems if it has been significantly involved in designing and establishing those systems.

In principle it should be management that initially identify the need for control systems (including RM systems) and management who should design and operate them. Internal auditors then provide independent assurance that these systems are fit for purpose and cost-effective.

The dilemma over the potential role of internal audit is particularly marked in respect of RM systems because of internal audit experience and expertise in actually applying RM techniques in the course of its normal work.

Could it be that internal audit is better placed than management to design (if not operate) effective RM systems? Some argue that while internal audit may have internal control process skills, their traditional accountants' perspective will cause internal audit to focus on financial controls and financial risk at the expense of a more appropriate wider view of risk and uncertainty. Certainly, internal auditing originated from a need for managers of large organisations to be assured that recorded information was complete and accurate. However, the role has steadily expanded to include 'operational auditing' which encompasses considerations of economy, efficiency and effectiveness of all organisation processes.

Many internal auditors disagree with this view, pointing out that their basic roles (see earlier list) are more about providing an overall view of management processes in general, not solely financial systems. In practice, the perspective adopted by internal audit depends on the skills and backgrounds of those employed as internal auditors, and the head of internal audit in particular.

However, even if one accepts that internal auditors are not biased towards a financial perspective, there still remains a clear focus on control systems in internal audit. The importance of this is not in doubt, but for RM purposes it leads to a restricted perspective of the nature of RM. For example, the IIA (1998a) Standards define risk simply as probability of threat: *'the probability that an event or action may adversely affect the organisation'*. As discussed in Chapter 1, this definition implies a rather narrow view of risk and therefore of the potential roles for risk management.

A further factor which must limit internal audit's ability to contribute to the establishment of RM systems is the ubiquity of RM. Organisations which are making effective use of RM will have embedded RM within all decision-making processes and systems (including control systems). Additionally, different RM systems may be operated for different contexts and purposes, albeit within a framework provided by corporate guidelines. This ubiquity of RM suggests the need for separate, dedicated, (and informed), oversight of the development and operation of RM in the organisation. This need also arises out of the existence of pockets of specialisation in various areas of risk (including internal audit) which may not be sufficiently well linked or practised in RM techniques. While responsibility for this oversight rests ultimately with the CEO and board, in practice it warrants the appointment of a Chief Risk Officer (CRO) whose role is to facilitate the development of RM.

The Role of Individuals

In most organisations RM is carried out every day by every employee. It is an implicit aspect of most people's jobs. There are problems to be faced and resolved, opportunities to be identified and exploited where possible, and uncertainties to be tolerated or managed. Sometimes the issues involved are small with limited impact, sometimes they are large with widespread, long-term implications. But not all of these situations warrant the application of formal risk management processes. For short-term, localised issues informal, ad hoc, situation specific RM may be entirely adequate and effective. However, all individual employees should:

- understand their accountability for particular risks;

- understand how they can enable continuous improvement of risk management;

- understand that risk management is a key part of the organisation's culture;

- report systematically and promptly to senior management any perceived new risks or failures of existing control measures.

(Adapted from AIRMIC, ALARM, IRM Standard, 2002)

Specialist Risk Management Functions

Typically, the division of organisation tasks and associated specialisation lends itself to learned ways of managing risk and uncertainty which naturally focus on the scope of the relevant tasks. This is particularly pronounced in organisation units whose main responsibility is to manage some aspect of risk. Examples of such units include: insurance management, health and safety, legal department, the treasury function, internal audit, quality control, security, public relations. In addition, various operating units or functions may develop formal approaches for RM in support of their activities. Examples might include project managers, human resources, management, and strategic planning. This diversity of separate RM activities is often referred to as a 'risk silos' approach to RM. Co-ordination of RM activities and cooperation in sharing analyses and information may be quite limited between different silos. The extent of any co-ordination and co-operation between one particular silo and another will depend on a variety of factors including:

- the visibility of RM activity in the other silos;

- perceptions of the relevance of skills and RM activity in other silos;

- operational separation between the silos;

- incentives for cooperation;

- the people involved.

Even in the same type of function there may be different levels of RM. For example, individual project managers may develop their own individual approaches to addressing risks in the projects they are responsible for. In such circumstances, it becomes very clear that sharing information about approaches and identifying best practice can result in increased quality of RM across all projects. More generally, cooperation between different silos of RM need not be about adopting a uniform approach to RM (which in any case may not be appropriate), but might be more about sharing information and expertise, co-ordinating RM activities, and ensuring a consistent approach.

The increasing need for more visible, formal RM has resulted in most large organisations establishing a specific RM function, typically reporting to top management. Depending on size the organisation RM function may range from a single risk champion, a part-time risk manager, to a full-scale RM department. The role of the RM function might be to:

- assist the board in setting policy and strategy for RM;

- build a risk aware culture within the organisation including appropriate education;

- establish internal risk policy and structures for business unit;

- design and review formal processes for RM;

- co-ordinate the various functional activities which advise on RM issues within the organisation;

- support the development of risk response processes including contingency and business continuity programme formulation;

- prepare reports on significant risk issues for the board and stakeholders.

The role of the corporate risk manager is discussed in more detail in Chapter 9.

2.3   GUIDING PRINCIPLES

Guiding principles relate to the fundamental nature of an organisation's business and associated risks. These principles should be based on the following (Banks and Dunn 2003: chap. 8):

1. Understanding what business areas the organisation will focus on and recognising the main sources of risk associated with these.

2. Deciding what risks are central to the firm's core business strategy and which are not. For example, a manufacturing firm might be prepared to take on commodity and demand risks as inherent to the core business, but wish to avoid all currency risk by appropriate hedging.

3. Understanding shareholder expectations in terms of corporate risk-taking and the firm's strategy.

4. Deciding the organisation's tolerance to risk based on:

    – the maximum amount of money the firm is willing to risk losing,

    – what resources are available to support potential losses,

    – consideration of whether the firm's return on capital employed is adequate given the risks being taken.

Banks and Dunn (2003) argue that all four of these aspects of guiding principles should be deliberated by the board and then communicated to internal and external stakeholders.

2.4   STRATEGY FOR RISK MANAGEMENT DEVELOPMENT

In addition to guiding principles related to an organisation's particular context, RM activity needs to be informed by a corporate statement of about when and why RM is to be employed. This involves specifying corporate strategy for RM in terms of the dimensions in Table 1.1. This will be heavily influenced by corporate management's view of whether RM should be concerned with just threats, both threats and opportunities, or uncertainty (the 'what' dimension in Table 1.1). In general, the widest interpretation should be placed on the what, when, and why dimensions if the full benefits of RM are to be aspired to. A statement which limits perceptions about the potential objectives and scope of RM can have serious consequences for subsequent development and growth of RM practice in an organisation. Chapter 3 discusses the interpretation of the term risk and its implications. Chapter 6 discusses in detail the range of benefits and objectives that might be pursued by RM.

2.5 POLICIES AND GUIDELINES FOR RISK MANAGEMENT

As with any formal organisational systems and procedures, formal RM systems require a clear RM policy to be formulated. This policy needs to address the following aspects of RM activity:

- the purpose of RM;

- what form RM should take;

- who should do it;

- how RM should be carried out, supported, and monitored;

- when RM should be undertaken;

- what resources should be applied.

In particular for corporate governance or control purposes, the policy needs to ensure:

- RM processes are repeatable;

- there are mechanisms for monitoring the application of the policy (including reports to the board, at least annually);

- that internal control mechanisms are in place for independent assessment that the policy is operated and is effective;

- there are clear escalation criteria for when to refer decision making upwards.

The OGC MoR guide (2002: p35) refers to policy being articulated at a strategic level in a high-level statement setting out how the management of risk will be handled throughout the organisation with guidance on roles, responsibilities, processes and procedures.

Possible components of a risk management policy/guidelines are listed in Table 2.1.

Table 2.1 Possible Components of a Risk Management Policy Statement
(Adapted from OGC, 2002: p35)

- the level and nature of risk which is acceptable for particular business activities or programmes

- responsibilities for the management of particular risks and associated risk financing arrangements

- roles and responsibilities for carrying out various RM activities

- mechanisms for monitoring and reviewing RM activities

- mechanisms for monitoring and reviewing RM principles, policies, and guidelines

- rules for reporting significant risks higher up the hierarchy

- RM processes in various contexts

- use of standard documentation for risk analysis and reporting

- use of particular tools and techniques for ranking and evaluating sources of risk

- treatment of interdependencies between risk contexts

Such policies and documentation may be set out as formal requirements or as guidance on recommended good practice. Clearly there is scope for varying the level of detail on these aspects. Even rather general statements, endorsed by the board, can have useful symbolic value by flagging top management support for RM, and by giving designated risk managers broad authority to operate. Some companies with RM capability well integrated into investment decision making and project management can have quite extensive documentation, which incorporates corporate objectives for RM, procedures, guidelines, and general advice on RM issues and carrying out different forms of analysis.

There are clear difficulties here in deciding on an appropriate level of detail to incorporate in policy statements. To some extent this can be driven by distinguishing practice that is company policy and therefore mandatory, and what are better regarded as guidelines or advice. Even policy statements will warrant some explanation of the underlying rationale and supporting guidance to facilitate implementation. Requirements of corporate governance and other regulatory requirements need to be defined as policy, although even here it is always useful to explain the reasons for requirements or policies.

Given the variety of contexts that RM may be applied in, it is not usually practical to specify policy in too much detail, as some degree of flexibility in processes is desirable. Quite apart from being inappropriate in a given context, over-specified policy can stifle initiative and development of RM expertise, not to mention motivation. Also in organisations with a high degree of decentralisation, it may be unrealistic to attempt to dictate policy on RM processes in too much detail.

2.6 INFORMATION SYSTEMS AND DECISION SUPPORT

Efficient and effective RM needs appropriate information systems and decision support. However, it is difficult to generalise about what is appropriate apart from observing basic principles that information needs to be relevant, timely, reliable and appropriately detailed.

Much depends on the nature and scope of RM practice and on intentions about future RM development. As discussed later in Chapter 6, documentation to support formal processes can bring important benefits that may be worth pursuing in their own right. One example is the provision of a corporate knowledge base that can facilitate corporate learning and build competitive advantage. Consequently, information systems should be designed with the specific intention of achieving these benefits.

In principle, information systems design could revolve around what is needed to carry out particular steps in a generic RM process framework. At a basic level this might involve the collation of information about identified sources of risk in a risk register. However, this raises questions about how this information will be used and by whom, what information to include related to individual sources of risk, how much detail to record, and how frequently this information will be updated. Additional issues include the extent to which information from particular RM applications will be made available for other future applications and how this pooling of information will be organised and coordinated. An intranet data facility centrally controlled is an obvious approach, but the cost-effectiveness and reliability of such a system requires careful assessment. Proprietary software databases can be useful, but care needs to be taken in considering the facilities such packages offer. The problem is that facilities provided, such as risk ranking, may drive an organisation's

RM processes and perceptions of what RM is about. This can pre-empt future deployment of alternative, perhaps more sophisticated methodologies.

A further consideration in deploying RM information systems is the desirability of linking this information with other information systems. If RM is to become 'integrated' in the sense defined in Chapter 1, wholly separate RM information systems may be inappropriate. Indeed, the feasibility and value of augmenting existing information systems and associated decision making procedures should be a primary consideration. An obvious priority is linkage with information systems to support strategic planning.

The deployment of decision support software is less problematic. Such software might include spreadsheets plus simulation software to help quantify and evaluate risk and sources of uncertainty. This is readily deployed for local use in particular RM applications. However, effective and efficient risk analysis requires specialist knowledge and sometimes, expert assistance to construct appropriate models for a given context. This can warrant significant corporate investment in centralised analytical support. Ad hoc reliance on bought-in consultants to undertake specific analyses is always an option. However, given the potential in most organisations for expanding RM activity, developing an in-house capability is likely to be much more efficient and effective. Such investment needs to be guided by individuals who understand the scope for RM and the full range of benefits that RM can bring (see Chapter 6).

2.7 A CORPORATE RISK MANAGEMENT MANUAL

There is a strong argument for supporting RM with a corporate RM manual which includes, but goes much further than setting out corporate policy. The central benefits are that a RM manual:

- signals the importance of RM and illustrates the scope of RM activity;

- provides a focal point for communicating an organisation's RM guiding principles, strategy, policies, and guidelines throughout the organisation;

- acts as a one-stop-shop for practical information relevant to effective RM;

- can operate as a repository of corporate experience and acquired knowledge.

If an internal website is established, then information provided can be extensive, but organised in a hierarchical fashion with appropriate links to external websites and internal data sources to facilitate efficient, effective access to relevant material. Table 2.2 lists possible contents of a corporate RM manual/website.

Table 2.2 Possible Contents for a Corporate Risk Management Manual or Intranet Site

Purpose of the RM manual   Who should use it, why, and for what purposes, how to make best use of this resource.
Corporate philosophy on RM   A statement of top management's fundamental beliefs about the nature of RM and its potential for contributing to organisation performance. This might include statements about what management is interested in, in terms of threats, opportunities, or uncertainty and a recognition of the linkages between them and their importance to achieving performance (shareholder value).
Guiding principles   The organisation's (top management's) attitude to risk and uncertainty. Clarification of extent of willingness to accept risk. What is not acceptable. Limits on the organisation's activities. Support for risk taking by management under appropriate conditions.
Objectives expected from RM   How RM can help deliver performance by identifying long-term aims, benefits in the short-term and medium-term, and immediate benefits in supporting decision processes and improved control of operations. Some explanation of motives driving the development of RM would be appropriate. Relationships with corporate strategy, associated objectives and relative priorities. Personal benefits expected for those who undertake RM.
RM strategy   A statement of current capability and practices. Articulation of the organisation's intentions for extending RM practice and building capability. This might outline plans for investment in developing capability, priority areas with the underlying rationale, directions in which existing practice will be developed. Use (if any), of bench-marking.
Regulatory requirements influencing RM strategy and policies   A statement summarising the regulatory requirements influencing RM strategy and policies, their scope, significance, and compliance implications.

RM policies

Basic rules and procedures within which all RM activity should operate as a minimum. These might relate to any or all of the six W's: what, why, whichway, who, when, and wherewithal. In particular, an outline of compliance procedures for corporate governance and other regulatory requirements could be described (e g risk reporting and review procedures to the board and audit committee). Policies in respect of risk retention and risk ownership.

Roles and responsibilities for RM

A statement of roles and responsibilities in respect of RM of: the board, Risk Committee, Chief Risk Officer (CRO), unit risk managers, project managers, unit managers, all employees, specialist functions (legal, treasury, risk financing, personnel, customer relations, health and safety, maintenance, business continuity, corporate security, etc). The desirability of communication, co-ordination of RM efforts, scope of these, existing corporate mechanisms, possible options for ad-hoc co-ordination.

Contexts for RM

Potential locations and applications of RM: formulation, evaluation and implementation of strategy; project management; operations management (continuous improvement, operational controls, business continuity, crisis management); environmental assessment; asset recognition, development and utilisation; investment appraisal; improving the quality of decision-making, etc.

Sources of risk and uncertainty

Summary descriptions of key areas of uncertainty and related risk drivers (sources of uncertainty). For example, senior management's current top ten concerns/issues (regularly updated). These might relate to key assets (tangible and intangible), aspects of corporate culture, strengths or weaknesses in the organisation's operations, or developments in respect of: technology, the business environment, global events, competition, markets, government policies, etc.

RM processes

General advice on undertaking RM, recommended process frameworks, sources of information (internal and external). Specific recommendations and general advice about good or best practice in respect of phases in a generic RM process. For example, advice on tools, techniques and issues to address in risk identification (use of frameworks, prompt lists, group processes), structuring (minor/major risks, links between risks), response development (specific/general responses, generic forms of response), risk analysis (estimating, combining risks, importance of recognising dependency).

Documentation to support RM processes
Mandatory, recommended, or illustrative pro-forma documents for different phases of RM process applications. In particular, risk identification could involve updating a central risk register and selective downloading for particular contexts and applications. Advice about ad hoc modifications to pro-forma documents for particular context applications. Pro-forma documents for self-assessment, and reporting purposes.

Risk ownership and incentives for RM
Importance of clear decisions about risk allocation (including risk sharing). Implications for effective RM especially where multiple parties are involved in cooperative work.

Examples of RM in action
To promote interest and increase motivation to employ RM, include examples of RM in action, both from within and outside the organisation. This offers an opportunity to learn from other organisations as well as demonstrating the use of RM internally. Examples could include recent incidents or decisions in the organisation where a more structured approach to RM could have avoided loss or exploited a missed opportunity. Other examples could include stories of effective RM applications in the organisation, or suggestions of ways in which RM could contribute operationally and strategically to decision making.

Useful Contacts
List of all individuals with responsibility for supporting/facilitating/advising on RM. Membership of risk committees, working groups, risk forums, etc.

Recent developments in RM
Latest developments internally and externally likely to give rise to changes in RM practices.

Sources of useful information
Corporate knowledge bases. External websites including government sites, professional bodies, educational institutions, journals, books and other literature.

Table 2.2 is not definitive either in terms of the specific content or the structure employed. For example, the structure could be elaborated to give more prominence to RM processes in particular specialist functions, or particular contexts (such as crisis management), and more extensive explanations of analytical techniques could be appended. Effective website design enables useful pathways through the material to be defined by a thoughtful use of links. Few organisations yet have manuals or websites as extensive in scope as Table 2.2. In practice organisations are likely to adopt different strategies for manual or website development depending on management's priorities, interest in RM, and the expertise of RM support staff. Whether in the form of a colour-coded loose-leaf binder, or accessible intranet site, such information and advice still has to be accessed, read and applied. This may be a 'chicken-and-egg' situation where lack of use may be due to scepticism as to the practical value of the information, but this may be difficult to demonstrate until the policies and advice become sufficiently well used. A more fundamental problem is persuading management to apply RM in the first place.

Starting with simple, well-defined processes with limited objectives may be an attractive strategy, particularly where investment in resourcing RM effort is itself limited. The problem with this approach is that RM may never develop much beyond this, or if it does, it is at a very slow pace. Yet for many organisations, modest investment in creating resources to support RM activity could facilitate the development of an important core competence in a relatively short time period.

3

RISK THREATS, OPPORTUNITIES, OBJECTIVES AND UNCERTAINTY MANAGEMENT

3.1 INTRODUCTION

In the 'what' dimension of Table 1.1, the choices for risk management (RM) development were expressed in terms of 'threat management', 'opportunity and threat management', or 'uncertainty management'. This chapter considers the limitations of a threat management focus for RM, and arguments for combined attention to both opportunities and threats. However, the main purpose of this chapter is to outline the desirability of an uncertainty management focus for RM. This facilitates consideration of a much wider set of uncertainty related issues than RM focused only on opportunities and threats. A key obstacle to adopting this wider approach is narrow or restrictive definitions of risk that induce a restricted approach to RM, and may obstruct RM development. This chapter argues that risk is best defined as *the implications of significant uncertainty about the level of performance achievable.*

A further issue is that risk is always relative to one or more performance objectives. Therefore, formulating and modifying objectives should be regarded as an important, even fundamental aspect of RM. This aspect of RM is more naturally addressed by taking an uncertainty management perspective that considers all significant sources of uncertainty confronting an organisation.

3.2 DEFINITIONS OF RISK

For RM development purposes the popular, dictionary definition of risk as: hazard, chance of bad consequences, loss, exposure to chance of injury or loss, will not do. Such definitions illustrate one problem with the term 'risk' – its ambiguous use as a synonym of probability or chance in relation to an event or outcome, the nature of an outcome, or its cause. In an entertaining and well referenced paper, involving a discussion with Humpty Dumpty, Dowie (1999) argues persuasively for abandoning use of the term 'risk' altogether. "It is simply not needed". Dowie argues that the term 'risk' is:

'an obstacle to improved decision and policy making. Its multiple and ambiguous usages persistently jeopardize the separation of the tasks of identifying and evaluating relevant evidence on the one hand, and eliciting and processing necessary value judgements on the other.'

'(The term) 'risk' contaminates all discussions of probability because of the implicit value judgements that the term always brings with it, just as it contaminates all discussions of value assessment because of the implicit probability judgements that it contains.' (Dowie, 1999)

Dowie's argument is appealing, but most people would have difficulties with abandoning use of the term 'risk' completely. Instead, a more precise definition is needed.

The issues involved in determining an appropriate definition of risk become evident from an inspection of possible alternative definitions. The list of definitions in Table 3.1 is only a small selection of the various definitions that have been published in various standards, guidelines, and texts. However, these examples have been selected to illustrate the nature of variations and to highlight the main ways in which recent definitions vary.

The first point to note is that nearly all the definitions refer to effect on objectives, or more precisely, effect on achievement of objectives. That is, risk or risks are associated with potential changes in performance measured in terms of particular performance objectives. In some definitions risk is the effect on performance (definitions 1, 2, 3, 7, 8), although sometimes somewhat vaguely expressed as a 'combination' of probability of an event and its consequence in definitions 1, 3, 7. Definitions 4, 5, 9 define 'a risk' as the cause of an effect on performance, while definitions 6 and 10 refer to the chance or possibility of an event or something happening. Thus we see the scope for defining risk as a probability or chance in relation to an event or outcome, the nature of the outcome, or its cause. However, despite Dowie's (1999) argument summarised above, such differences in focus are not particularly important for RM as long as one recognises the need to explicitly distinguish and address the sources or causes of possible variations in performance, possible consequences, and the chances of different levels of variation in performance.

Table 3.1 Definitions of Risk

1	Combination of the probability of an event and its consequence.... consequences can range from positive to negative. (British Standard BSI PD ISO/IEC Guide 73: 2002, and UK AIRMIC/ALARM/IRM Risk Management standard 2002)
2	Uncertainty of outcome, whether positive opportunity or negative threat. (Office of Government Commerce, 2002)
3	Uncertainty of outcome, within a range of exposure, arising from a combination of the impact and probability of potential events. (HM Treasury, 2001)
4	An uncertain event or condition that, if it occurs, has a positive or negative effect on a project's objectives. (Project Management Institute, 2000)
5	An uncertain event or set of circumstances that should it occur, will have an effect on the achievement of... objectives. (Simon, Hillson and Newland, PRAM Guide, UK Association for Project Management, , 1997)
6	The chance of something happening that will have an impact on objectives. (Australia/New Zealand Standard, 1999)
7	A significant uncertain occurrence... defined by the combination of the probability of an event occurring and its consequences on objectives. (UK MoD, 2002)
8	Potential inability to achieve overall programme objectives. (US DoD DSMC, 2000)
9	Something happening that may have an impact on the achievement of objectives... it includes risk as an opportunity as well as a threat. (National Audit Office, 2000)
10	The possibility that an event will occur and adversely affect achievement of objectives. (Opportunities: the possibility that an event will occur and positively affect the achievement of objectives.) (PricewaterhouseCoopers 2004)

3.3   THREATS AND OPPORTUNITIES

In terms of influence on RM development, a key aspect of any definition of risk (as a source or its effect) is whether it is associated with both positive and negative effects on objectives (performance) or just negative effects. In Table 3.1 only definitions 8 and 10 (both US based) relate risk to just adverse effects on the achievement of objectives. These two definitions imply an approach to RM that is focused on identifying and managing threats to performance. With this perspective identifying and exploiting opportunities for enhancing performance are outside the scope of the RM process (see for example, COSO, 2004). This is unfortunate because it creates a situation where the scope of RM is inappropriately restrictive, separated from main stream decision making, and where the largest potential benefits from a broad approach to RM will be missed.

If RM is regarded as a means of improving organisation performance, there is no reason why RM should not also consider possible opportunities, as well as threats. Recognising this, all the definitions of risk in Table 3.1 (except definitions 8 and 10), associate risk with both positive and negative effects on objectives (performance). In some definitions this is explicit (definitions 1, 2, 4, 9), in others this is implicit (definitions 3, 5, 6, 7). The intention is to signal that RM needs to address both potential threats to performance and potential opportunities to enhance performance. In spite of this, there is still a tendency for practitioners to think of risk in largely down-side, threat terms and to regard RM as primarily threat management. This may reflect a fundamental difficulty in throwing off the commonly understood, dictionary definition , meaning of 'risk'.

In the face of a general tendency for managers to set challenging objectives, a focus on threats and threat management is reasonable, and can be very useful. For example, if a 'tight' budget for a project is set, then by definition this implies a preponderance of threats to keeping to budget over opportunities for coming in below budget. This reinforces the notion that risk is a 'bad thing' that needs to be neutralised. However, in any given decision situation, both threats and opportunities are usually involved, and both should be managed together. A focus on one should never be allowed to eliminate concern for the other.

Often opportunity and threat are inseparable, two sides of the same coin, and it does not make sense to focus on one and not the other. The entrepreneur's understandable enthusiasm for the potential benefits of a perceived opportunity should be balanced by appropriate attention to the possible disadvantages of the venture or adverse consequences of potential problems or threats. This recognises that opportunities to improve performance usually have associated potential for an overall reduction in performance if things don't work out as planned, or hoped for. Conversely, a focus on potential threats and their associated possible adverse consequences should not only consider ways of reducing adverse consequences, but also consider ways of managing threats to create benefits. Courses of action are often available which reduce or neutralise potential threats while simultaneously offering opportunities for positive improvements in performance. This is the idea of making a virtue out of a vice, or turning a weakness into a strength.

Unfortunately, RM operating as threat management is often practised as an activity focused on reducing or at best neutralising the potential adverse consequences of 'pure risks', sources of risk that can only impair performance. The result is that potential opportunities to enhance performance by creatively managing threats are never even looked for, let alone evaluated.

To emphasise the desirability of a balanced approach to opportunity and threat management, the term 'uncertainty management' is increasingly used in preference to the terms 'risk management' and 'opportunity management'. However uncertainty management is not just about managing perceived threats, opportunities, and their implications. It is also about identifying and managing the sources of uncertainty that give rise to and shape perceptions of threats and opportunities.

3.4 UNCERTAINTY AS VARIABILITY AND AMBIGUITY

Uncertainty is in part about 'variability' in relation to performance measures like cost, duration, or 'quality'. It is also about 'ambiguity' associated with lack of clarity because of the behaviour of relevant project players, lack of data, lack of detail, lack of structure to consider issues, working and framing assumptions being used to consider the issues, known and unknown sources of bias, and ignorance about how much effort it is worth expending to clarify the situation.

For example, in a project context Ward and Chapman (2003: p7) argue that an uncertainty management perspective should address not just particular threats or opportunities, but uncertainty about:

- the variability associated with estimates of project parameters;
- the basis of estimates of project parameters;
- the completeness and feasibility of plans;
- objectives and associated priorities;
- relationships between project parties.

All these areas of uncertainty are important, but generally items become more fundamentally important to project performance as we go down the list. Potential for variability is the dominant issue at the top of the list, but ambiguity rather than variability becomes the more dominant underlying issue towards the bottom of the list. Uncertainty about variability associated with estimates involves the other four areas, each of them involving dependencies on later areas in this list.

An obvious area of uncertainty in any organisation concerns estimates of time, cost, and quality related to particular planned activities. For example, we may not know how much time and effort will be required to complete a particular activity. The causes of this uncertainty might include one or more of the following :

- lack of a clear specification of what is required;
- novelty, or lack of experience of this particular activity;
- complexity in terms of the number of influencing factors and associated inter-dependencies;
- limited analysis of the processes involved in the activity;
- possible occurrence of particular events or conditions which might affect the activity.

Only the last of these items is directly related to specific events or conditions. The other sources of uncertainty arise from a lack of understanding of what is involved. This uncertainty is compounded by any uncertainty about who produced the estimates, what form they are in, why, how and when they were produced, from what resources and experience base, and what assumptions underpin them.

3.5   RISK, UNCERTAINTY, AND OBJECTIVES

As noted earlier, most definitions of risk are associated with potential changes in performance measured in terms of particular performance attributes. Defining 'risk' as the implications of uncertainty about performance achievable, and 'source of risk' as a factor that produces that uncertainty, clearly links risk with how we define performance and associated performance objectives. This has four important implications.

1. Setting Objectives is Part of Risk Management

RM cannot be undertaken without reference to performance objectives of some kind. Defining objectives for particular performance attributes affects the nature of associated risk. For example, setting a difficult to achieve, 'tight' budget for a project makes the project more risky by definition, in the sense that the chances of exceeding the budget are increased. Conversely, setting an easily achievable, 'slack' budget makes the project less risky because the chances of exceeding the budget will be decreased. Consequently, selecting relevant performance attributes, formulating objectives for these attributes, and modifying objectives, should be regarded as important, even fundamental aspects of RM.

2. Performance and Risk are Multi-Dimensional

Organisational performance is a multi-dimensional concept. Typically, in any given context, there is more than one performance attribute and associated attribute objective, often even a hierarchy of attributes/objectives. The implication is that variations in performance on each attribute are possible and measurable, and hence that uncertainty exists in respect of these performance attributes. A simple example is the common presentation of project performance in terms of cost, time and quality related objectives. The cost attribute might be addressed in terms of capital cost or 'whole life' cost, and the quality attribute might be divided into technical specification, functionality, reliability, and appearance, each of which may be 'at risk' to different degrees. Objectives may be set for each of these performance attributes, and the project will be 'at risk' to different degrees with respect to each objective. Risk is multi-dimensional to the extent that the referent performance is multi-dimensional.

3. Risk Management Should Recognise Trade-Offs Between Performance Objectives

Active management for performance usually involves making trade-offs between objectives as different courses of action involve different combinations of uncertainty in respect of the various performance attributes. Failure to recognise these trade-offs and articulate preferred trade-offs can result in ineffective and often inappropriate management of risk. For example, to ensure that a project is completed on time is it really sensible to adopt any course of action whatever the cost?

In the extreme, performance attributes that are not readily quantified may be treated as inviolate constraints for management purposes. This may lead to neglect of uncertainty in these performance attributes and failure to manage associated risk, even though they represent important aspects of performance.

4. Different Stakeholders Will Adopt Different Approaches to Risk

Most organisational activities involve more than one party working together, whether it be a team of individuals from same organisation unit, cooperation between different functional units, or inter-organisational ventures involving formal contractual arrangements. In any of these ostensibly cooperative situations, the different parties involved are likely to have different performance objectives, or at least different priorities and perceptions of objectives. As a consequence, different parties will have different perceptions of risks associated with these objectives, and consequently, may wish to adopt different strategies for managing uncertainty. This divergence may be aggravated if different parties also have different knowledge and perceptions of the nature of sources of uncertainty and different capabilities for managing risk (Chapman and Ward, 2002, 2003). This suggests that in any RM activity it is important to consider explicitly who the uncertainty owners could be, and to make conscious decisions about how uncertainty and associated issues should be allocated to various parties (see the 'clarify ownership' phase in Chapter 8).

Major difficulties arise in organisations if there is uncertainty about performance objectives, the relative priorities between objectives, and the nature of acceptable trade-offs. These difficulties are compounded if this uncertainty extends to the objectives and motives of different stakeholders and trade-offs stakeholders are prepared to make between their objectives. The emergence of 'value management' to encompass these issues (Green, 2001), is perhaps indicative of past failures of RM practice to address such issues.

3.6   UNCERTAINTY MANAGEMENT

Effective RM needs to address uncertainty in a broad sense, with the early consideration of all sources of significant uncertainty and associated responses. RM processes that adopt a focus on threats will not address many of the above sources of variability and ambiguity. RM processes concerned with threats and opportunities will do better, but will still tend to be focussed on uncertain events or circumstances. This does not facilitate consideration of aspects of variability that are driven by underlying ambiguity.

In terms of addressing both variability and ambiguity, definitions 1, 3-7, 9, 10 in Table 3.1 are all deficient because they imply a restricted and limiting focus on 'events', 'conditions', or circumstances which cause effects on the achievement of objectives. In this respect, a better definition of 'a risk' or 'source of risk' is: *'a circumstance, action, situation or event (CASE) with the ability or potential to impact (inhibit, enhance, or cause doubt) the key dependencies that support the core processes of the organisation'* (Hopkin, 2002).

However, to address uncertainty in both variability and ambiguity terms, we need to adopt a more explicit focus on uncertainty management. To this end, it is more useful to define risk as an *uncertain effect* on performance, rather than as a cause of *(uncertain) effect* on performance. Such a definition of risk is: *'the implications of significant uncertainty about the level of performance achievable'* (Chapman and Ward, 2003). Using this broad definition of risk we can then associate 'downside risk' with the *implications* of significant 'threats', or unwelcome consequences, and 'upside risk' with the *implications* of significant 'opportunities' or welcome consequences. Consideration of significant threats and opportunities then becomes part of uncertainty management.

Present use of the term 'risk' is ambiguous. Current best practice regards risk as encompassing both threat and opportunity, but associated guidance on RM is frequently couched in threat management terms, related to possible 'events' or 'circumstances'. An obvious first step towards uncertainty management is to remove this ambiguity by using the term 'uncertainty' in the everyday sense of 'lack of certainty' instead of the word 'risk'.

Replacing 'risk' with 'uncertainty' as a starting point could significantly broaden thought processes. In particular, 'risk identification' would become '*uncertainty* identification'. A process involving *uncertainty* identification (rather than risk identification), would draw attention in a natural way to uncertainty about planning choices, uncertainty about objectives and priorities, and uncertainty about fundamental relationships between the organisation and its stakeholders. Additionally, an uncertainty identification process would induce identification of a wider set of possibilities for managing a particular source of uncertainty. For example, a risk identification process, focussing on potential threats, might highlight 'unavailability of a key resource' as a risk, prompting possible responses such as 're-schedule activities', 'obtain additional resource'. However, an exercise seeking to identify sources of *uncertainty* encourages a more open-ended, neutral description of factors, which facilitates a less constrained consideration of response options. Thus instead of the risk 'unavailability of a key resource', an exercise identifying sources of uncertainty would express this as 'uncertainty about availability of a key resource', prompting questions about all factors influencing availability, essential characteristics of the resource, and the possibility of excess as well as shortage of the resource. In particular, how to make good use of excess resource has to become an issue.

After simple substitution of 'uncertainty' for 'risk' in all terminology, an additional step would be to modify wording in RM guidelines wherever this associates risk (uncertainty) with threat (Ward and Chapman, 2003). For example, a risk response of 'mitigation' could be described as 'effect modification' rather than 'impact reduction', and the generic response of 'prevention' as 'changing the probability of occurrence' (rather than 'reducing impact'). Decisions about the transfer of risk would become decisions about sharing significant uncertainty, considering both upside and downside effects. Not only would this terminology induce a more considered view of the wisdom of risk (threat) transfer, it would also stimulate consideration of the wider implications of transfer strategies.

In a project context, an uncertainty management perspective highlights the need to take a programme or corporate view of some aspects of project related uncertainty as part of managing the project infrastructure. Also an uncertainty management approach should facilitate integration of RM with project management earlier in the project life cycle than a threat orientated RM process. The need to explore and understand uncertainty (and avoid a largely pessimistic threat orientated perspective) is greatest in the earliest stages of a project's life cycle, that is, during conception when uncertainty is at its greatest. An uncertainty management perspective more naturally focuses attention on this stage of the project than threat orientated RM. Comprehensive uncertainty management should operate as an important extension of conventional strategy and project development, with the potential to influence strategy and project design on a routine basis, occasionally influencing very basic issues like the nature and choice of stakeholders and their objectives.

3.7   CONCLUSION

This chapter began with a brief discussion of definitions of risk adopted by various influential institutions. The definitions reviewed are by no means exhaustive of possible variations, but the sample in Table 3.1 is sufficient to illustrate the key issues in defining risk. A basic point is that terminology needs to be able to distinguish between probability in relation to an event or outcome, the uncertain effect on one or more performance attributes, and the source or cause of an effect on performance. Use of the word 'risk' to refer to any of these inter-changeably, is not helpful.

Definitions of risk are important because they drive the focus of attention in subsequent RM. A narrow definition of risk will imply a correspondingly narrow focus of attention in RM. A perspective that views risk solely in terms of adverse effects on the achievement of objectives, is not without value in seeking to increase the chances of meeting objectives, but it is unnecessarily limited. A focus on possible events, conditions, or circumstances which could effect levels of performance is a more useful perspective. This leads to a focus on the management of opportunities as well as threats, including the possibility of obtaining positive improvements in performance by creative management of apparent threats.

However, defining risk in terms of events, conditions, or circumstances, does not facilitate consideration of potential variability in performance that is driven by underlying ambiguity. Sources of ambiguity related to the quality of estimates, gaps in plans, the nature of objectives, and working relationships between different parties, can have major implications for performance, and they require careful management. To address uncertainty in both variability and ambiguity terms, we need to adopt an explicit focus on the management of uncertainty.

Uncertainty management implies exploring and understanding the origins of uncertainty before seeking to manage it, with no preconceptions about what is desirable or undesirable. Key concerns are understanding where and why uncertainty is important in a given organisational context, and where it is not. This is a significant change in emphasis compared with most established RM processes.

4

SOURCES OF UNCERTAINTY

4.1   INTRODUCTION

This chapter considers the broad scope and nature of sources of uncertainty facing the organisation. The approach taken is to consider sources of uncertainty from a variety of perspectives. The aim is to highlight the value of different perspectives that focus on different aspects of uncertainty and risk. Nonetheless the approach is necessarily selective, and the perspectives chosen are not the only ones that could be adopted. But taken together, these different perspectives highlight the wide scope of sources warranting attention, and the desirability of using one or more different perspectives, depending on the context and focus of a given risk management (RM) application. Five basic perspectives are adopted:

- a corporate strategy perspective,

- an asset management perspective,

- a people perspective,

- a project perspective,

- a systems perspective.

A further perspective, focusing on decision processes, is explored in Chapter 5. While presented separately, it is important to recognise that these perspectives are interdependent.

4.2   A CORPORATE STRATEGY PERSPECTIVE

Taking a corporate strategy perspective of RM involves the greatest challenge for uncertainty identification, not least because the factors capable of influencing performance are so numerous. To make any analysis of sources of uncertainty tractable at a corporate level requires sources to be broken down into broad categories or areas which taken together, completely cover the range of uncertainties facing the organisation. These categories then serve as prompt lists for identifying sources of uncertainty in more detail. The simplest kind of framework can be just a list of major categories such as the examples shown in Table 4.1.

Table 4.1 Simple Frameworks for Categorising Sources of Risk

Example 1 (OGC, 2002: p19) Strategic/commercial risks Economic/financial/market risks Legal, contractual and regulatory risks Organisational management/human-factors Political/societal factors Environmental factors/Acts of God (force majeure) Technical/operational/infrastructure risks
Example 2 (PricewaterhouseCoopers, 2004) External factors: economic and business; natural environment; political; social; technological. Internal factors: infrastructure; personnel; process; technology.

Such lists demonstrate the wide range of factors that might be identified, but offer limited guidance without additional, more detailed sub-categories. The logic and completeness of simple lists of this kind can also be questioned.

Some corporate perspective frameworks provide diagrammatic structure to add supporting logic for the categories of risk identified. An example of this kind is shown in Figure 4.1.

This diagrammatic framework offers a richer perspective of sources of uncertainty both in terms of the structure and scope of sources included. However, it is easy to question the completeness of the factors included here, and in some respects the positioning of factors.

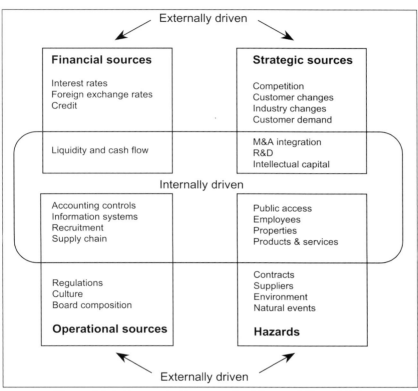

Figure 4.1 A Corporate Framework of Areas of Uncertainty (Adapted from the AIRMIC, ALARM, IRM Standard, 2002)

Other corporate perspective frameworks categorise sources of risk in hierarchical frameworks. For example Arthur Andersons Business Risk Model (reproduced in full in ICAEW, 1999) allocates business risks into three main categories of environment, process, and information for decision-making. Process uncertainties are divided into operations, empowerment, information processing technology, integrity, and financial. These categories are then further divided to facilitate a more detailed analysis. Another example is Ernst and Young's Risk Universe based on four first level categories of: operations, financial, strategic, and knowledge, followed by more detailed second and third level divisions of these categories into narrower (but still broad) areas of uncertainty (Motorshead and Godfrey, 2001).

Such hierarchical frameworks can vary significantly in the categories adopted at each level, and it can be difficult to make a compelling case for one structure over another. In practice organisations might choose to develop their own hierarchical frameworks, recognising particular features of their line of business. For example, Banks and Dunn (2003) structure their discussion of risks in financial institutions into 'operating' risks which have a direct and continuous impact on earnings, and 'balance sheet' risks which are discrete events which affect book value equity immediately and directly. The focus of their discussion is on the 'universe' of balance sheet risks categorised as shown in Table 4.2.

Table 4.2 'Balance Sheet' Risks (Banks and Dunn, 2003)

Market risk	– movements in the market value financial assets
Credit risk	– the inability or unwillingness of a counter party to pay on its financial obligations
Liquidity risk	– risk of loss due to a mismatch between cash inflows and outflows arising from an inability to sell or fund a position
Model risk	– use of inappropriate models and analytic tools to value financial assets
Suitability risk	– counterpart claims for financial injury due to lack of suitability of financial transactions provided
Legal risk	– risk of loss due to failures in legal documentation of financial transactions
Process risks	– risk of losses from failure of internal business and control processes due to: • failings in disaster recovery • slow recovery from temporary interruptions • availability of key personnel • front office errors • operational errors • software errors • weaknesses in authorisation procedures • inadequate collateral • violations of compliance regulations.

For financial institutions whose every day business involves trading in financial instruments, Table 4.2 offers a useful list of core risk factors that should be addressed on a corporate basis. For non financial organisations such factors should still be important, related as they are to the fundamentals of doing business with customers and suppliers. But how many of these would appear on a board's top ten list of risks?

Likely very few. The reason for this might be a presumption that such risks are recognised, understood, and adequately managed by the appropriate functional departments in the organisation. Uncertainty about whether this is the case or not should certainly be an item in the board's top ten list.

The list of factors in Table 4.2 is compelling as a list of key factors for financial institutions because they are related to the essential aspects of doing business. In particular, the list of process risks follows the chronological order in which business is done. A basic starting point for doing business is that the entire basic infrastructure of the institution has to be available ('ensure disaster recovery capability'), and working smoothly with a minimum of interruption ('rapid recovery from interruptions' and 'key personnel available'). After a transaction has been agreed to, it needs to be correctly uploaded into the organisation's computerised information system from which documentary evidence of the transaction is created and sent to the customer, records updated, and details fed into the organisation's financial, operational, and regulatory compliance controls systems (all remaining process risks addressed) (Banks and Dunn, 2003).

This suggests that any framework for identifying and structuring sources of uncertainty for organisations in general will be more effective if it is related to key features of core business processes, rather than to some arbitrary categorisation scheme. Indeed, the use of an arbitrary categorisation scheme, or even worse, simple brainstorming, to generate lists of risk sources, is likely to encourage an undesirable separation of risk identification (and therefore RM) from key decision making processes and the management of core operating procedures. Taking a corporate perspective in risk identification suggests using source frameworks that inform the process of formulating and planning strategy, and relate to the key features of core operating processes. Some such frameworks are already well-known in the strategic management literature, although some are more useful than others. These frameworks tend to relate to internal and external factors influencing performance. Examples of frameworks that focus on external factors are summarised in Table 4.3.

Table 4.3 External Factor Frameworks

PEST or PESTEL analysis of the business environment (political, economic, social, technological, environmental, and legal factors)
Ansoff's (1987) characterisation of environmental turbulence via six factors: changeability of the market environment, speed of change, intensity of competition, fertility of technology, discrimination by customers, pressures from governments and influence groups.
Supply chain analysis: nature of suppliers, distributors, and customers, and relationships with the organisation.
Competition analysis in terms of five forces: rivalry of competitors, power of buyers, power of suppliers, threat of entry, threat of substitute products (Porter, 1985).
Pros and cons of generic strategies: cost leadership, differentiation, market penetration, product development, market development, horizontal diversification, vertical integration, (see for example, Porter, 1985; Ansoff, 1987; Johnson and Scholes, 2002)

One approach is to employ a framework based on the key operations that contribute to the achievement of corporate objectives. For example an operations framework might focus on the uncertainty associated with:

Marketing: how products and services are positioned in relation to the competition, priced, advertised, and distributed;

Manufacturing: production processes, locations, utilisation of technology, key skills;

Finance: sources of funding, financial control systems, information for decision-making and reporting;

Research and development: level of investment, planning horizons, ability to develop new products, scope of activities;

Human-resources: recruitment, selection, reward systems, retention, appropriate mix of skills and experience;

Organisation infrastructure: co-ordination, control mechan-isms, information systems, disposition of power in the organisation, levels of cooperation.

A well-known refinement of this approach is the value chain framework developed by Porter (1985). This framework breaks an organisation's activities down into primary activities and linked support activities. The primary activities are: inbound logistics, operations, outbound logistics, marketing and sales, and service. These represent the activities of physically creating a product or service, transferring it to a buyer, and providing after-sales service. The support activities are: procurement, technology development, human resource management, and the firm's infrastructure. The scope of these activities is summarised in Table 4.4.

Table 4.4 Activities in the Value Chain (Porter, 1985)

Primary activities	
Inbound logistics	Receiving, storing and distributing internally the inputs of raw materials, components, information, additional resources for the production of products or services.
Operations	The production process of transforming inputs into finished goods and services.
Outbound logistics	The dispatch and distribution of finished goods and services to customers.
Marketing and sales	A product promotion and advertising, pricing, sales force activity.
Service	Installation, warranties training in private use, maintenance contracts, advice.
Support activities	
Procurement	The acquisition of any inputs used in the value chain.
Technology development	Research and development activity, product design, process improvements, use of information technology, development of skills and capabilities, knowledge acquisition.
Human resource management	Recruitment, training, development and rewarding of employees.
The firm's infrastructure	The structure of the organisation, planning, control systems, information systems, policies and procedures.

Analysis of the value chain can be used to identify cost drivers, cost structures, the potential for lower costs, and possibilities for (further) differentiating the firm's products and services. In carrying out this analysis it can be useful to subdivide the primary and support activities into their component parts, and to consider inter-relationships between activities. Often it is the effective management of inter-relationships between activities that can create core competences for organisation. These are particular competences and capabilities which enable an organisation to respond to threats and exploit commercial opportunities, preferably in distinctive ways which are appreciated by customers but not readily copied by rivals (Johnson and Scholes 2002). Eden and Ackerman (2000) argue that often the most important distinctive competencies are emergent patterns between component competences. They also argue that unless competences are considered as patterned or linked attributes of an organisation, then it is likely that strategy making will miss significant sources of effective strategic management. Recognising these distinctive competences, exploiting them, and protecting or strengthening them, is important from either a strategic management or RM perspective.

4.3   AN ASSET MANAGEMENT PERSPECTIVE

In common with any audit of resources for strategic planning purposes, an uncertainty identification framework based on different aspects of operations should also consider the resources employed in the different aspects of operations. This would include consideration of the types, amount, quality, and uniqueness of resources possessed by an organisation and otherwise available, together with methods of deployment in the organisation, utilisation of these resources, and the controls used to manage them.

In broad terms, the resources available to any organisation can be classed as either tangible or intangible. The tangible physical resources include: buildings, plant, financial assets, material stocks, people, operating systems, and intellectual property. Intangible resources include assets such as customer goodwill, reputation, corporate image, employee loyalty, the corporate culture, core competences and so on. Intangible assets are by definition less visible than tangible assets, difficult to value, and consequently potentially less well recognised and proactively managed than tangible assets.

The protection of an organisation's assets is a vital aspect of successfully operating and maintaining the organisation, and must be an important part of any RM effort. However, asset protection represents a limited, threat perspective on risk and uncertainty management. A threat perspective involves a focus on: 'how can we preserve and retain the use of the assets we have?' A wider, and managerial more useful perspective, involves opportunity management, with a focus on: 'how can we make the most effective and efficient use of existing assets?'; 'how can we improve the quality of these assets?'; and 'in what ways should we develop assets?' An opportunity perspective incorporates the desirability of asset protection, but involves a more proactive, decision support role for risk and uncertainty management. This is the perspective adopted in strategic analysis and strategy formulation.

Asset management in this wider, opportunity sense, means understanding the true value to the organisation of its assets. It also requires an awareness of what the assets of the organisation actually are, not just quantitatively and qualitatively in respect of obvious tangible assets, but also in respect of intangible assets. Without an understanding of what these assets are, and their relative importance to the organisation's survival and success (however measured), RM efforts run the risk of being inadequate in scope, let alone substance.

In general, the management of tangible assets, essentially the organisation's physical resources including finances, buildings, plant, material stocks, information systems, data, people, intellectual property, have all been the subject of detailed scrutiny ever since organisations began. Current best-practice techniques for effectively managing these assets are highly developed, and often very sophisticated, requiring the involvement of specialised and experienced professionals. In particular, effective asset protection requires specialised knowledge of the asset characteristics, its acquisition and deployment. To discuss even briefly, how these assets can be best used, how they can fail, and how they can be maintained, would serve little purpose here.

In recent years it has become increasingly difficult for firms to gain sustainable competitive advantage through the acquisition of tangible assets, and attention has turned to the opportunities that intangible assets may create. Intangible assets can often represent a major asset and competitive advantage for an organisation because they are difficult for competitors to imitate or acquire.

RM has an important role to play here in ensuring that recognising and protecting all important intangible assets is emphasised as much as the opportunities they may present. To illustrate the kinds of issues that can be involved, several key intangible assets that organisations cannot afford to be without are discussed briefly below.

Reputation

A particularly significant intangible asset is an organisation's reputation. Rayner (2003) defines reputation as: *'a collection of perceptions and beliefs, both past and present, which reside in the consciousness of an organisation's stakeholders – its customers, suppliers, business partners, employees, investors, analysts, communities, regulators, governments, pressure groups, non-government organisations, and the public at large.'*

As Rayner (2003: p2) points out, reputation is fundamentally about perception and beliefs, whether well-founded or not. Reputation is also potentially transient: *'although a good corporate reputation can take many long years to build, it can be destroyed in an instant through an ill-considered off the record remark, a lapse in personal behaviour, an ethical blunder in the supply chain, or an inadequate response to a crisis'*. Thirdly, reputation can be influenced by virtually anyone in the organisation or anyone in its supply chain. Rayner (2003) distinguishes seven drivers of reputation, with desirable components summarised in Table 4.5.

Table 4.5 Drivers of Reputation (Based on Rayner, 2003)

Financial performance and long-term investment value
- long-term shareholder value
- honest and transparent accounts
- directors accountable for the honesty and integrity of accounts
- international comparable accounting standards

Corporate governance and leadership
- compelling and clearly communicated vision and strategy
- leadership is responsible, of good integrity, and dynamic but not autocratic
- an effective board which is balanced in terms of adequately representing different stakeholders, and in terms of skills, experience and personalities
- directors' remuneration and incentives are appropriate
- relevant and effective board committees
- comprehensive and coherent risk management and internal control systems
- robust oversight of management
- full and transparent disclosure of corporate governance practices
- directors available and responsive to stakeholders
- management embraces a principles-based best-practice approach to corporate governance rather than mere compliance.

Regulatory compliance
- compliance with laws and regulations
- compliance with the spirit, not just the letter of the law.

Delivering customer promise
- quality and fair pricing
- live up to promises implicit in brands
- products and services reliably available
- responsive and flexible in dealing with customers' requirements and concerns
- innovation in line with evolving market needs
- act responsibly in supply chain and marketing practices
- awareness of any threats to reputation from the customer base

Workplace talent and culture
- fair pay and conditions
- employees valued, trusted and respected
- effective recruitment, training and development of employees
- the corporate culture protects and enhances reputation

Corporate social responsibility
- corporate social responsibility embedded in all strategy, decisions, and activities
- a clear tone set by top management on ethics, integrity, fairness, accountability and transparency

Communications in crisis management
- communications are honest, accurate, complete, transparent, prompt, and responsive to changing needs of stakeholders
- there is co-ordination and consistency across separate communications
- crisis plans developed and rehearsed, and effectively implemented

---

An important issue for managing reputation risk is recognising which stakeholder groups are most concerned with each of the seven drivers of reputation. Not all stakeholders will be equally concerned with each driver. This is a clear example of the point made in Chapter 3 about different stakeholders (parties) having different objectives and consequently, different perceptions of risk leading to different approaches to RM.

Satisfied Customers

It is self-evident that no business can be successful without satisfied customers. However, understanding the full implications of failure to deliver customer satisfaction can help to identify useful strategies for proactive management of customer satisfaction. Based on a survey of the literature, Connell (2003) identified five problems retailing organisations face as a direct result of a failure to offer good customer service and customer satisfaction.

1. Customer Defections

Customers are lost, perhaps permanently, with the loss of any potential for that customer to generate revenue. If the customer defects to a competitor, the organisation loses twice over. An important source of uncertainty arises in respect of an organisation's ability to identify when and why customers are lost. Cook (2002) suggests that most organisations lose significantly more than 30% of their customers before, or at the time of a repurchase decision, mainly through poor service.

2. Additional Costs of Replacing Customers

The cost of lost customers is compounded by the additional costs involved in marketing and generating sales from replacement customers. The return on investment for marketing expenditure on existing customers is often much higher than the return from a similar expenditure on prospective customers. It can cost five to ten times as much to generate business from new customers as it does to get more business from existing customers (Nash and Nash, 2001). The impact can be even more severe if the organisation is financially weak. Additional expenditure to replace customers may mean reduced funding of initiatives to boost levels of customer service leading to further customer losses.

3. Negative Word-of-Mouth Advertising

Potential customers are more likely to be persuaded to use, or avoid, a retailer based on the personal statements of people they trust. A report of a negative experience from friends or family can be enough to dissuade a customer from making a purchase from a specific retailer. One dissatisfied customer can tell a lot of people personally of their negative experience. The impact of this type of advertising can be particularly damaging to retailers because of their reliance on positive word-of-mouth advertising.

4. Failure to Maintain Competitive Advantage

In addition to having a negative effect on a retailer's business, offering poor customer service can also improve the position of a competitor's business. Offering good levels of customer service and customer satisfaction will help any organisation in retaining existing customers and preventing competitors from gaining market share (Cook, 2002).

5. *Inability to Offer Higher Prices*

A failure to offer good levels of customer service and satisfaction will reduce a firm's ability to increase profitability by raising prices for quality service.

Employees and the Corporate Culture

An organisation's employees, or its 'human capital' is perhaps the most significant intangible asset any organisation possesses. This human capital embraces the skills, experience and knowledge of employees, their degree of loyalty to the organisation, their level of motivation, their networks of professional relationships, as well as their knowledge and understanding of the way things are done which contribute to the corporate culture.

The term culture is a convenient umbrella term that encompasses the implicit beliefs, values, convictions, and associated 'ways we do things around here' that are taken for granted and which pervade all organisations. Usually, this culture is indirectly visible via physical manifestations such as routines, control systems, administrative structures, power structures, symbols, and company stories which make-up what Johnson (1992) has termed the cultural web. The usefulness of the concept of organisational culture is nicely summarised by Martin and Siehl (1990: p71):

> *'First, cultures offer an interpretation of an institution's history that members can use to decipher how they will be expected to behave in the future. Second, cultures can generate commitment to corporate values or management philosophy so that employees feel they are working for something they believe in. Third, cultures serve as organisational control mechanisms, informally approving or prohibiting some patterns of behaviour. Finally, there is the possibility, as yet unsupported by conclusive evidence, that some types of organisational cultures are associated with greater productivity and profitability.'*

Of course, however one defines 'organisational culture', there are likely to be many sub-cultures within an organisation associated with different formal or informal groups of employees, different levels, and/or different locations. Martin and Siehl (1990) argue that *(sub)-cultures can express conflicts and address needs for differentiation among organisational elements*. They explore the relationships that might exist between the dominant culture and three different types of sub-culture: enhancing, orthogonal, and counter-cultural sub-cultures. Appreciating the existence of these different sub-cultures, and their implications for the organisation as a whole, can be an important part of RM.

Deal and Kennedy (2000) argue persuasively that top management's enthusiasm for short-termist cost cutting through downsizing and re-engineering ('corporate lobotomy'), and outsourcing ('corporate amputation'), has failed to recognise the damage done to the human capital and corporate culture. Deal and Kennedy (2000: p106) argue that outsourcing produces cultural alienation:

> *'In the case of outsourced workers who return to a workplace on shortened hours, co-workers no longer want to hang out with them. They are afraid they may contract the 'disease' themselves and be shoe-horned out of their jobs. Outsourcing alienates both those who are outsourced and those who remain. This has a destructive effect on corporate culture.'*

Deal and Kennedy argue that downsizing has had equally unfortunate consequences, company loyalty has become obsolete and self-interest now dominates (Deal and Kennedy, 2000: p79):

> *'Trust was the first victim of the downsizing. As successive waves of downsizing swept over companies (and it did over most), this lack of trust turned into cynicism about the process as well as the integrity of senior management. When record pay packages were announced for the senior executives who were the architects of these upheavals, cynicism turned into outright hostility. Everything that management espoused was tainted.'*

In addition to this destruction of the basic commitment between employee and employer, Deal and Kennedy (2000: p85) point to the loss of key 'informal players' *whose presence and efforts glue a company together*. With this loss goes the loss of much business-specific knowledge and 'corporate memory'. Deal and Kennedy cite Challenger (1996) who describes corporate memory as *the collective business experiences, dramas, visions, successes and failures of real people who work for the company.* Challenger goes on to say that:

'(corporate memory) is the knowledge, nuances and intuition we bring to day-to-day decision-making. A little bit of this invaluable corporate memory disappears each time an individual is laid off. In the final analysis, cutting out the memory of an organisation may do more harm than good to the company's bottom line. If, after lay-offs are made, the company can no longer perform at the level it once did, customers will take their business elsewhere and the business will be left in worse condition than before the lay-offs.'

There is much to be said for taking a customer perspective on employees, and considering the five core problems resulting from a failure to offer good customer satisfaction noted in the previous section: defections, cost of replacement, word-of-mouth advertising, maintenance of competitive advantage, an inability to increase profitability. Badly treated employees can become 'ill-will ambassadors' for the organisation (Furnham, 2003). Failure to identify, and adequately nurture and reward good people can result in loss of important human assets. As with the organisation's customers, the cost of losing good employees can be far greater than the cost of finding and recruiting replacements. Good managers take pains to identify and nurture key employees, and to develop their staff. As Furnham (2003: p11) notes:

'Good managers take seriously the process of injecting new employees into their organisations. They explain the written and unwritten rules, and the taboos and unusual quirks of the company. They introduce new people to all those who will be important to doing their job well, regardless of their rank.'

4.4   A PEOPLE PERSPECTIVE

Virtually everything that goes on in organisations involves people, so a people perspective on uncertainty in organisations is an obvious choice of focus. However, the psychological, sociological and physiological aspects of human performance that could be considered as part of RM is vast. Recognising this, Fortune and Peters (1995) take a selective, illustrative approach which looks briefly at human factors on three levels: the organisation, the group or team, and the individual. Depending on the context of a RM application, a focus on one or more of these levels may be very appropriate. For example, both the group and individual levels may be very appropriate when considering the performance of the management team in a particular business unit. The discussion here takes a different approach by looking briefly at some basic drivers of human performance.

While employees and other agents are essential to the achieving of organisation performance, they also contribute to uncertainty about future performance. This uncertainty arises from several factors, including:

- uncertainty about the level of performance that will be achieved;

- the individual's level of motivation;

- the quality and reliability of work undertaken;

- the extent to which personal objectives are aligned with organisation objectives, and the scope for moral hazard where the individual is motivated to do things which are not in the best interests of the organisation;

- the actual abilities of the individual;

- the continued availability of the individual.

This list provides a useful starting point for managing risk and uncertainty associated not just with individuals who play a significant role in a given RM context, but also with sets of similar employees, teams, departments, business units, or external suppliers.

Building on the above list, there are many possible reasons why individuals (all organisational units) may fail to perform.

Task Perception

Individuals fail to realise the extent of their responsibilities. Instructions are misinterpreted. Inappropriate priorities are adopted, such as taking short cuts through safety rules to save time.

Capability and Experience

Individuals may lack education, training, or appropriate experience. They may be unable to learn from experience or adapt to the environment. Individuals may lack skills in analysis, planning, prioritising work, and be unable to work quickly. This may result in jumping to conclusions about the nature of a situation and inappropriate choice of actions. Furnham (2003: p241) has suggested that it seems particularly important for managers to learn skills in: listening, writing, speaking, providing feedback, assertiveness, and conducting meetings.

An individual may be ill-suited for the job they are in. This may be due to poor selection or poor promotion decisions. Following the Peter principle: *'in any hierarchy, individuals tend to rise to their levels of incompetence'*, an individual may have been promoted beyond their level of competence (Peter, 1985). Alternatively, and perhaps additionally, the nature of an incumbent's job may have changed due to changes in organisation, technology, or the working environment.

Individuals may be failing to perform because of inappropriate personality traits. For example, they may be obsessive, impulsive, impatient, lacking in self-confidence, afraid of failure etc (see Furnham, 2003 for an extensive discussion of psychological factors).

Mistakes

Individuals can make errors in the form of random slips, incorrect assessments of the situation, or failure to detect very unusual situations or rare events. Therefore individuals may not take appropriate actions. (Reason, 1990)

Motivation

Individuals may lack sufficient incentives to aspire to high levels of performance. They may also be pursuing personal objectives which are not aligned with organisational objectives. Individuals may be distracted by problems related to their personal lives such as: relationship issues, illness, addictions (gambling, smoking, alcohol, drugs) etc. Individuals may have become disaffected, lacking in involvement or commitment (Furnham, 2003: p249).

Work Environment

The individual may be failing because the task is overwhelming, impractical, inadequately defined, or it is impossible to achieve laid down performance objectives. Task overload impairs ability to monitor developments and formulate adequate reactive or proactive responses. Information overload makes it difficult to identify important pieces of information and easier to ignore or delay scrutiny. The working environment may be impairing performance due to inefficient or ineffective equipment and procedures.

Actions of Others

An individual's performance may be dependent on quality support from senior management, suppliers, service providers, colleagues etc. Other parties may fail to communicate information, and frustrate actions. Other parties may supply insufficient resources, incorrect or faulty materials or components.

Incompetence

In the world of management, Furnham (2003) argues that incompetence is more often the rule than the exception. Usually, this incompetence is associated with flaws in interpersonal skills and lack of ability. In a book entitled Managing by mistake, Courtis (1986) noted that: *basic and essential management principles are being flouted everywhere. Mistakes made by incompetent managers fall crudely into five categories:*

1. *Errors of omission (failure to act or communicate).*

2. *Errors of commission (doing things you ought not to have done).*

3. *Qualitative errors (doing the right thing inadequately or by the wrong method).*

4. *Errors of timing (doing the right thing too early or too late).*

5. *Credibility errors (doing the right thing, at the right time, but in such a way as to irritate everyone or discredit the action).* (Courtis, 1986: p ix)

Signs of managerial incompetence noted by Courtis (1986) include:

- tendency towards scapegoating culprits for personal errors;

- focusing on finding scapegoats to blame for problems rather than diagnosing the causes of failure;

- poor delegation – tasks rather than objectives are delegated, and accountability is blurred so as to make it impossible for subordinates to use their initiative;

- forgetting that their job is to take a longer view;

- belief in luck, rather than the value of forward planning or problem analysis to make your own luck;

- underestimating the role, importance, and intelligence of support staff;

- management by crisis rather than reason;

- failing to plan, monitor, and ask difficult questions.

Furnham (2003: p28) notes *'organisations do not create incompetence: they may foster it, even reward it; (but) its origins lie in the individuals: those high and low- flyers that end up being managers.'*

Principal – Agent Issues

Principal-agent relationships are an inherent part of any organised activity whether involving formal contracts, or informal agreements between two cooperating parties. Organisational hierarchies consist of a chain of principal-agent relationships between manager and subordinate. Principal-agent relationships also arise between customers and suppliers of products or services, whether inside the same organisation or spanning two or more organisations. The principal-agent relationship, is prone to three fundamental problems: adverse selection; moral hazard; and risk allocation (Eisenhardt, 1989).

Adverse selection refers to misrepresentation of ability by the agent and the principal's difficulty in selecting an agent with appropriate skills. The agent may claim to have certain skills or abilities when hired, but the principal cannot completely verify these skills or abilities either at the time of hiring or while the agent is working. A 'selection' problem can also arise where a contractor misrepresents the work that will be done or the likely final price. Once a contractor has been hired, it may be difficult for the client to ensure that costs are contained and work promised is what is actually delivered.

Moral hazard refers to an agent's failure to put forth the contracted effort. This can be of greatest concern to the principal when it is particularly difficult or expensive for the principal to verify that an agent is behaving appropriately, as when task specifications are inadequate or the principal lacks knowledge of the delegated tasks.

Risk allocation concerns the manner in which responsibility for project-related issues (sources and responses) is allocated between principal and agent. Risk allocation is very important because it can strongly influence the motivation of principal and agent, and the extent to which uncertainty is assessed and managed. Insofar as principal and agent perceive risks differently, and have different abilities and motivations to manage uncertainty, then their approach to risk management will be different. In particular, either party is likely to try to manage uncertainty primarily for their own benefit, perhaps to the disadvantage of the other party. In particular, there can be significant issues in allocating risk in a hierarchical structure or between different units in the same organisation. Chapman and Ward (2002: chap. 6) explores 'internal contracts' to address such issues.

The uncertainties arising from problems of adverse selection, moral hazard, and risk allocation are more likely to arise where principal and agent are separate organizations, as in most client-contractor relationships. Where principal and agent belong to the same organization it might be expected that such problems would be less likely to arise, to the extent that the parties can share information, responsibilities and objectives more readily. Unfortunately, this is not always the case. Much depends on the level of trust between parties, their motives, and the incentives operating.

The relationships between the various parties involved in an undertaking is another major source of ambiguity and uncertainty. For example, the involvement of multiple parties in a project introduces uncertainty arising from ambiguity in respect of:

- specification of responsibilities;
- perceptions of roles and responsibilities;
- communication across interfaces;
- the capability of parties;
- formal contractual conditions and their effects;
- informal understandings on top of, or instead of, formal contracts;
- mechanisms for coordination and control. (Ward, 1999)

In particular, ambiguity about roles and responsibilities for bearing and managing project related uncertainty can be a crucial issue.

4.5   A PROJECT PERSPECTIVE

Projects are a major part of all organisational activity, and an ability to pursue and effectively manage projects can be an important core competence for any organisation. In some ways, projects should be easier to manage than ongoing operations of a business unit or organisation, because the scope and duration of the task is more constrained. On the other hand, projects can be difficult to manage because of their novelty, limited resources and their temporary nature.

The need to manage uncertainty is inherent in most projects which require formal project management, using 'uncertainty' in the plain English 'lack of certainty' sense. Consider the following illustrative definition of a project:

an endeavour in which human, material and financial resources are organised in a novel way, to undertake a unique scope of work of given specification, within constraints of cost and time, so as to achieve unitary, beneficial change, through the delivery of quantified and qualitative objectives. (Turner, 1992)

This definition highlights the change-inducing nature of projects, the need to organise a variety of resources under significant constraints, and the central role of objectives in project definition. It also suggests inherent uncertainty related to novel organisation and a unique scope of work, which requires attention as a central part of effective project management.

Much good project management practice can be thought of as effective uncertainty management. For example, good practice in planning, coordination, setting milestones, and change control procedures, seeks to manage uncertainty directly. However, most texts on project management do not consider the way uncertainty management should be integrated with project management more generally, in terms of a wide view of what a coordinated approach to proactive and reactive uncertainty management can achieve.

The scope for uncertainty in any project is considerable, and most project management activities are concerned with managing uncertainty from the earliest stages of the project life cycle (PLC), clarifying what can be done, deciding what is to be done, and ensuring that it gets done. Uncertainty is in part about 'variability' in relation to performance measures like cost, duration, or 'quality'. It is also about 'ambiguity' associated with lack of clarity because of the behaviour of relevant project players, lack of data, lack of detail, lack of structure to consider issues, working and framing assumptions being used to consider the issues, known and unknown sources of bias, and ignorance about how much effort it is worth expending to clarify the situation.

Many important sources of uncertainty are associated with the fundamental management processes that make up the PLC. A fair number of sources are implicitly acknowledged in lists of project management 'key success factors'. Potential sources typically identified in this way are listed in Table 4.6 against the various stages of the PLC.

In major projects, careful attention to formal RM is usually motivated by the large scale use of new and untried technology, where there are likely to be significant threats to achieving objectives. A threat perspective encourages a focus on these initial motivating factors. However, key performance issues are often unrelated to these motivating factors, but rather are related to sources of ambiguity introduced by the existence of multiple parties and the project management infrastructure. Such issues need to be addressed very early in the project and throughout the project life cycle, and should be informed by a broad appreciation of the underlying 'root' uncertainties. Chapman and Ward (2003) offer a six Ws framework for this purpose based on the following six questions about the project:

1. Who are the parties ultimately involved?
2. What do the parties want to achieve?
3. What is it that each party is interested in?
4. Which way (how) is each party's work to be done?
5. What resources are required?
6. When does it have to be done?

Understanding the uncertainty associated with each of these basic questions, and the implications of interactions between them, is fundamental to effective identification and management of both threats and opportunities. Use of the six Ws framework from the earliest stages of the PLC could usefully inform development of project design and logistics by clarifying key sources of uncertainty. Stakeholder expectations associated with a conceive stage which is not

Table 4.6 Typical Uncertainty Management Issues in each Stage of the PLC (Chapman and Ward, 2003; Copyright John Wiley & Sons Ltd., used with permission.)

Stages of the PLC	Uncertainty management issues
Conceive the product	Level of definition Definition of appropriate performance objectives Managing stakeholder expectations
Design the product strategically	Novelty of design and technology Determining 'fixed' points in the design Control of changes
Plan the execution strategically	Identifying and allowing for regulatory constraints Concurrency of activities required Capturing dependency relationships Errors and omissions
Allocate resources tactically	Adequate accuracy of resource estimates Estimating resources required Defining responsibilities (number and scope of contracts) Defining contractual terms and conditions Selection of capable participants (tendering procedures and bid selection)
Execute production	Exercising adequate coordination and control Determining the level and scope of control systems Ensuring effective communication between participants Provision of appropriate organizational arrangements Ensuring effective leadership Ensuring continuity in personnel and responsibilities Responding effectively to sources which are realized
Deliver the product	Adequate testing Adequate training Managing stakeholder expectations Obtaining licences to operate
Review the process	Capturing corporate knowledge Learning key lessons Understanding what success means
Support the product	Provision of appropriate organization arrangements Identifying extent of liabilities Managing stakeholder expectations

subjected to formal risk management until the end of the plan stage can be a major issue, as can performance objectives in terms of relative priorities.

A common source of project risk inefficiency is a failure to carry out steps in the design and plan stages thoroughly enough. Thus a project proceeds through to execution with insufficiently well-defined specifications for production. During execution this gives rise to difficulties necessitating additional design development and production planning, and consequently adverse effects on the performance criteria of cost, time and quality. Related risk inefficiency associated with 'premature definition' is also difficult to avoid entirely, except on very routine, repeated projects. The problem is most acute in novel, one-off projects involving new technology. The basis of both problems is that it is extremely difficult to specify in advance how every part of the execution and termination phase will take place; neither is it cost effective to seek to do so. In any case, some uncertainty about operating conditions and related factors outside the control of project management will always remain. Inevitably, judgments have to be made about the degree of detail and accuracy practicable in the design and plan stages. However, these judgments should be supported and informed by appropriate risk analysis that is undertaken no later than the end of the plan stage.

The allocate stage is a significant task involving decisions about project organization, identification of appropriate agents, and allocation of tasks between them. As noted in the previous section, the introduction of an agent is prone to the three problems of adverse selection, moral hazard, and risk allocation. Even if client and agents all work for the same organization, the problems presented by these uncertainties can be substantial. When agents are different organizations, these problems can be particularly challenging.

During the execute stage, the essential process issue is the adequacy of coordination and control procedures. Thus coordination and control ought to include risk management practices as 'good project management practices' which amount to:

- milestone management;

- adequate monitoring of activities likely to go wrong;

- ensuring realistic, honest reporting of progress;

- reporting problems and revised assessments of future issues.

A common source of risk inefficiency in the execution phase is the introduction of design changes. Such design changes can lead to disruption of schedules and resourcing, and affect cost, time and quality measures of performance directly. A potentially serious concern is that changes are introduced without a full appreciation of the knock-on consequences. Apart from direct consequences, indirect consequences can occur. For example, changes may induce an extension of schedules, allowing contractors to escape the adverse consequences of delays in works unaffected by the change. Changes may have wider technical implications than first thought, leading to subsequent disputes between client and contractor about liability for costs and consequential delays (Williams *et al,* 1995a,b; Cooper, 1980). Standard project management practice should establish product change control procedures which set up criteria for allowable changes and provide for adequate coordination, communication and documentation of changes.

Looking forward to the deliver and support stages, and developing appropriate responses for key sources of uncertainty while still in the plan stage, can reduce or eliminate potential later problems at relatively low cost. The key here is identifying which issues need this attention in the plan stage, and which do not.

4.6   A SYSTEMS PERSPECTIVE

A systems perspective on uncertainty and risk is useful for considering systemic features of the organisation. This is not so much about taking in the 'big picture' for strategy formulation and assessment purposes. It is about appreciating the organisation as a coherent and effective system with properties which are distinct from those of its component parts. It is about seeing the wood rather than the trees in organisation process terms, and appreciating the cumulative, combined effects of participants, policies, procedures, directives and initiatives on the day-to-day operations of the organisation. Viewing an organisation as a system that needs to operate successfully in a wider environment leads to the identification of seven basic problems which all organisations need to address (Georgopoulous, 1973):

1. Adaptation

Organisations need an ability to adapt to and effectively interface with the external environment. This includes an ability to respond to changes, obtain resources, maintain useful relationships with stakeholder groups and a favourable reputation, and influence the environment to the benefit of the organisation and its members.

2. Resource Deployment

Organisations need an ability to deploy and allocate resources effectively. This includes appropriate distribution of authority, rewards and information, and appropriate allocation of tasks to organisational units and personnel.

3. Co-ordination

Organisations need an ability to articulate and co-ordinate in time and space the diverse activities necessary to achieve organisational objectives.

4. Self Integration

Self integration involves all necessary activities to secured the co-operation and compliance of organisational participants, the development of common organisational values and shared norms, attitudes and mutual understandings.

5. Tension Management

Organisations need an ability to manage and control organisational tensions and conflicts between interacting groups.

6. Productivity

Organisations need an ability to attain high levels of output performance. This involves maximising efficient and reliable performance in all organisational units.

7. Preservation of Identity and Integrity

Organisations need an ability to preserve the organisation's identity and integrity as a distinct and unified problem-solving system. This includes an ability to maintain the organisation's basic character and viability in the face of potential disruptions and threats to the survival and well-being of the organisation.

The above categorisation of an organisation's problems might be regarded as somewhat conceptual, but it has the advantage of being comprehensive and applicable to any organisation or part of an organisation (subsystem). It also offers a useful framework for objectives setting which extends well beyond the scope of most objective setting frameworks, even variants of Kaplan and Norton's (1992, 1993, 1996) balanced scorecard. The scorecard is conventionally constructed using four groups of measures, which represent shareholder interests arising from an external customer perspective and internal business processes, both of which are influenced by a company's ability to learn and improve (Kaplan and Norton, 1992). It allows managers to look at the business from four different perspectives by requiring answers to the following questions:

- how do customers see us? (customer perspective);

- what must we excel at? (internal business process perspective);

- can we continue to improve and create value? (learning and development perspective);

- how do we look to shareholders? (financial perspective).

The balanced scorecard management process is a continuous cyclic process. Its task is not directly concerned with the mission of the organisation, but rather with internal processes and external outcomes. The system's control is based on performance metrics that are tracked continuously over time to look for trends, best and worst practices, and areas for improvement. The main concern of the balanced scorecard is not individual performance, but collective organisational performance.

The broader, 'balanced' scope of performance criteria addressed is part of the appeal of the balanced scorecard. It is also less complex in terms of the groups of measures employed than for a performance assessment scheme based on the seven system's needs. However, from a RM perspective, a system's needs perspective offers a powerful framework for focusing management attention on fundamental processes and abilities that underpin successful organisational performance.

System Weaknesses

In considering what makes organisation's effective, another fruitful approach is to consider why organisations fail, or somewhat more generally, what causes managed systems to fail. Following this approach, much effort has gone into understanding the causes of major accidents or disasters associated with managed systems. Such events usually demand and receive close scrutiny to answer the question - how did this happen; to discover who was responsible; and to identify actions which will reduce the chances of such events occurring again. However, the findings of these investigations usually provide important lessons for management in general because *'some disasters are caused by inadequacies of management, or by poor or unprofessional behaviour, whereas other disastrous events arise as by-products of the normal functioning of larger managerial and technical systems'* (Turner, 1994: p215).

Understanding how disastrous events arise can help not merely to avoid or reduce the chances of similar major failures in the future, but also to highlight a whole range of factors that either might contribute to 'near-misses', or, more likely, operate to surreptitiously reduce system performance. No organisation is perfect, but an understanding of the causes of major failures can throw a strong light on areas of system weakness where most organisations could improve performance. Numerous case-studies of managed systems indicate that major accidents (systems failures), usually arise from the *'unforeseen and usually unforeseeable concatenation of several diverse events (or conditions), each one necessary but singly insufficient'* (Reason, 1990: p197). It is as if major accidents have a large number of preconditions in the form of a multiplicity of minor events, misperceptions, misunderstandings and miscommunications which accumulate unnoticed over a lengthy incubation period. Reason (1990: p197) has likened this build-up of latent causal factors to the build-up of resident pathogens in the human body. Turner (1994) has argued that these preconditions, or 'pathogens', *'stay in place in the organisation or in managerial practice, ready to contribute to major failure unless something happens to neutralise them by bringing them out into the open. Until the point at which they combine and react in undesirable ways, the misconceptions about the world which such 'pathogens' embody merely provide elements which are available to contribute to a disaster. They constitute an accident waiting to happen. If they are not uncovered, the preconditions are brought together by some trigger event which sets off a disaster.'* (Turner, 1990: p216)

This suggests that management needs to watch for signs that preconditions for system failure are building up. Turner (1994) identifies the following signs:

- toleration of gaps in important information;

- failures to reveal information;

- information being available only to members of the organisation who do not understand its significance;

- perennial problems of communication between different (specialist) departments;

- rigid hierarchies that inhibit the flow of information;

- multiple groupings attempting to deal with complex, ill-defined, and prolonged tasks;

- shifting goals, roles, and administrative arrangements;

- out of date regulations;

- professionals who are preoccupied because of pressure of work or for other reasons.

Turner (1994: p217) further argues that *'one of the most dangerous kinds of inadequate management, and one with the greatest potential for disaster, is a situation where senior management have a blinkered, unrealistic view of their organisation, its operations, its environment and its vulnerabilities, and use their authority to reinforce this closed view of the world. This condition, which has been called 'groupthink' (Janis, 1982), is particularly dangerous because such a management not only has power to influence events, but is also in a position to appoint staff to reflect its own prejudices and to overrule objections, warnings or complaints originating from those outside the organisation who are not under their control.'*

Additionally, prior to major accidents, managers are typically found to have been working with incomplete information, poor communications, or with complacent work practices. In addressing such organisational weaknesses, it is important not to over-react. As Turner (1994: p217) notes: *'poor or incomplete information conditions are not removed merely by communicating everything, because this just sets up a bewildering barrage of noise. Lax regulations can be tightened up, but over-rigid, rule-bound management is inflexible and may also be potentially dangerous.'* Whatever the system, it should be efficient and cost-effective. Inevitably, trade-offs have to be made between the cost and complexity of a system and the reliability and effectiveness of the system. Some of the key trade-off issues are most readily highlighted by considering systems in high reliability organisations where high levels of reliable and safe operation are required in very complex and risky technological systems. In such organisations, trade-offs are necessary because of mutually incompatible demands on a system between:

- the need for quick decisions but also a need for accurate decisions (Halpern, 1989);

- the desire for decision making to be informed by large amounts of information and the need to avoid information overload;

- the desirability of loosely coupled systems to avoid the rapid transmission of failure from one part of the organisation's operations to another, and the desirability of tightly co-ordinated groupings to improve reliability (Weick, 1976);

- the need for a well defined hierarchy to deal with technological complexity and the need to improve people at the lower levels of the organisation. (Turner, 1994)

Such trade-offs are not easy to manage. Managing the first two trade-off problems is discussed briefly in Chapter 5. There is some evidence to suggest that effective organisations handle the third dilemma by establishing a managerial unit with the sole task of managing and overseeing dependencies in a system (Roberts and Gargano, 1989), or by the use of active co-ordinators to link specialists for effective action (Lawrence and Lorsch, 1967). Such concern for inter-dependencies resonates strongly with possible roles for a corporate risk manager (see Chapter 9).

In respects of the fourth dilemma, it appears that effective complex organisations handle this problem by overlaying and modifying a basic hierarchical structure with flexible arrangements for communication and co-ordination (Rochlin, 1989). These flexible arrangements are facilitated by the availability of plenty of support staff provided with continuous training and updating.

The Problem of Fine-Tuning

The continuing managerial quest for increased efficiency and effectiveness makes investment in RM activities, such as those just mentioned, problematic. An important question is how much resource should be expended on monitoring and control of systems, or in designing systems to operate at very high levels of reliability. This issue is the focus of one particular study of the 1986 Challenger space shuttle disaster by Starbuck and Milliken (1988) entitled *'Challenger: fine-tuning the odds until something breaks'*. Drawing on testimony before the Presidential Commission and reports in newspapers and magazines, Starbuck and Milliken examine the decision making behaviour of engineers and managers on the project and the progression of their beliefs about the shuttle's reliability. Starbuck and Milliken's analysis has some useful lessons for the reliability management of all kinds of socio-technical systems, particularly those involving high complexity and new technology. Starbuck and Milliken suggest that *'both repeated successes and gradual acclimatisation alter decision makers' beliefs about probabilities of future success, and thereby, they may strongly influence decisions concerning high risk technologies'*.

Few people would argue with the idea that if failure is encountered, estimates of the probability of future success might be revised downwards or upwards depending upon whether deficiencies can be identified and corrected. In respect of success, participants in a socio-technical system might readily adopt the view that previous success makes subsequent success appear more likely. Previous success suggests competence and experience provides opportunities for learning to improve. For example, experience may allow operators to make fewer mistakes or make incremental improvements in equipment, procedures or personnel. Additionally, experience may provide more information upon which to update estimates of probabilities of future success. Repeated success also makes for greater efficiency as procedures can become more formalised and routine. In particular, repeated successes can motivate engineers and managers to 'fine tune' systems to render them less redundant, more efficient, cheaper, or more profitable.

The intention is that fine-tuning should improve performance without making future success less likely. However, Starbuck and Milliken suggest a number of conditions under which fine-tuning actually might make subsequent failure very likely. An example of fine-tuning is the incremental reduction of safety margins. As successful experience mounts, safety margins may look more and more unnecessary and therefore reducible. The rationale is: 'we can reduce margins a bit because we got away with it last time'. Any tendency on the part of managers to pare safety margins may be increased where other parties, engineers perhaps, are perceived to emphasise safety and reliability and managers are expected to pursue cost reduction and capacity utilisation. *'Because managers expect engineers to err on the side of safety, they anticipate that no real risk will ensue from incremental cost reductions or incremental capacity expansions. And engineers, expecting managers to trim costs and to push capacity to the limit, compensate by making safety factors even larger'* (Starbuck and Milliken, 1988).

The concern is that following a series of successes, managers will continue fine-tuning of safety margins until these margins become inadequate and something 'breaks'. This issue has been prominent in enquiries in the UK following, for example, rail disasters or alleged cases of negligence on the part of over-worked junior hospital doctors. Other situations where fine-tuning might involve reducing safety margins and failure could be disastrous come easily to mind. However, the wider relevance of excessive fine-tuning is apparent if we think in terms of contingencies, or slack (Bourgeois, 1981), rather than safety margins. A contingency represents a resource or capability that is intended to help managers cope with uncertainty. Back-up systems, safety margins, spare capacity, long lead times, a third shift capability, additions to cost and time budgets, and financial reserves all represent organisational contingencies or slack. Any of these may be subject to incremental reduction by management as successes accumulate over time. The same general concerns apply to contingencies or slack as to safety margins.

Fine-tuning of contingencies is even more likely if (a) contingencies are visible, (b) the rationale for their particular size or nature is unclear (or unconvincing), and (c) their impact on success criteria is considered significant. For example, high manning levels capable of dealing with peak workloads, or contingent cost allowances in a competitive bid may involve additional costs which management is not willing to carry. If conditions like (a) – (c) apply, those concerned to retain adequate slack may seek to make them less visible, or overstate the case for contingency allowances. Either way this can result in fine-tuning which amounts to real-life experimentation in the face of uncertainty and consequently an increased chance of future failure.

A further factor that can lead to fine-tuning until something breaks is the illusion of control. Repeated success naturally tends to increase confidence in managerial ability, existing procedures and technology. Managers assume performance is essentially under their control and so attribute success to themselves rather than to good luck. For example, fund managers can be prone to this belief, or so say financial market theorists. Following continued success, especially with new or risky technology, managers may become complacent and overconfident about their chances of future success. It may be increasingly assumed that existing procedures are adequate to flag developing problems (or opportunities) when in fact they are not. Future risks are underestimated, and (excessive) fine-tuning is encouraged.

A genuine difficulty arises with socio-technical systems that are complex and/or involve new technology. Determining what contingencies (such as safety margins) are actually appropriate may be problematic because a full understanding of how such systems will behave is difficult if not impossible to obtain. This increases the likelihood of conditions (a)- (c) above, inappropriate fine-tuning and a greater chance of future failure.

Choices about fine-tuning very often involve making trade-offs between performance criteria like time, cost and quality. Unfortunately management often lacks the means to make such tradeoffs in a rational or consistent way. Excessive and potentially disastrous fine-tuning may be prevented by ensuring that there are clear reasons for maintaining slack at particular levels. This implies that sources of slack need to identified, levels of slack estimated, any rationale for its existence laid bare, and the impact of this slack on performance assessed.

4.7   CONCLUSION

A very large number of factors can affect the performance of an organisation. Some can be influenced directly by the organisation's management but many cannot. Understanding the nature of these factors and the way they influence performance, let alone managing them, is a major task. This task is particularly difficult because:

- factors influencing performance are numerous;

- there is uncertainty about the nature of factors and their potential effect on performance;

- these factors are usually inter-related, often in complex and uncertain ways;

- these factors, their inter-relationships, and their effects on performance, are constantly changing;

- typically, there is limited time and resources to understand and analyse the relative significance of different factors.

This chapter has considered the sources of uncertainty facing organisations from a number of different perspectives. Each of these perspectives is useful in its own right, but taken together they facilitate a deeper insight into sources of uncertainty that warrant management attention. It is tempting to relate the different perspectives to different levels of management: top management takes the corporate strategy perspective, marketing takes the customer perspective, human resources takes the people perspective, project managers take the project perspective, and operations management takes the systems perspective. However, this would be a gross over-simplification because each perspective discussed here involves sources of uncertainty that pervade all aspects of an organisation. Managers at all levels could usefully consider all perspectives.

A basic aspect of RM is seeking to understand the nature of factors that can have a significant, but uncertain effect on organisation performance. This implies making a comprehensive effort to identify sources of uncertainty, some attempt to distinguish significant sources from insignificant ones, and a dynamic identification process that involves continuous review of operations and the organisation's environment to ensure an up-to-date appreciation.

The challenge is to devise efficient and effective processes for identifying key sources of uncertainty that make intelligent use of different perspectives in different contexts. Relying on simple brainstorming techniques to identify broad areas of risk is haphazard at best.

A fundamental problem for management is how much detail to go into at different levels in the hierarchy. Paradoxically, the higher one goes in the organisation hierarchy, the greater the need to take a systemic and strategic perspective involving a wider range of factors, but the less the ability or inclination of management to go into 'details'. But very often, 'the devil is in the detail', particularly if the detail actually concerns fundamental processes and behaviours that everything depends on.

5

DECISION PROCESSES

5.1   INTRODUCTION

This chapter focuses on the quality of decision making processes and the scope for embedding risk management (RM) in decisions. An understanding of the nature of decision processes and associated sources of uncertainty is important because this can help to motivate RM efforts, and guide the focus of RM efforts, ultimately making RM more efficient and effective.

Decision-making is a fundamental process in organisations and no activity, including RM, is possible without decision-making. In Chapter 1 it was suggested that RM will be most effective when it is 'integrated' or 'embedded' into all aspects of organisational decision making and individual decisions, particularly important ones. One way to achieve this is to consider how RM might be used within individual decision processes to help address the subject matter of the decision. To understand the potential roles that RM might play it is necessary to examine the components of a decision process, to understand where uncertainty can arise, and what the implications of this uncertainty can be for the decision process.

However, RM also has a potential role in managing the decision process itself. This second role is concerned with enhancing the quality of the process, partly by adopting good practice, but also by highlighting and minimising bad practice. This implies considering how decision-making is supported and organised, the role that participants play in any particular decision process, and how their motivation and attitude to uncertainty can drive decision processes.

Consistently making decisions which have successful outcomes is extremely difficult, some might say impossible. The fact that a previous decision had a good outcome does not of itself help much in making the next decision, particularly if we just got lucky and events just happened to unfold in our favour. What does help is an understanding of what makes a good decision process. We can never be sure our decisions will turn out for the best, but we can increase the odds in our favour and reduce the chances of 'post-decision regret' by endeavouring to follow a high quality decision process.

5.2 A BASIC DECISION PROCESS FRAMEWORK

To facilitate further discussion it is useful to consider the stages involved in any decision process as set out in Table 5.1. This simple characterisation implies that decisions arise from a monitoring of the environment and current activities for issues that require resolution. These issues may be problems, perceived threats, or possible opportunities, or merely the need to decide on a future course of action. The next stage, 'scope the decision', is necessary in order to put boundaries on the factors relevant to the decision. Subsequent stages involve identifying relevant performance criteria which will be used to select a preferred course of action, identifying possible courses of action, evaluating and comparing them on the chosen performance criteria, and selecting the most preferred alternative.

The final two stages, 'implement the chosen alternative' and 'monitor and review performance', might be regarded as outside the decision process. However, if the concern is issue resolution then it is important to recognise these two steps and consider them in earlier stages of the decision process.

Table 5.1 Stages in the Decision Process (Chapman and Ward, 2002)

Monitoring the environment and current activities
Issue recognition
Scope the decision
Determine performance criteria
Identify alternative courses of action
Assess the outcomes of courses of action
Compare outcomes and choose a course of action
Implement the chosen alternative
Monitor and review performance

Most decision processes are not adequately described in terms of this simple sequence of separate stages. In any context, the distinction between separate stages becomes blurred by simultaneously working on more than one stage at a time, and by iterative loops between various stages to incorporate revised perceptions and additional information. For example, the determination of performance criteria may be merged with the identification of alternative courses of action, or their evaluation, because views about what performance criteria are relevant are initially ill-defined, and need to be developed in the light of what alternatives are identified. However, Table 5.1 is a useful portrayal of what is involved in outline.

A high quality decision process would involve careful attention to each of the decision stages in Table 5.1. Specifically, it would involve:

- appropriate scoping of decision area and participants;

- all relevant performance criteria identified, and relative priorities and trade-offs identified;

- a wide range of possible alternative courses of action identified;

- careful weighing of both positive and negative consequences of each alternative, assumptions tested, and implications of uncertainty fully taken into account;

- plans for implementation made, including contingency plans.

Unfortunately achieving a high quality decision process can be very difficult for several reasons, including:

- the decision is complicated by interactions and interdependencies with other decision situations;

- performance criteria are multiple, conflicting, and some are difficult to quantify;

- it is impossible to examine a wide range of alternatives because of ignorance of alternatives or because their consequences are difficult to assess;

- there is insufficient time for a careful search for alternatives and full evaluation of those identified;

- there are limited resources available for gathering information, undertaking analysis, and deliberating.

Such difficulties and constraints on decision-making are a fact of life. One implication is that in practice all decisions, particularly significant ones, must involve a higher level 'meta decision' about how much effort to invest in a given decision. Deliberations here need to consider how far to simplify matters by making assumptions or introducing constraints to narrow degrees of freedom, who to involve (or not), what decision support is available and how this can be best deployed, and how much effort to put into each stage of the decision process. For minor decisions such deliberations are often intuitive and quickly completed informally using judgement and experience. For major, one-off decisions or significant, often repeated decisions, such deliberations can be very important and may warrant some degree of formalisation. In the case of often repeated decisions, organisations typically develop carefully designed decision routines, computerised decision support, and information systems to facilitate rapid, efficient decision-making. For example, Chapman and Ward (2002: Chap. 3) describe the design of repeatable processes to facilitate competitive bidding decisions for a contracting organisation. Major one-off or novel decisions such as significant investment decisions, may warrant careful consideration of all stages in the decision process, but with a deliberate iterative element to allow reconsideration of earlier decision stages if analysis suggests this will be useful.

For decisions that are important, and where time and other resources permit, decision makers may use formal decision support processes incorporating explicit, documented models to assist with various stages in the decision process. Such models can include cognitive mapping or influence diagramming to clarify issues and scope decisions, multiple criteria decision analysis to determine performance criteria and associated trade-offs, creative nominal group techniques to assist in the identification of alternative courses of action, and investment appraisal techniques, decision analysis, and risk analysis to estimate and evaluate outcomes from alternative courses of action. 'Decision support' need not imply formal computer based information system support, though it often does. The key is formal models and associated analysis and synthesis to help make decisions more efficiently and effectively, without attempting to exclude any relevant decision maker input and associated uncertainty (Chapman and Ward, 2002).

5.3 UNCERTAINTY IN THE DECISION PROCESS

The scope for uncertainty in any managerial decision situation is considerable. Much of this uncertainty is associated with the information used in each stage of the decision process. In this respect, suppliers of such information often have a significant influence on the quality of the decision process. For example, cost estimators can fundamentally drive choices by the way they select and interpret data to formulate estimates (Gilovich et al 2002; Morgan and Herion, 1990). The extent of this influence can be substantially underestimated and very difficult to assess.

As Table 5.2 shows, each stage in the decision process presents sources of uncertainty that may or may not be recognised and managed. Failure to deal with these sources can lead to poor-quality decision making. Clearly, the more significant the decision, the more important it becomes to address sources of uncertainty associated with each decision stage.

Table 5.2 Sources of Uncertainty in the Decision Process
(Chapman and Ward, 2002, Chap. 1; Copyright John Wiley & Sons Ltd., used with Permission)

Stage in the decision process	Uncertainty about .....
Monitoring the environment and current activities	Completeness, veracity, accuracy of information received, meaning of information, interpretation of implications.
Issue recognition	Significance of issues, urgency, need for action.
Scope the decision	Appropriate frame of reference , scope of relevant organisation activities, who is involved, who should be involved, extent of separation from other decision issues.
Determine performance criteria	Relevant performance criteria, whose criteria, appropriate metrics, appropriate priorities and tradeoffs between different criteria.
Identify alternative courses of action	Nature of alternatives available (scope, timing and logistics involved), what is possible, level of detail required, time available to identify alternatives.

Stage in the decision process	Uncertainty about .....
Assess the outcomes of courses of action	Consequences, nature of influencing factors, size of influencing factors, effects and interactions between influencing factors (variability and timing), nature and significance of assumptions made.
Compare outcomes and choose a course of action	How to weigh and compare predicted outcomes.
Implement the chosen alternative	How alternatives will work in practice.
Monitor and review performance	What to monitor, how often to monitor, when to take further action.

The first stage in the decision process involves continuous monitoring of the environment and current operations in the organisation. At some point issue recognition occurs, when those with sufficient influence realise there is a need to make one or more decisions to address an emergent issue. However, uncertainty associated with ambiguity about the completeness, veracity and accuracy of the information received, the meaning of the information, and its implications, may make ambiguity associated with the emergence of issues important. Further, defining issues may not be straightforward. Different parties in an organisation may have different views about the significance or implications of an existing situation, and differing views about the need for action. Issues may be recognised as threats or opportunities which need to be addressed either reactively or proactively. Alternatively, issues may be expressed in terms of weaknesses in organisational capability which need to be remedied, or particular strengths which could be more extensively exploited. Issues may involve relatively simple concerns within a given ongoing operation or project, but they may involve the possible emergence of a major organisational change programme or a revision to a key aspect of strategy. The decisions involved may be 'first order' decisions, or they may be 'higher order' decisions, as in making choices about the design of organisational decision and planning processes, that is, deciding how to decide. Ambiguity about the way issues are identified and defined implies massive scope for uncertainty.

The 'scope the decision' stage will depend on how an issue is defined. It involves determining which organisational activities are relevant to addressing the issue, who is already involved with the issue, who should be involved, and importantly, the extent to which other areas of decision making need to be linked with this decision process. There may be considerable uncertainty about the answers to these questions.

The 'determine the performance criteria' stage involves identifying the performance criteria of concern, deciding how these will be measured, and determining appropriate priorities and tradeoffs between the criteria. As with previous decision stages, the tasks comprising this stage can present significant difficulties, particularly if multiple parties with differing performance criteria or priorities are involved. As is well known, individuals may seek to impose their own objectives and priorities, prejudices and viewpoints on a decision.

An aim of improving organisation performance presupposes clarity about performance objectives, the relative priorities between objectives, and acceptable trade-offs between various objectives. Attempting major investment decisions or RM when this clarity is lacking is like attempting to build a tower on shifting sand. The implications of uncertainty related to the nature of objectives and relative priorities need to be managed as much as uncertainty about what is achievable. Morris and Hough (1987) argue for the importance of setting clear objectives and performance criteria which reflect the requirements of various parties, including stakeholders who are not always recognised as players (regulatory authorities, future customers, for example). The different objectives held by interested parties, and any inter-dependencies between different objectives need to be appreciated. It is perhaps indicative of a perceived failure of conventional RM and management decision making in general to address objectives and trade-offs, that the concept of 'value management' has been introduced to encompass this concern (Kelly and Male, 1993).

The 'identify alternative courses of action' stage of the decision process may involve considerable effort to search for or design feasible alternatives. For example, identification of alternatives and their evaluation is often an iterative process involving search and screening processes to produce a shortlist of alternatives which are developed and evaluated in more detail. In the case of major investment decisions, often only one alternative is fully developed and evaluated because alternative courses of action and alternative design choices have been dismissed in earlier iterations through the 'choose a course of action' stage.

The 'predict outcomes of courses of action' stage builds on this to identify the factors that are likely to influence the performance of each identified course of action, estimating their size and estimating their combined effect.

An important area of uncertainty relates to the basis for estimates produced by those who contribute information to the decision process. For example, it is often necessary to rely on subjective estimates for probabilities of various possible outcomes in the absence of sufficient relevant statistical data for determining probabilities 'objectively'. The basis for such subjective judgments may be unclear, but articulating them at least makes these estimates available for scrutiny and comparison with other estimates. Uncertainty about the basis of estimates may depend on who produced them, what form they are in, why, how and when they were produced, from what resources and experience base, and the extent of any bias in estimates (Chapman and Ward, 2002: Chap. 4).

The 'choose a course of action' stage then involves comparing the evaluations obtained in the previous stage, often by comparing relative performance on more than one performance criteria. This presents significant challenges where relative performances are uncertain and best presented as cumulative probability distributions (Chapman and Ward, 2002).

Ambiguity about how best to manage all these decision stages from 'monitoring the environment' through to 'choosing a course of action', and uncertainty about the quality of the output from each of these stages are further major sources of uncertainty.

Experience, as well as this brief overview of sources of uncertainty in a generic decision process stage structure, tells us that the scope for making poor quality decisions is considerable. Difficulties arise in every stage. The uncertainties listed in Table 5.2 indicate the nature of what is involved. Have we correctly interpreted information about the environment? Have we correctly identified issues in a timely manner? Have we adopted the most appropriate scope for our decision? Are we clear about the performance criteria and their relative importance to us? Have we undertaken a sufficiently thorough search for alternatives? Have we evaluated alternatives adequately in a way that recognises all relevant sources of uncertainty? And so on.

In order to manage all this uncertainty, decision makers seek to simplify the decision process by making assumptions about the level of uncertainty that exists, and by considering a simplified version or model of the decision components.

5.4 CHARACTERISTICS OF AN INDIVIDUAL DECISION MAKER

In addition to the inherent difficulties in addressing a given decision situation and associated uncertainty, limitations in the information processing abilities of decision makers can impair the quality of decision processes. For example, consider the problem facing most managers who typically have to deal with a range of potentially inter-related, contemporaneous issues. Isenberg (1984) found in a study of senior managers' decision making that they typically dealt with a portfolio of problems, issues and opportunities by forming problem categories based on how individual problems were inter-related. This allows a manager to seize opportunities more flexibly and to use progress on one problem to achieve progress on another, related issue. Isenberg also found that how problems were defined and ranked was heavily influenced by how easy problems were to solve. In this respect considering what is a possible solution often precedes and guides the process of conceptualising a problem. In this way problems can be defined in terms that already incorporate key features of solutions, and thus make it easier to take action. A variant of this is to simplify a problem by introducing non-essential constraints to reduce the degrees of freedom.

With such approaches, the potential for inappropriately scoping decision areas and prematurely narrowing the range of options considered is clear.

Janis and Mann (1977) have argued that the information processing capabilities of a decision maker are affected by the level of stress associated with a decision. The amount of stress here is proportional to the risk of loss resulting from the decision. Janis and Mann argue that in conditions of extremely low or high stress information processing will be defective, while moderate stress leads to what they term 'vigilant information processing' and high quality decision processes. Confronted with a problem or opportunity, if the risks in not responding are not serious there is low stress and insufficient concern about overlooking unfavourable consequences or about taking care over a decision. Similarly, if the risks in responding are not serious, there is again low stress, and limited concern for vigilant information processing. For example, a low risk, incremental response could be adopted which is capable of gradual modification in the light of experience. There is then no need to undertake high quality decision making. When a decision is required but all options involve serious risks, a high stress situation, Janis and Mann argue that decision makers will adopt 'defensive avoidance' involving behaviours such as:

- selective inattention, ignoring defects of the least objectionable option;

- selective forgetting;

- distortion of the meaning of warning messages;

- construction of wishful rationalisations that minimise negative consequences;

- buck-passing – rationalising that others know better how to make the right choice or that a problem is in someone else's area of operations.

In extremis, where there is also little time to deliberate, Janis and Mann suggest that decision-makers' thinking becomes disrupted – 'hyper vigilant'; immediate memory span is disrupted, and thinking becomes simplistic. Effects include: perseverance in thinking about a limited number of alternatives, rather than a wider set – thinking 'in a rut'; failure to use remaining time to adequately evaluate those alternatives identified; a tendency to 'clutch at straws' by latching on to hastily contrived solutions and to overlook serious consequences of such snap judgments.

However, if a decision involving high risk is required, but there is high confidence in finding a satisfactory solution and sufficient time to identify and deliberate alternatives, then the moderate stress involved encourages 'vigilance' and high quality decision making.

There are clear implications for managerial decision making in Janis and Mann's framework, the main one being that high-stress situations should be avoided by ensuring that there is sufficient time for critical decisions and that there is a capability for rapid, efficient and effective identification of decision options and evaluation of those options. This implies a need for proactive RM to anticipate the need for decisions and reduce the chances of 'surprises', for awareness of the dangers in setting unrealistic, excessively tight time constraints on planning and decision-making activities, and for the establishment of decision support including formal RM processes to facilitate efficient and high quality deliberations.

More generally the quality of decision deliberations can be influenced by a decision maker's personality, personal (recent) experience, predispositions, prejudices, and biases. For example, individuals may:

- structure issues and scope decisions based on their own experience;

- preferentially seek out information that is consistent with their own beliefs, and pay less attention to information that is not;

- accept a sufficient or satisfactory explanation rather than seek out the most correct explanation such as focusing on people as the cause of the behaviour and events;

- seek out confirming data which supports their preferred choice and downplay or disregard evidence which does not support this choice;

- once committed to a course of action, perceive and evaluate alternatives in a more biased, subjective manner which tends to confirm the initial choice.

Gilovich, Griffin and Kahneman (2002) provide an in-depth review of such factors.

5.5 ATTITUDE TO RISK

A key driver of individual decision making behaviour is attitude to risk. It is often suggested that decision makers are risk averse. The meaning and significance of this needs to be considered carefully. In particular, the common interpretation that 'risk averse' means preferring less risk to more risk, lacks precision and is not very helpful. To illustrate, consider three increasingly risky options A, B, and C which are risky in the sense that their outcomes, measured solely in financial terms, are uncertain. A delivers £100 for sure, and therefore involves no risk. B offers a 50% chance of £400 and a 50% chance of nothing (expected pay-off £200); C offers a 50% chance of £2000 and a

50% chance of nothing (expected pay-off £1000). All risk averse decision makers would prefer £200 for sure to option B, and strongly risk averse decision makers would prefer the certain outcome of A to the uncertain outcome of B, even though B has a higher expected pay-off. However, many risk averse decision makers would prefer C to A, and all would prefer C to B. It is incorrect to say that risk averse decision makers always prefer the least risky option. Rather decision makers evaluate trade-offs between the level of uncertainty and expected pay-offs, not just the level of uncertainty or size of the lowest pay-off.

'Risk preferring' decision makers would have different preferences between options A, B, and C. Specifically, any risk preferring decision maker would prefer B to A, and option B to a pay-off of £200 for sure, even though there is a 50% chance of nothing from B. Only a risk neutral decision maker, who is indifferent to risk, would be indifferent between £200 for sure and option B. Most people behave like risk averse decision makers most of the time when choosing between alternative combinations of potential (positive) pay-offs. However, many people become risk preferring when choosing between alternative combinations of potential cost. This has important implications for how managers make choices about investment decision options with uncertain outcomes.

To appreciate these implications, it is useful to describe an individual decision maker's attitude to risk in a utility function framework. Risk aversion and risk preference behaviour suggest that the value or utility a decision maker places on financial returns does not increase linearly (uniformly) with the level of return. Figure 5.1 portrays the general shape of a utility function for a risk averse decision maker, with the characteristic that the additional increase in utility from gaining an extra £1 decreases as the total wealth increases. Figure 5.1 shows one particular example of a risk averse decision maker's utility function, for convenience assigning a utility of 1 to a pay-off of £2000 writing U(2000) = 1, and zero to a pay-off of zero, writing U(0) = 0. For this decision maker option C will have an expected utility of:

$$U(C) = 0.5 \ U(2000) + 0.5 \ U(0) = 0.5$$

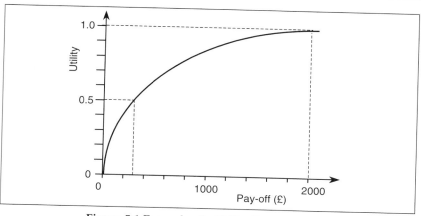

Figure 5.1 Example of a Utility Function for a
Risk Averse Decision Maker

As the diagram shows, for this decision maker a utility of 0.5 corresponds to a payoff of £300. Consequently, this decision maker will regard the risky option C (which involves an expected pay-off of £1,000) as equivalent to a certain sum of £300. Therefore any *certain* sum greater than £300 will be preferred to option C, and option C will be preferred to any *certain* sum less than £300.

Figure 5.2 illustrates the general shape of the utility function of a risk preferring decision maker, again for convenience setting U(2000) = 1, and U(0) = 0. The shape of this utility function shows that the additional increase in utility from gaining an extra £1 *increases* as the total wealth increases. To such a decision maker option B will have an expected utility of 0.5. Given the illustrative curve in Figure 5.2, a utility of 0.5 corresponds to a payoff of about £1720. This risk preferring decision maker will regard the risky option C as equivalent to a certain sum of £1720. Therefore any certain sum greater than £1720 will be preferred to option C, and C will be preferred to any certain sum less than £1720.

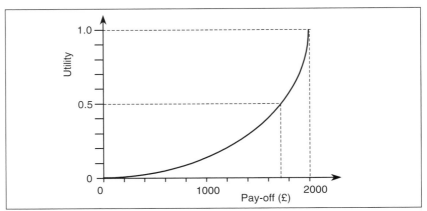

Figure 5.2 Example of a Utility Function for a Risk Preferring Decision

More realistically, a decision maker's utility function will exhibit aspects of risk aversion and risk preference over different ranges of profit and loss. Figure 5.3 shows a plausible representation of a typical decision maker's utility function over all values of profit and loss (cost). Apart from a limited range around the break-even point, most decision makers exhibit risk aversion in the range of (large) profits and risk preferring behaviour in the range of (large) losses (Kahneman and Tversky, 1979; Swalm, 1966). In the range $-R < m < R$, the utility function is very shallow and linear implying a risk neutral attitude to risk and very little change in utility for monetary amounts m between $-R$ and R. In the ranges $m < -S$ and $R < m < T$, the decision maker is risk preferring, while in the ranges $-S < m < -R$ and $T < m$, the decision maker is risk averse. The utility curve for losses is generally steeper than for profits, indicating a greater sensitivity to losses than for profits.

Figure 5.3 is consistent with the purchase of lottery tickets for small cost where this is only a small chance of winning a very large sum of money. It is also consistent with the risk averse payment of insurance premiums to insure against the small chance of very large losses. However, of particular significance for risk management is the implications of risk preferring behaviour in respect of significant losses (costs). As Figure 5.3 shows, the *incremental* loss of utility for each additional £1 loss or spent *decreases* as the total amount lost or spent increases. Initial losses/costs just below $-S$ are regarded as much more serious than a similar additional loss on top of an existing loss which is much greater than $-S$. For illustrative purposes, suppose $-S$ in Figure 5.3

corresponds to a loss or cost of £10 000 for a particular decision maker. Next, suppose this decision maker must choose between an option D costing £34 000 for sure, or an option E involving a 60% chance of incurring a cost of £50 000 and a 40% chance of incurring a cost of £10 000. The expected cost of E is £ (0.6x50 000 + 0.4x10 000) = £34 000 the same as for D, but because of the risk preferring shape of the decision maker's utility function below £10 000, the expected utility of the risky option E will be greater (less negative) than the expected utility of option D. (The reasoning is similar to that used with option C in Figure 5.2). Consequently, our decision maker will prefer the risky option E to the zero risk option D.

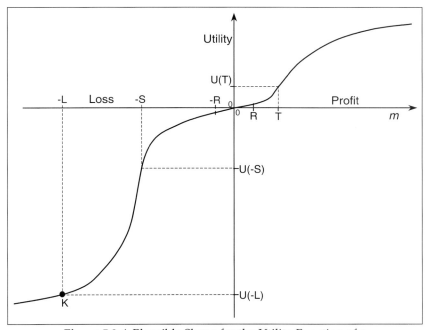

Figure 5.3 A Plausible Shape for the Utility Function of a Typical Decision Maker

5.6   FRAMING EFFECTS

Figure 5.3 suggests that attitude to risk is different for potential gains and losses relative to an initial starting position, the zero point on the monetary value axis in Figure 5.3. This raises the possibility that the way a decision is presented or 'framed', can cause a given situation to be presented either as a choice between alternative gains, or as a choice between alternative losses, and consequently influence the decision maker's choice. Framing a given situation as a choice between losses can induce a risk preferring selection, while framing the same situation as a choice between gains would induce a risk averse, and hence different, selection.

Bazerman (1998) offers the following example to illustrate the problem. A large car manufacturer has been recently hit with a number of economic difficulties, and it seems that three plants will need to be closed and 6000 employees laid off. The production director has been exploring alternative ways to avoid this outcome. She has developed two plans:

Plan A will save one of the three plants and 2000 jobs.

Plan B has a 33% probability of saving all three plants and all 6000 jobs, but has a 67% probability of saving no plants and no jobs.

Informal empirical investigation demonstrates that a large majority of individuals when asked to choose between plans A and B choose plan A (Bazerman, 1998).

Now reconsider this example, replacing plans A and B with the following choices:

Plan C will result in the loss of two of the three plants and 4000 jobs.

Plan D has a 67% probability of losing all three plants and all 6000 jobs, but a 33% probability of losing no plants and no jobs.

In this framing of the choices, a large majority of individuals when asked to choose between plans C and D choose plan D (Bazerman, 1998).

Objectively, the two pairs of alternative plans are the same. Plan A produces the same outcome as plan C, and plan B the same as plan D. However plan A and B are framed as gains relative to a reference point of all three plants lost, inducing the risk averse, low uncertainty choice A. Conversely, plans C and D are framed as losses relative to a reference point of all three plants continuing to operate, inducing the risk preferring, high risk choice D.

While this is a simple example, it does illustrate the importance of guarding against framing effects by focusing on end state positions, and framing options in different ways to test decision choices.

A further framing issue arises when, in making a series of decisions, a decision maker does not regard past losses as 'a sunk cost', that is, irrelevant to future decisions. Suppose a decision maker has incurred a significant loss -L < -S in Figure 5.3 as a result of previous decisions. Next suppose the decision maker now has an option G available which involves a 50% probability of a *further* loss -L, and a 50% probability of a gain of (L-S). The expected monetary value of this risky option is 0.5(L-S-L) = -0.5S , suggesting this is an unattractive option which should be declined. However, *relative to the point* K in Figure 5.3, the potential gain in utility from reducing cumulative losses back to -S is much larger than the potential loss of utility from a *further* loss of -L. The expected utility from the option is positive and our risk preferring decision maker will happily accept the chance the risky option offers to recoup some of his/her losses.

Of course, if our decision maker were prepared to cut his/her losses and treat them as truly 'sunk', 'water under the bridge', then the decision maker would evaluate the option G relative to the zero reference point in Figure 5.3. Now it is easy to see that the option not only has an unattractive expected monetary value of -0.5S as before, but also an expected utility of (0.5U(L-S) + 0.5U(-L)) < 0, and the option is not worth taking up.

A reluctance to treat previous losses as 'sunk', can lead to an increasing tendency, as losses mount, to prefer risky choices and 'throw good money after bad'. More generally, such behaviour has been described as 'escalating commitment', or persistence, with a failing strategy (see for example, Brockner, 1992; Staw, 1981; Staw and Ross, 1987).

Examples of risk preferring escalating commitment can arise in a wide variety of situations involving a sequence of investment decisions including:

- (rogue) trading in financial securities;

- lending additional funds to an existing debtor;

- continuing to watch a bad theatre play you paid see;

- continuing with a high cost capital project which is in difficulties;

- drilling further exploratory wells in the hope of proving an oilfield;

- committing further resources in a major conflict; and so on.

Staw (1981) has argued that individuals may escalate commitment rather than cut their losses because they are strongly motivated to justify previous decisions and demonstrate competence. Continuing commitment allows the possibility of being able to rectify past losses and prove to others that the decision maker was not wrong or incompetent in making an earlier decision, and that resources expended have not been wasted. Senior managers in particular may be under pressure to show consistency and clear conviction to a particular strategy. Such factors can also encourage over-optimism about the chances of being able to turn the situation around, particularly if there is a prevailing corporate culture of 'macho' management and an individual has experience of having turned round previous failing strategies. A further factor driving persistence can be administrative inertia, where there is a wish to avoid disruption of existing operations and procedures, and there are uncertain costs associated with 'pulling the plug', which may include damage to corporate reputation in the case of highly visible projects.

Being aware of the dangers of escalation can obviously help reduce the chances of inappropriate decisions to persist with failing strategies. But more specifically, decision makers should be encouraged to frame decision choices in a variety of ways in order to investigate the stability of preferences. Decision makers should be instructed not to evaluate decision alternatives in terms of gains or losses from a neutral reference point as they are inclined to do. Instead, they should be encouraged to formulate decision choices in terms of final states for outcomes (Kahneman and Tversky, 1981; 1984). Unfortunately, sometimes the only real cure for escalating commitment to a dubious corporate strategy appears to be the appointment of a new CEO who has less personal kudos invested in the previous strategy.

5.7 GROUP DECISION PROCESSES

Group decision processes present more complex decision contexts than individual decision-making processes, not least because participants will have:

- differing information bases;
- differing past experiences;

- varying perceptions of the decision context and alternative courses of action;

- differing views of relevant performance criteria and priorities;

- other agendas relating to personal objectives and relationships with other participants.

Very often decision making is undertaken by a group precisely because of these differences between potential participants. Employing group decision making is also expensive in terms of the opportunity cost of participants' involvement, and in terms of the additional time that group decision making typically entails. Accordingly, a key issue is whether the benefits of using a group process will outweigh the costs. This is not always an easy issue to address, but this higher level, 'meta-decision', about whether to use a group process or not, needs to be informed by a proper appreciation of the relevant advantages and disadvantages of a group process. Additionally, and as is well known, meta-decision makers can strongly influence the quality and direction of decision making by dictating procedures, timing, and participation in given decisions. Often it is clear that a decision needs to be made by an individual because for example, there is a need for an immediate response, there is a need for confidentiality, or a decision requires a particular individual's expertise. However, there is sometimes a danger that meta-decision makers will use these arguments as an excuse to retain control over a decision process and avoid the scrutiny and deliberations of a group.

Potential Benefits of Group Decision Processes

Decisions about when to use group decision making should be guided by the following potential benefits of a group process.

1.   *Increased Creativity*

In principle, group discussion can stimulate creative thinking, particularly about alternative courses of action. A tentative suggestion from one member may spark off a productive discussion that develops the suggestion and generates further lines of thought.

2. Increased Knowledge and Information

The quality of each stage of the decision may be enhanced by a sharing of information and expertise of a variety of participants from different technical backgrounds or from different stakeholder groups.

3. Co-ordination of Different Perspectives

Co-ordination will be an important motivation for the use of group decision processes where issues and decisions are complex, and affect or involve different units of an organisation and other core operating organisations. Key concerns will be the desirability of understanding the reasons behind differing perceptions of issues and related context, together with associated differences in objectives and priorities. An important purpose of the group is then to develop a full understanding of decision context and issues, a coherent set of objectives, and priorities across these objectives.

4. Participation Increases Comprehension and Acceptance

Group decision making allows for the views of different interest groups to be aired. This can increase the potential for conflict, but provides an opportunity to take differing interests into account and resolve differences. This increases the acceptability of decisions, and hence reduces resistance. In any event, resistance may be reduced because of improved comprehension of how and why a decision was made.

5. Increased Motivation of Group Members

Participation in a particular group can increase an individual's sense of belonging and self-esteem, particularly if the decision is an important one or involves important information. The social pressure of the group can also provide more immediate motivation by stimulating greater efforts to contribute to deliberations.

6. Learning and Development of Participants

Group decision processes can provide an opportunity for participants to learn from one another. This is often thought of in terms of less experienced personnel developing their knowledge and decision process skills by observing other, more experienced members of a decision group. However, even experienced participants can learn from other group members about alternative approaches to different aspects of the decision process, or about the way others think, operate, and communicate. Increasingly, organisations are recognising the value of employing a facilitator to guide consideration of complex issues and co-ordinate coherent output from deliberations (Eden and Radford, 1990; French, Kelly and Morrey, 1992; Marples and Riddle, 1992). Such situations acknowledge not only the need to learn about a given decision context, but also the value of learning about more effective and efficient decision processes.

Effective Group Decision Making

In thinking about how to decide, 'meta-decision' makers ought to consider the above potential benefits of group decision processes as possible objectives and so design group decision processes accordingly. This includes deciding how much time and resources to allocate to the process, the methods to be used to address all the stages and associated uncertainties of the decision process listed in Table 5.1, and appropriate membership of the group. There is a large literature on effective group decision making, but only a brief overview of some important work can be given here.

Tuckman (1965) addressed the idea that groups generally need to go through a process of socialisation before they are able to perform to their full potential. Tuckman argued that this socialisation involves three phases: 'forming', 'storming', and 'norming', but that some groups may get stuck in one of these phrases and never reach the full effectiveness of the final 'performing' phase. Tuckman's phases are briefly summarised in Table 5.3.

Table 5.3 Phases of Group Socialisation (Tuckman, 1965)

the Phase 1. Forming
Testing acceptable behaviour, and finding out about the other members of the group. Clarifying what the group is expected to achieve. Appointment or emergence of a leader.
Phase 2. Storming
Establishing roles and priorities. Possible formation of sub-groups and individuals are 'jockeying for position'.
Phase 3. Norming
Emergence of a consensus about the group's objectives and the roles of individual members. Trust and cooperation developed. Information flows more freely.
Phase 4. Performing
Constructive collaboration. Effective issue definition and decision making are possible. Differences between group members respected. There is rational discussion rather than coercion. Any conflict is confined to issues facing the group rather than related to interpersonal issues.

Important research by Belbin (1981), identified a range of roles that need to be performed in an effective group as follows:

– the chairman – the company worker – the resource investigator

– the shaper – the team worker – the completer

– the monitor-evaluator – the plant – the specialist.

Belbin's work indicated that different personalities will be suited to different roles and that individuals tend to adopt the same one or two roles fairly consistently. Accordingly, selecting participants in group decision making might usefully be guided by the desirability of including participants who can provide complete coverage of the above roles.

It is often argued that the leader of a decision making group is a key factor in determining the effectiveness and efficiency of a decision making group. Vroom and Yetton's (1973) contingency model of decision making stresses that leadership style needs to be matched to the context if effective decision processes are to be achieved. Vroom and Yetton (1973) formulated a model of contingency leadership styles which distinguished five styles of leadership representing a continuum from authoritarian approaches, to consultative, to a fully participative style. Vroom and Yetton then suggested a set of questions that managers could ask themselves to help determine which style to adopt. Vroom and Jago (1988) extended this approach by hypothesising that the effectiveness of decision processes is dependent on:

- the quality of the decision process;

- the commitment made to the decisions;

- the time expended on the decision process.

Consequently, they argue that the effectiveness of leadership is a function of the effectiveness of decisions minus the cost of making the decisions, *plus* the value realised in developing participants' abilities by means of committed decision making. Vroom and Jago's perspective is a reminder that effective decisions *per se* are not enough; it is also important that decision processes are cost-effective and should recognise the desirability for an organisation of developing the decision-making abilities of employees.

From an opportunity management perspective, it is important that the potential benefits of group decision making are recognised and proactively pursued. It is also important to appreciate how thoughtful selection of appropriate leadership and design of the decision process can increase the quality of group deliberations in addressing all the sources of uncertainty listed in Table 5.1.

Potential Problems with Group Decision Processes

From a threat management perspective, it is important that potential problems of group decisions are appreciated and actively managed. Ideally, this should involve proactive avoidance and reduction of adverse effects on decision processes. However, it may also involve recognising problems with existing group decision mechanisms, and taking steps to remedy both problems and obstacles to high quality decision making. This may be easier said than done, especially if the group decision processes involve senior management teams (boards and government cabinets, for example).

Group decision processes have at least five major disadvantages:

1. *Tendency for Premature Decision-Making*

Members of the group suggest various possible explanations for a situation or alternative options, and these receive both initial support and criticism. Often the first explanation or solution to receive significant support prevails over other potentially superior alternatives. This effect is compounded by the tendency of groups to become prematurely committed to a course of action, much as individuals often do (Bazerman et al, 1984). One problem is that such pre-emptive support may have been the result of particularly skilful and repetitive presentation of proposals, and/or because the course of action reflects conventional thinking (Hoffman and Maier, 1964). Additionally, some members of the group may have committed to a particular interpretation of the decision issues and appropriate courses of action, even before the group starts to deliberate.

2.   *Individual Domination*

Groups may be dominated by a formal or informal leader whose problem-solving abilities may or may not be good. If time is pressing, and progress through the decision process stages is lacking, the group leader may take responsibility for making a decision. The danger is that such an outcome is engineered, and/or that other managers outside the group are deluded into believing that a group decision has been made. Some individuals in the group may be naturally more assertive or garrulous, not necessarily more able. Such individuals may become more influential, especially if other members become frustrated or 'tune-out'. A further possibility is that a small minority of the group so vehemently opposes the majority view that the majority is forced to consider inappropriate levels of compromise, resulting in reduced quality decisions.

3.   *Concern with Winning the Argument*

Group members who become committed to a specific view or proposal frequently become more concerned with winning the argument than with improving the quality of the decision process.

4.   *Lack of Acceptance of Responsibility for a Decision*

Collective responsibility for a decision may be interpreted as meaning no individual blame. Actions agreed may not be followed through with the same priority, rigour, and commitment as if there were individual responsibility.

5.   *Compromise Decisions*

Group decision making which involves significant compromise tends to preclude the acceptance of radically different courses of action or perspectives on an issue. Yet in a competitive environment such radical thinking may be what is needed to improve the competitive position of the organisation.

Conflict and Conformity

It is generally accepted that some level of conflict or difference of opinion increases the quality and quantity of analysis in decision processes. Intra-group conflict is only a problem when it operates as a barrier to exchanging information, views, and rational deliberation. Similarly, some degree of conformity, as in Tuckman's (1965) norming phase in Table 5.3, is desirable to achieve effective decision making. Such conformity may extend to individuals going along with the majority view but not fundamentally altering their own point of view. However, problems arise where there are excessive pressures on individuals to conform, and groups exhibit concurrence-seeking tendencies. When this tendency is a dominant feature of group decision processes, the quality of decision making is impaired and groups exhibit symptoms of what Janis (1973) has termed 'groupthink' – a collective pattern of defensive avoidance. Janis (1973) defines groupthink as the *'deterioration of mental efficiency, reality testing, and moral judgment'* in the interests of group solidarity. Grounded in a study of foreign policy decisions made by several US presidential administrations, Janis (1973) identifies eight major symptoms that characterise groupthink:

1. An illusion of invulnerability shared by most members of the group which creates excessive optimism and encourages taking extreme risks.

2. Collective efforts to rationalise in order to discount warnings which might lead group members to reconsider their assumptions.

3. An unquestioned belief in the group's inherent morality, inclining the group to ignore the ethical and moral consequences of their decisions.

4. Stereotyping rivals and enemies as too evil to warrant genuine negotiations or as too weak or stupid to counter the group's actions.

5. Direct pressure on individuals not to dissent from the group's stereotypes, assumptions, or commitments.

6. Self-censorship in which the individual minimises the importance of those doubts and arguments they have that run counter to the apparent group consensus.

7. A shared illusion of unanimity partly resulting from self-censorship, but also from a false assumption that silence implies consent.

8. The emergence of self-appointed 'mind guards' – members who protect the group from adverse criticism or information that would contradict the group's thinking.

Janis (1973) suggested that strong concurrence thinking is likely to become dominant in policy-making groups, giving rise to groupthink and defective decision making, under the following main conditions:

- high group cohesiveness increases the individual's psychological dependence on the group, and increases willingness to adhere to group norms.

- insulation of the group, so that members have little or no opportunity to discuss issues outside the group, and therefore are more likely to rely upon judgements of the group.

- lack of methodical procedures for search and appraisal encourages conformity because of the absence of procedural safeguards against cursory or biased analysis.

- directive leadership increases the likelihood that the leader will exert pressure on individuals to conform to the leader's decisions.

- high-stress along with a low degree of hope for finding a better solution to the one favoured by the leader or other influential members. Here individuals are motivated towards defensive avoidance behaviour and to reduce the stress of decisional conflict by collectively bolstering the least objectionable alternative.

The implications for managerial decision making are clear. While not all cohesive management teams will necessarily suffer from groupthink, most are likely to display the symptoms from time to time. Obvious counter-active strategies involve directly addressing the above antecedent conditions, including the adoption of more systematic techniques for managing uncertainty in each stage of the decision process. Moorhead, Ference and Neck (1991) have used the groupthink hypothesis to review the decision to launch the ill-fated space shuttle Challenger in January 1986. As a result they propose a revised framework in which time and leadership style operate as moderators of the manner in which group characteristics lead to symptoms of groupthink. Leadership style can either promote or reduce the development of groupthink symptoms. For example, the group leader may not promote a preferred solution, but they may allow, or even assist the group in seeking agreement by not forcing the group to critically appraise all alternative courses of action. When there is pressure to make decisions quickly, there will be more pressure to agree, with increased tendency to discourage dissent, self-censorship, avoidance of expert opinion, and assumptions about unanimity. However, an assertive group leader may be able to gain the group more time by negotiating an extension.

Groups Make More Risky Decisions?

The preceding discussion has focused on the factors that might affect and impair the quality of group decision processes. This has implications for RM which seeks to improve the quality of decision making under uncertainty. A somewhat different issue is whether group decision processes lead to more or less risk taking than would be embarked upon by individual decision makers. As noted above, Janis (1973) has argued that groups suffering from groupthink may exhibit excessive optimism and extreme risk-taking. This is sometimes referred to as the 'risky shift' phenomenon. However, Whyte (1989) has argued that *'the groupthink hypothesis is a less than comprehensive explanation for why groups may make excessively risky decisions. The main theme of groupthink is concurrence-seeking but concurrence-seeking occurs generally in group decision making, and it is not unique to groups that perform poorly...'*

Whyte offers a different perspective to explain the occurrence of policy decision fiascos, which he calls 'prospect polarisation'. In addition to the pressures for uniformity of groupthink, Whyte's perspective employs the notions of framing effects, risk seeking in the domain of losses, and group polarisation. Whyte suggests that decision fiascos are the result of choices that have been framed as losses so that risk preferring behaviour is elicited. In group decision making, pressures for concurrence will encourage a group choice that is consistent with the initial risky preferences of a majority of members. Group discussion would also reinforce the preference for the risky option via a process of polarisation (Myers and Lamm, 1976). The net effect of these processes is that groups whose members frame the choice as one between different loss distributions, will show an inappropriate preference for risk even more frequently and to a greater degree than would the group's average member (Whyte, 1989). As Whyte notes, this explanation is intended to apply equally to business decision making as well as to military or political decisions. Moreover, it is consistent with previously advanced views that firms performing below target are more likely to pursue risky options than those that are not (Singh, 1986).

Whyte's perspective implies that strategies for reducing the occurrence of group decision fiascos should include not only those used to reduce antecedent conditions of groupthink, but also those outlined earlier to reduce the effects of framing.

5.8   CONCLUSIONS

This chapter began with a discussion of the basic nature of decision processes characterised by the nine stage structure in Table 5.1. This provides a framework for understanding what needs to be considered in achieving a high quality decision process. In particular, it is important to recognise the full scope for uncertainty in each stage of a decision process if major errors, inappropriate assumptions, omissions, and simplistic deliberations are to be avoided. Depending on the importance of a decision, the implications of the sources of uncertainty in Table 5.2 need to be understood and managed. A key issue is deciding how much effort to invest in a given decision or type of decision. Important, one-off decisions, or often-repeated decisions may warrant carefully designed decision support incorporating formal modelling and analysis. This decision support may be particularly helpful in identifying and managing the various sources of uncertainty present at each stage of a decision process.

Much of this chapter was concerned with the considerable, ever present threats to high quality decision making due to the way individuals and groups engage in decision making and think about uncertainty. These limitations need to be recognised and managed just as much as the uncertainty associated with the context and subject matter of a particular decision.

Experience and psychological studies show that the quality of an individual's thinking is reduced under conditions of high-stress and limited time to deliberate. Additionally, individuals habitually exhibit bias and selective attention to information in order to reduce complexity and uncertainty during decision processes. An important driver of most decisions involving significant uncertainty and risk is the decision maker's attitude to risk. The issues involved are most conveniently described in a utility function framework. While this does not explain the underlying reasons why individuals exhibit the preferences indicated, a utility framework illustrates that choices between alternative risky options are influenced by whether choices are framed as losses or gains, and by trade-offs between expected (average) outcome and the level of uncertainty associated with each option. All of these psychological factors can be addressed by appropriate formal modelling and analysis to support decision processes (see for example, Dickson, 2003; Goodwin and Wright, 2003).

A key issue for organisations is ensuring high quality group decision making. This is particularly important at senior management levels, where decisions often involve high levels of uncertainty and risk. While groups have important advantages over individual decision makers, a group decision context can result in the foibles of individuals being compounded by group dynamics. This is most clearly evident when the quality of high-level decisions are impaired by 'groupthink'. In particular, a combination of framing effects, risk seeking in the domain of losses, and concurrence-seeking behaviour amongst group members can combine to cause groups to take more risky decisions than individuals.

6

OBJECTIVES FOR RISK MANAGEMENT

6.1   INTRODUCTION

In Chapter 1 the purpose of risk management (RM) was considered in terms of the level of anticipation adopted, ranging from a purely reactive approach characterised broadly as 'crisis management', through to a highly proactive approach characterised by 'strategy formulation'. Choices in this 'why' dimension of RM development shape expectations of what RM is intended to achieve in terms of different kinds of response to risk. A 'crisis management' focus implies a concern for effective crisis recognition and decisive, rapid responses. This may include an element of contingency planning. A less passive 'business continuity' focus involves attempting to change the probability of events and modify their effects. A 'proactive control' focus extends the RM agenda to include the setting of appropriate performance targets. 'Strategy formulation' involves the highest level of proactive management. Here RM has a basic influence in the design of strategies, the players involved, and the choice of relevant performance criteria.

This 'level of anticipation' perspective is useful in considering the underlying philosophy of a RM approach. However, a more detailed set of objectives needs to be considered to refine our understanding of what RM can achieve, and how it might be operationalised. This chapter describes a multi-level structure of possible objectives for RM that relate to: quality of the RM process, purpose in a given application, RM performance criteria, and the development of strategic capability. The use of documented formal RM processes can contribute at all four levels of objectives.

6.2   BENEFITS OR OBJECTIVES?

Effective RM can bring substantial benefits in terms of improved organisational performance both in the short and long term. However, these benefits are not automatic, they depend very much on the scope and quality of RM carried out. So much so in fact, that potential benefits should be identified up front, and proactively sought out by designing RM processes accordingly. In this manner, potential benefits are best regarded as potential objectives for any RM activity.

Surprisingly, the implications of this fundamental point are typically not explored in most guidelines on RM. If benefits are addressed at all, they are typically identified as a list of separate items with little or no further comment. Even if they seem entirely plausible, such lists of benefits are of limited use unless they are used to clarify appropriate objectives for RM activity, objectives which are then actively pursued.

Sometimes the problem is that objectives for RM are rather broadly expressed as in:

- *The objective (of good RM) is to add maximum sustainable value to all the activities of the organisation* (AIRMIC, ALARM, IRM Standard, 2002).

- *Enterprise RM enables management to operate more effectively in environments filled with risks* (PricewaterhouseCoopers, 2004: p2).

- *Enterprise RM... enhance(s) the likelihood that management will make better decisions* (PricewaterhouseCoopers, 2004: p11).

The UK Office of Government Commerce publication *'Management of Risk: guidance for practitioners'* (2002: paragraph 1.3), states that effective management of risk helps to improve performance by contributing to:

- increased certainty and fewer surprises;

- better service delivery;

- more effective management of change;

- more efficient use of resources;

- better management at all levels through improved decision making;

- reduced waste and fraud, and better value for money;

- innovation;

- management of contingent and maintenance activities.

These are all feasible objectives for suitably designed RM processes, but no further explanation or clarification is provided of the mechanisms which link RM to these objectives. However, a similar set of objectives for RM which does provide some additional explanation is shown in Table 6.1.

Table 6.1 How Risk Management Can Help Improve Performance (National Audit Office, 2000: p37)

Area of activity	*How RM can help*
Service delivery	Avoid or arrange to deal with delays; poor-quality, reliability, accessibility of services; sudden increases in demand; joining up complementary services at the point of delivery.
Managing change	Assess the likelihood of major changes that might impact on resource requirements and service delivery. Develop contingency plans to maintain services if things go wrong, and consider ways of responding to increased expectations in service standards and levels.
Efficient use of resources	Identify areas that may be over-controlled or over-regulated so that resources can be released to priority areas.
Project management	Risk assessment at feasibility and appraisal stages can help to meet project objectives by developing forecasts, optimising allocation of risk, and helping to clarify responsibilities for managing identified sources of risk.
Minimising waste, fraud, and poor value for money	Regular assessment of performance measures, processes and systems to help assess their reliability and how they might need to be enhanced.
Innovation	Assessment of the likely opportunities for improved service delivery and what needs to be done to manage sources of risk associated with each option. This can provide a framework for adopting a more innovative approaches.

The explanations in Table 6.1 clearly signal a requirement to address both opportunities and threats if the listed objectives are to be achieved. Indeed, if an organisation's RM activity is primarily threat orientated with a focus on improved control and neutralisation of threats, it is difficult to see how some of the above objectives could be pursued (improved decision-making and innovation, for example).

Further insights into what RM might achieve involves specifying potential benefits (objectives for RM), in more operational detail. For example, Table 6.2 lists 43 potential benefits of RM associated with different aspects of an organisation's activities (OGC, 2002: Annex A).

Table 6.2 Examples of Benefits of Risk Management (OGC, 2002: Annex A; Crown copyright 2002, used with permission)

A1 Strategic benefits
1. Corporate decision-making is improved through the high visibility of risk exposure, both for individual activities, and major projects, across the whole of the organisation.
2. A progressive management style and a culture of continuous improvement are enhanced by the encouragement of openness in relation to risk.
3. The organisation's image in the eyes of managers, major stakeholders, partners, suppliers and the public is enhanced through the visible and highly professional approach.
4. Ensures that threats to cost, time and performance are managed with the clear aim of meeting the objectives of the organisation and its stakeholders.
5. Creates an awareness of the risks in making business decisions at all levels in the organisation.
6. Embedding the processes provides a clear message and direction in meeting the needs of corporate governance.
7. Clear ownership and accountability for risk and its management.
8. Enhances an awareness of the balance between costs and benefits which should lead to making appropriate business and operational decisions.
A2 FINANCIAL BENEFITS
1. Provides financial benefit to the organisation through improved 'value for money' potential.
2. Improves management of project finance.
3. Provides visibility and strict management of contingency plans.

A3 PROGRAMME BENEFITS

1. Management of project risk is carried out within the wider context of programmes, thus minimising the risk of individual project failure through the impact of other projects.

2. Consistency of approach can be achieved throughout the programme by high-level monitoring and direction.

3. Forward thinking is promoted through the programme, fostering greater confidence in project and programme success through commitment to risk management activities.

4. A culture of openness and teamwork is generated through the collective participation in identification, management and reporting of risk activities.

5. A wide range of data may be collected for detailed analysis, enhancing the ability to forecast outcomes and provide accurate estimates.

6. Clarity of vision is engendered for uncertain or unknown work challenges, via the use of structured management of risk techniques.

7. The organisation is prepared for most eventualities, and being assured of adequate contingency plans.

A4 BUSINESS PROCESS BENEFITS

1. Improves likelihood of supporting the agenda for the organisation as laid down by major stakeholders such as top management.

2. Improves understanding of the project through the identification of risks and proper consideration of mitigation strategies.

3. Creates an understanding of the relationship between risks, cost, programme timescale and price.

4. Creates an environment for the conscious acceptance of business risks on an informed basis.

5. Assists in the establishment of criteria for the inclusion of risk contingency.

6. Reduces the need for costs to be hidden within individual elements of the cost estimate.

7. Demonstrates clear corporate governance procedures.

A5 OVERALL MANAGEMENT BENEFITS

1. Facilitates 'ownership' of both risks and their causes, so that they are effectively monitored, and practically managed.

2. Provides management with clear visibility of the risk and actions being taken to resolve them.

3. Makes the relative importance of each risk immediately apparent.

4. Improves contingency plans and the organisation's business continuity plans.

5. Enables decision making to be more systematic and less subjective.

6. Reduces the need for time or cost escalation.

7. Reduces product performance shortfalls and maintenance expenditure.

8. Brings realism into consideration of the trade-offs between performance, cost and time.

9. Allows comparison of the robustness of projects to specific uncertainties.

10. Assists in moving towards a 'no surprises' environment and so managing expectations.

11. Facilitates selection of options alongside consideration of the fallback positions.

12. Emphasises to project teams the importance of clear criteria for performance measurement.

13. Provides a framework for encouraging lateral thinking in searching for better ways to mitigate risks.

14. A creates an open and candid approach to risks that encourages staff to assist in overcoming them.

15. Encourages a considered and decisive style of management, resulting in proactive decisions and proper handling of the risks themselves, rather than later reactive decision making (management of crisis).

16. Filters and prioritises risks so that management may have clear visibility of the important risks.

17. Provides for acceptance and ownership of risks at the correct management level.

18. Creates awareness in all personnel of the cost and benefit implications of their actions in managing risk.

The list in Table 6.2 shows that RM might be undertaken at various levels of decision making to achieve corporate-wide, ongoing strategic benefits, improvements in project and programme performance, and improvements in the quality of operating decisions. Aside from the evident lack of structure to this list, the benefits listed range from the very broad to the very specific, corresponding to long term, strategic objectives for any RM activity, down to specific operational objectives that virtually define the required content of RM activities. For example, benefits A1.2, 3, 6 concern broad corporate benefits which are consequential on effective RM, but convey no suggestion of how RM might be carried out. At the other extreme are benefits that suggest specific operational steps in any RM process. Benefits A3.5, A5.1, 2, 3, 9, 11-13, 16, 17, are all examples of this kind. They translate easily into operational steps to be included in the RM process. In between these two extreme groups of benefits are benefits that could form performance objectives for any RM activity. Benefits A3.3, 4, 7, A4.7, A5.4, 5, 6, 7, are examples in this category. Still other benefits listed in Table 6.2 imply a purpose for individual applications of RM. Benefits A4.5, A5.1, 8, 9, 17 are examples in this category.

Table 6.3 presents this distinction between different levels of benefit or objective in a more helpful format. The objectives shown in Table 6.3 are by no means a complete set, but they are sufficient to illustrate the range of objectives that might be associated with RM activity. Table 6.3 indicates four levels of objective for RM activity, focused on process, application context, performance, and strategic capability.

Table 6.3 A Multi-level Structure of Possible Objectives for Risk Management (adapted from Ward, 2004; Copyright PMI, used with permission)

1. Process objectives (related to phases in the RM process)	2. Application objectives	3. RM performance criteria	4. Strategic capability objectives
Clarify risky contexts	Crisis management	Demonstrate clear corporate governance procedures	Enhance culture of continuous improvement
Identify risks	Contingency planning	Higher profitability	Good management distinguished from 'dumb luck'
Size risk from various sources	Business continuity	Objectives achieved more often	Bad management distinguished from simple 'bad luck'
Determine the significance of sources of risk, and likely effects on performance	Proactive control	Fewer surprises and crises	Enhanced competitiveness
Assess appropriateness of performance criteria	Strategy formation	More effective management of change	Enhanced corporate reputation via an image of competence
Identify options for treating risk, assess these options, select appropriate options, and plan for implementation	More effective use of resources		Development of a RM culture where risk is welcomed as an opportunity, and organisation learning is commonplace
Monitor risk, assess the effectiveness of treatment, and review relevance of plans	Improved project evaluation and design		A culture of openness and teamwork generated
	More effective exploitation of opportunities		
Documentation of analysis	Clearer thinking	A record of decisions	A knowledge base
	Clearer communication		A framework for data acquisition
	Familiarisation		

6.2 PROCESS FOCUSED OBJECTIVES

Process focused objectives are the most limited kind of objective, concerned with achieving particular phases in a particular project RM process application. In crude terms a RM process might be described in terms of six phases such as: 'define the context', 'identify risks', 'estimate risks', 'evaluate risks', 'treat risks', 'monitor and review'. The process objectives entries in Table 6.3 column 1 then relate directly to achieving the output of these phases. Given this correspondence, it is not necessary to undertake a comprehensive RM process to achieve one or more of the process objectives. For example, a given application of RM might be primarily concerned with the identification of risks, and so stop the RM process once the 'identify risks' phase is complete. Such an approach to RM would preclude pursuit of all the other process objectives listed in column 1, and consequently severely limit ability to pursue objectives in subsequent columns of Table 6.3. In principle, the process objectives in column 1 could be elaborated to reflect more sophisticated phase structure descriptions of the RM process, and therefore more specific process objectives. Indeed, this is a primary motive for articulating formal process frameworks in more detail than the simple six phase characterisation above (Chapman and Ward, 2003). Chapters 7 and 8 consider this issue in more detail.

6.3 APPLICATION FOCUSED OBJECTIVES

Application focused objectives in column 2 of Table 6.3 relate to the purpose for which RM is undertaken in a particular application context. Objectives like those in column 2 could be appropriate in a variety of different contexts including, operations, projects, programmes and strategies.

To give this characterisation of application contexts and associated objectives for RM more precision, it is useful to envisage operations, projects and programmes of projects, as embedded in a parent strategy whose development can be described in terms of a 'strategy life cycle' (SLC). Table 6.4 conceptualises the SLC as a seven stage process, each stage involving a number of component steps and associated decisions. Essentially this follows Chapman and Ward's (2003) characterisation of the project life cycle, with some modifications. Thus a strategy's life cycle begins with conceptualisation of an ill-defined idea beginning with a 'trigger event' (Lyles, 1981), when an opportunity or need is perceived. If considered worth pursuing, elaboration of the idea follows in a strategy formulation stage. This stage could involve fairly opaque, intuitive and complex decision processes (Mintzberg, 1994), but is likely to involve development of design and associated performance criteria in an iterative process. Assuming an acceptable strategy is formulated, the next stage involves decisions about planning for implementation (or programming as Mintzberg terms it), followed by detailed allocation of internal resources and personnel to implement the plan (Table 6.4b). As with the strategy formulation stage, planning and allocation decisions could involve a number of iterations with potential looping back from allocation or planning to earlier stages. This process may break the parent strategy down into a series of component strategies or projects for more detailed development, implementation and control purposes. It may also prompt the abandonment of a strategy or the conception of further strategies. The next stage, implementation of a strategy, could be of lengthy duration without a clear end point for the parent strategy (unless it fails or is abandoned), but with clear end points for component strategies or projects. The review stage involves a documented audit following substantive implementation of the strategy or its components. The purpose of this activity is to capture lessons for the future and to inform the development of future strategies. Ongoing operations is shown as a final stage to depict the basic operations of the organisation which are the product of all previously implemented or emergent strategies.

This stage and step characterisation of the SLC highlights potential primary roles for RM in different decision contexts as indicated in the right hand column of Table 6.4. At every stage of the SLC, organisational performance and the management of uncertainty are key concerns, but the focus of attention will vary as the cycle progresses. Most organisations are likely to apply RM in a piecemeal fashion, to some SLC stages and steps, but not to others. In particular, RM is most often applied in the 'maintenance of operations' by specialists in insurance, health and safety, legal department, finance, quality control, internal audit etc., as noted earlier. Elsewhere, for example in strategy planning and implementation, explicit RM may be relatively weak.

Table 6.4a Applications of Risk Management in the Strategy Life Cycle (Ward, 2003: Copyright Perpetuity Press, used with permission)

Stages	Steps	Roles for risk management

Strategy conception	Trigger event
	Concept capture
	Clarification of purpose
	Concept elaboration
	Concept evaluation
		Possibility and issue
		  identification
		Identification of stakeholders
		  and their expectations
		Identification of appropriate
		  performance objectives

Strategy formulation	Basic design
	Development of
	  performance criteria
	Design development
	Design evaluation
		Testing reliability of design
		Testing the feasibility of design
		Setting of performance criteria
		Assessing the likely cost of
		  a design
		Assessing the likely benefits
		  from a design
		Assessing the effect of changes
		  to a design

Strategic planning	Base programme
	Development of targets
	  and milestones
	Programme development
	Programme evaluation
		Identifying and allowing for
		  regulatory constraints
		Assessing the feasibility of
		  a plan
		Assessing the likely duration of
		  a plan
		Assessing the likely cost of
		  a plan
		Determination of appropriate
		  milestones
		Estimation of resources
		  required
		Assessing the effect of changes
		  to the plan
		Determination of appropriate
		  levels of contingency funds
		  and resources

Table continued overleaf.

Table 6.4b Applications of Risk Management in the Strategy Life Cycle (Ward, 2003: Copyright Perpetuity Press, used with permission)

Stages	Steps	Roles for risk management
Resource allocation	Base design and plan detail Development of allocation criteria Allocation development Allocation evaluation	Evaluation of alternative procurement strategies Defining contractual terms and conditions Determining appropriate risk sharing arrangements Assessing the implications of contract conditions Assessment and comparison of competitive tenders Determining appropriate target costs and bid prices for contracts Estimation of likely profit
Strategy implementation	Coordinate and control Monitor progress Modification of targets and milestones Allocation modification Control evaluation	Identification of remaining execution risks Assessing implications of changes to design or plan Revising estimates of performance Assessing feasibility of meeting performance criteria Assessing reliability of testing equipment Assessing requirement for resources to modify programme deliverables
Strategic review	Basic review Review development Review evaluation	Assessing effectiveness of risk management strategies Identification of realised risks and effective responses
Ongoing operations	Maintenance of operations Development of performance criteria Performance evaluation	Identifying extent of future liabilities Reducing liability exposures Assessment of appropriate level of resources required Reducing the 'cost of risk'

In principle, RM should be a natural part of the 'strategy conception' and 'strategy formulation' stages of the SLC. Indeed, ideas like Ansoff's (1984) Strategic Issue Analysis and the ubiquitous SWOT analysis (Hill and Westbrook, 1997), follow the basic thrust of RM, albeit in rather broad conceptual terms. However, concepts and approaches to managing risk do not appear to be particularly well developed in the strategic management literature, and the various stages of the strategic life cycle could benefit substantially from more specific application of RM concepts and techniques.

6.5   PERFORMANCE FOCUSED OBJECTIVES

The performance focused objectives in column 3 of Table 6.3 extend beyond the way risk is addressed in individual RM applications and relate to improved performance over a stream of applications and improvements in corporate performance as a whole. In principle, performance in terms of objectives with this focus are more measurable than performance in respect of process and application focused objectives. Objectives in column 3 offer the most obvious ways of measuring the effectiveness of RM efforts.

6.6   STRATEGIC CAPABILITY OBJECTIVES

'Strategic capability' objectives in column 4 of Table 6.3 imply a longer term perspective of potential benefits from RM than even performance focused objectives. Strategic capability objectives go beyond short to medium-term improvements in organisation performance, in being concerned with fundamental qualitative improvements in RM capability and related benefits. This includes the achievement of a fundamental shift in risk thinking which makes subsequent use and development of RM easier, more efficient, and more effective, thereby facilitating a virtuous circle of continuous improvement. For example, a complacent, risk-averse culture based on a widely held view that 'uncertainty and risk are negative issues, and RM is just more bureaucracy', should give way to a new RM culture based on a shared view that 'uncertainty is the source of commercial opportunities, and we need to understand opportunities to exploit them effectively'.

Part of this shift involves understanding what is under a given party's control, what is not, and why it is not. The result is an ability to understand and reward management performance appropriately with obvious benefits in the form of employee motivation and commitment. Good managers are recognised and rewarded, rather than those who are merely lucky or skilled at 'presenting a good face'. Similarly, manages who experience plain bad luck in undertaking risky ventures can be distinguished from simply bad managers.

These kinds of culture change can make work more rewarding and make going to work more enjoyable. This in turn can lead to higher quality staff wanting to join (and stay with) the organisation, with obvious general long-term benefits (Chapman and Ward, 2003).

6.7   OBJECTIVES OF DOCUMENTATION

As with objectives set for any other management activity, achievement of the various levels of RM objectives is not automatic, but has to be consciously pursued. This requires management to first recognise the full scope of possible benefits obtainable, and then seek to achieve these by adoption of appropriate RM practices. As an example of this approach, consider the benefits of documentation for RM purposes shown in the lower part of Table 6.3.

Documentation is a key feature of all formal processes. This documentation is a key process output, but it also facilitates the operation of a formal process, and it provides a means of assessing the performance of the process. All managers are aware of the importance of documentation for effective management. Formal RM processes require appropriate documentation for all these basic reasons, but documentation is especially important because of the need to deal with uncertainty in terms of both variability and ambiguity. This can include information in a wide variety of forms: describing activities, sources of uncertainty, possible responses, decisions taken, identified trigger points for action, and so on. Such documentation might be regarded as a by-product of RM activity, rather than a central concern, but it serves a number of useful purposes which may be worth pursuing in their own right (Chapman and Ward, 2003: Chap. 3):

1. **Clearer thinking.** A focus on documentation can clarify the initial thinking process. If people have to set down their thinking in writing, this forces clarification of what is involved.

2. **Clearer communications.** Documentation can provide an unambiguous vehicle for communication at any given point in time. If people explain what they mean in writing terms of strategies, plans, risks and responses, the scope for misunderstanding is significantly reduced. This can be particularly important in communications between different organizational

units or in business partner situations. In such settings a number of questions concerning the RM effort need to be addressed. For example: who is responsible for which activities?, who bears the financial consequences of which sources of risk?, and who will respond to realization of shared risks? Clear documentation can also be an essential part of making all threats and opportunities and all key assumptions clearly visible to all interested parties. A key role for any formal analysis process is the collective use of team input to a joint decision, drawing on a range of expertise as appropriate. Communication is a vital aspect of this process.

3. **Familiarization.** Documentation can provide a record to assist new personnel to 'get up to speed' quickly. Staff turnover can be a significant source of risk, which documentation helps to mitigate. RM documentation is a very valuable training tool specific to the activities to which new staff are attached.

4. **A record of decisions.** Documentation can provide a record which explains the rationale for key decisions. In some industries (and for some careers), this may become a very important document if a decision goes badly wrong due to bad luck.

5. **A knowledge base.** Documentation can provide a record which captures corporate knowledge in a manner useful for successors, and subsequent initiatives. For example, if the kernel of the thinking behind one project is available in a readily accessible form, for those doing the next project, the value of this information can be very great. For contracting organizations this information can amount to a competitive advantage over rival firms. Such information can also be the basis of ongoing training as well as an individual learning tool, and a basis for continuous improvement.

6. **A framework for data acquisition.** When organizations first introduce a formal RM process, appropriate data is usually difficult to come by. However, the use of a formal RM process clarifies the nature of appropriate data, and generally leads to the systematic collection and appreciation of such data, as part of the documentation process. The importance of this development is difficult to understand for organizations which have not been through the process of introducing formal RM, but it is recognized as a major benefit by those who have introduced such processes. It is important to ask whether this issue is relevant up-front, because

it means a current lack of data which could be collected in the future does not distort the development of an approach which best serves long-term needs.

If only the first of these six purposes is of interest, limited documentation may be appropriate. However, the other purposes deserve careful prior attention, even if the design of the documentation has a fairly free format. The key underlying purpose of documentation is to integrate the expertise of teams of people so they can make effective, collective decisions based on clearly articulated and consistent premises.

6.8   LINKS BETWEEN LEVELS OF OBJECTIVE

The example objectives in Table 6.3 form a tentative hierarchy of objectives for RM. Pursuit of 'process objectives' contributes to, or facilitates, the achievement of 'application objectives', which in turn contribute to the achievement of 'performance objectives' in the short to medium term.

A shortcoming of much current RM practice is the lack of recognition given to the different levels of objective for RM in Table 6.3. Partly, this may reflect a failure to identify the full range of potential benefits achievable. Partly, it may be due to a lack of clarity about how lower level objectives (to the left in Table 6.3) contribute to the achievement of higher level objectives (to the right in Table 6.3). Chapman and Ward (2003) discuss some of these linkages, but this is an area that would benefit from research with organisations that have been successful in pursuing level 3 and 4 objectives in their RM activity.

Whatever the precise mechanisms linking achievement of objectives in one (lower) level with the next, it is certainly the case that limited attainment of 'process objectives' will severely curtail performance in terms of higher level objectives. For example, much current RM practice does not progress, in 'process objective' terms, much beyond the fourth objective in column 1 of Table 6.3 ('determine the significance of sources of risk, and likely effects on performance'). Often this involves little more than plotting identified risk events on a probability impact grid, assigning notional priorities, and then assigning responsibilities for managing these risks. More sophisticated analysis employs Monte Carlo simulation to progress to the next process objective ('assess the appropriateness of performance criteria') to derive distributions of project performance in cost and time terms, but on its own this may not add a great deal.

The next process objective ('identify options for treating risk, assess these options, select appropriate options, and plan for implementation'), surely takes place in most RM applications, but beyond recording proposed actions there is often no formal analysis undertaken to assess and compare the cost effectiveness of alternative treatment options. This severely limits progress that can be made in pursuing higher level objectives, and attendant benefits. Specifically, Chapman and Ward (2003) have argued that effective RM should pursue risk-efficient approaches to project designs, plans, and treatment of sources of uncertainty that evaluate trade-offs between risk and expected performance associated with alternative courses of action.

6.9 FACTORS INFLUENCING RISK MANAGEMENT OBJECTIVES

Echoing the tendency to associate risk and RM primarily with the threat management rather than opportunity management, RM is often introduced in response to a perceived need to avoid poor performance rather than because of the opportunities it offers for enhancing performance.

The previous section argued for developing an appreciation of the potential benefits obtainable from effective RM, and then establishing RM processes capable of producing these benefits. Judging by the typically limited levels of investment by organisations in developing an operating RM processes, it appears that RM is often motivated by a need to demonstrate compliance with externally imposed requirements, (such as corporate 'governance guidelines'), or to address weaknesses in performance revealed by recent experience. Figure 6.1 illustrates these influences. Much of the pressure for RM originates from bad experiences: heavy commercial losses, substantial cost overruns on major projects, major accidents, fraud, terrorist attacks, natural disasters, and so on.

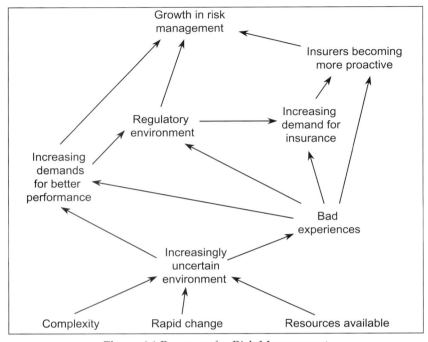

Figure 6.1 Pressures for Risk Management

These experiences can lead to substantial demands for better performance by particular organisations, from shareholders and management in the private sector, and from government and voters in the public sector. Such demands on a particular organisation need not be related to bad experiences of that organisation. The attacks in New York and Washington on September 11th, 2001 underlined for management everywhere the need to address physical threats to the organisation's activities and assets, including employees.

Bad experiences are also a key driver of developments in the regulatory environment, typically in respect of corporate governance and health and safety legislation. These developments can lead to increased demand for insurance, as in the case of Directors' and Officers' (D&O) liability. As is well known, bad experiences can stimulate demand for insurance and reduce the profitability of insurers. Together, these factors encourage insurers to become more proactive in enhancing their own RM practices and in encouraging the development of RM practices in client organisations. Of course, RM stimulated by these concerns will be largely concerned with reducing adverse effects on performance and associated threats to performance.

Taking a broader view of risk, the lower part of Figure 6.1 indicates that increasing uncertainty caused by complexity, rapid change, and limited resources, contributes to bad experiences and increasing demands for better performance. Focusing on these factors implies taking a broader perspective of RM objectives than a focus on bad experiences and their consequences. The need is then to improve performance (and reduce bad experiences) by managing uncertainty directly. Ways of doing this should include efforts to cope with complexity, rapid change, and make more effective use of available resources.

Figure 6.1 offers an outline explanation of why so much RM activity is focused on threats, and things that can go wrong. This is a very important role for RM and the benefits of effective threat orientated RM can be significant. However as indicated by Table 6.3, these benefits form only a small part of what could be achieved by a broader RM approach which addresses uncertainty and factors contributing to uncertainty. The factors in the lower part of Figure 6.1 should be no less motivators and generators of objectives for RM than the factors in the upper part of Figure 6.1. The problem is only that they are rather less visible, and perhaps less urgent, than the bad experiences and their knock-on effects.

6.10   CONCLUSION

A necessary condition for effective RM is a clear understanding of why RM is being undertaken. However, the full scope of benefits from RM will not be achieved unless the full range of related objectives is identified and actively pursued. This means pursuing objectives for RM on four levels:

1. Achieving particular aspects of the RM process;

2. Contributing to the management of particular application contexts;

3. Measurable improvements in corporate performance;

4. Fundamental improvements in RM capability.

These levels form a tentative hierarchy with achievement of level one objectives contributing to level to objectives and so on. Limited efforts at lower levels will make achievement of objectives at higher levels that much more difficult.

7

STANDARDS AND THE RISK MANAGEMENT PROCESS

7.1 INTRODUCTION

This chapter is the first of two that look in some detail at the 'whichway' dimension of RM development introduced in Chapter 1. In this dimension choices relate to the degree of formality and documentation in risk management (RM) processes, the scope of processes, the sophistication of tools and techniques employed, and the extent of quantification. Effective and efficient applications of RM require a formal process to provide a structure and to make explicit the tasks to be carried out in a given application.

Defining procedures is a common way of ensuring that people are clear what needs to be done, and that quality and consistency are maintained across different applications over time. Effective and efficient procedures need to be transparent and repeatable. The level of detail that is appropriate depends on the context and complexity of the overall task. For situations involving low uncertainty, formalisation can involve very well defined specific steps. In the limit, it can involve a rigid 'paint by numbers' procedure. Pre-flight safety checks on an aircraft often resemble this, at least until a fault is identified. Where high uncertainty is involved, it becomes much more difficult and inappropriate to specify procedures in much detail. Not only can this be inefficient and ineffective, it can also be counter-productive if attempts are made to persist with procedures that are too limited, or too inflexible to take into account important aspects of the application context. Therefore, a sensible approach is to define procedures in sufficient detail so that they can be usefully applied in a reasonably wide range of contexts and circumstances. A key issue is what constitutes sufficient detail.

Such considerations apply to the specification of a generic formal RM process. Given the variety of contexts in which RM might be employed, the range of objectives that might be pursued, and the complexity of issues involved, it is not appropriate to look for closely defined, inflexible procedures. Formality in RM processes needs to be more about making sure the right questions get asked, helping decision-makers to develop the right answers, and making sure that everyone who needs to know understands the answers.

7.2 STANDARDS AND GUIDELINES

RM is a developing discipline and there are many and varied views and descriptions of what RM involves, how it should be conducted, and what it is for. As a result, a number of standards or guidelines have been produced with a view to clarifying:

1   The terminology related to the words used ;

2   Objectives for RM;

3   The contexts in which RM might be used;

4   The processes by which RM can be carried out;

5   Administrative arrangements for operating and supporting RM processes.

A number of standards or guidelines are publicly available. These can be broken down into three groups: those published by national standards associations, those produced by professional institutions, and those issued by government departments. In the UK these include the Office of Government Commerce (OGC), the National Audit Office, HM Treasury, and Cabinet office. 'Standards' in respect of non-statutory activities like RM are often little different from summarised guidelines, and termed 'standards' because they are usually published by national standards associations such as the British Standards Institute, the Standards Association of Australia, and the Canada Standards Association.

This chapter considers how a selection of standards or guides describe the RM process. Five process frameworks are outlined and compared from:

*   the AIRMIC, ALARM, IRM Standard (2002);

*   the Australia/New Zealand standard 4360 (1999);

*   the UK Office of Government Commerce (OGC) Management of Risk Guide (2002);

- a representative project RM process framework (Chapman and Ward, 2003);

- the Enterprise Risk Management framework published by COSO, the Committee of Sponsoring Organisations of the Treadway Commission, (PricewaterhouseCoopers, 2004).

As with definitions of risk (discussed in Chapter 3), there have been many attempts to define a generic RM process framework. These can differ in detail, terminology, emphasis, and scope. This chapter summarises the process frameworks listed above and makes critical comparisons between them.

In considering the description of each RM process framework, the reader should note how definition of the term 'risk' drives the use of other terms employed, and even the scope and nature of the RM process. Accordingly, readers may find it useful to review the definitions of risk listed in Table 3.1 before reading this chapter.

7.3 THE AIRMIC, ALARM, IRM PROCESS FRAMEWORK

A key reference is the AIRMIC, ALARM, IRM *'Risk Management Standard'* (2002). Page 1 of the AIRMIC, ALARM, IRM (AAIRM) standard makes the very important point that: *'there are many ways of achieving the objectives of risk management and it would be impossible to try to set them all out in a single document. Therefore it was never intended to produce a prescriptive standard which would have led to a box ticking approach, nor to establish a certifiable process.'* Section 2 of the AAIRM standard provides diagrams summarising 'drivers of key risks', and a diagram showing a RM process framework. Subsequent sections outline the nature of risk analysis, evaluation, and treatment. Section 7 outlines the information needs at director, business unit and individual levels in the organisation, and for external reporting. The structure and administration of RM is outlined in Section 8, largely by setting down the roles for the board, business unit, RM functions, and internal audit.

The AAIRM standard RM process framework is shown in Table 7.1. This is a relatively simple specification which characterises the RM process in terms of identifying, estimating, evaluating, treating, and subsequently monitoring risks. Other than acknowledging that the whole process is intended to support the achievement of the organisation's strategic objectives, the framework makes no reference to the context and therefore the timescale within which the RM process operates. Implicitly, the AAIRM framework envisages RM as an organisation-wide activity which is on-going, with the sequence of phases in Table 7.1 being repeated periodically (AAIRM Standard, 2002: p2):

> *'RM is a central part of any organisation's strategic management. It is a process whereby organisations methodically address the risks attaching to their activities with the goal of achieving sustained benefit within each activity and across the portfolio of all activities. .....*
>
> *RM should be a continuous and developing process which runs throughout the organisation's strategy and the implementation of that strategy.'*

Table 7.1 The AIRMIC, ALARM, IRM (2002)
Standard Risk Management Process

Phase	*Purposes and tasks in outline*
The organisation's strategic objectives	
Risk assessment – risk analysis	
• Identification	Identify organisation's exposure to uncertainty.
• Description	Display identified risks in a structured format including consequence and probability of each risk for prioritisation purposes.
• Estimation	Establish probability of occurrence and possible consequence.
Risk assessment – risk evaluation	Compare estimated risks against the organisation's risk criteria to make decisions about significance of risk.
Risk treatment	Select and implement measures to modify risks (includes risk control/mitigation, avoidance, transfer, risk financing etc).
Risk reporting	Reporting risk assessment and treatment externally and internally to different levels.
Monitoring	Regular monitoring and review of assessment and treatment of risks, and of the RM process.

7.4 THE AUSTRALIA/NEW ZEALAND STANDARD 4360

The well known Australia/New Zealand Standard 4360 on RM (Australia/New Zealand Standard, 1999) is slightly more detailed than the AAIRM standard. Summarised in Table 7.2, the phases in the AS/NZ RM process framework are largely similar to those of the AAIRM standard, although some differences are worth commenting on. The most significant difference is the inclusion of an 'establish the context' phase to start the RM process off. This is very helpful because it acknowledges that RM may be carried out in many separate applications.

Table 7.2 The Australia/New Zealand Standard (1999) Risk Management Process

Phase	*Purposes and tasks in outline*
Establish the context	Describe the strategic, organisational, and RM context Establish criteria against which risks will be evaluated Define a structure for analysis
Identify risks	Identify 'what, why, and how things can arise'.
Analyse risks	Analyse risks in terms of the range of potential consequence and likelihood in the context of existing controls.
Evaluate risks	Rank risks in terms of estimated risk level against pre-established criteria.
Treat risks	Develop and implement plans to manage each risk.
Monitor and review	Monitor and review the effectiveness of risk treatments, the performance of the RM system, and the changes that might affect them.

'Establishing the strategic context' involves determining the crucial elements which might support or impair an organisation's ability to manage the risks it faces (page 9). Focusing on the environment in which the organisation operates, this step includes identifying the organisation's strengths, weaknesses, opportunities and threats.

'Establishing the organisation context' involves understanding the organisation and its capabilities, as well as the objectives and strategies that are in place to achieve them (page 9).

'Establishing the RM context' involves establishing: the goals, objectives, strategies, scope and parameters of the activity, or part of the organisation to which the RM process is being applied, and its relationship with other activities' (page 10). Appendix A of the AS/NZ standard lists 28 example application contexts including investigation of various liabilities sources, new ventures, particular threats, projects and operating systems. This step is also about outline planning of how to carry out the particular RM application. It involves setting up the scope and boundaries of a RM application, defining objectives for the process, resources required, duration and location of the process, who is to be involved, and the scope of associated studies.

In principle, most of these context related steps are included in the AAIRM framework's identification phase, but the added detail in the AS/NZ framework is useful. However, unlike the AS/NZ framework, the AAIRM framework does not incorporate any reference to planning for individual RM applications. Given the desirability of cost-effective RM, explicit consideration of planning the RM process for application in a particular context would seem to be a good idea.

The next step in Table 7.2 involves establishing criteria against which risks will be evaluated. This step is also included in the AAIRM framework (Table 7.1), but as part of risk evaluation.

The final step in the 'establish the context' phase of Table 7.2 is 'define the structure'. The AS/NZ standard describes this as *separating the (subject) activity or project into a set of elements... to provide a logical framework for risk identification and analysis'*. While important, it could be argued that this step is at a lower level of detail than the rest of the framework, and therefore of limited value in Table 7.2.

The next phase in Table 7.2, 'identify risks', corresponds directly with the 'identification' and 'description' phases in the AAIRM process in Table 7.1. However, the AS/NZ framework highlights the desirability of identifying not just the exposures to uncertainty (risk), but also of identifying *'why and how things can arise'*. The language here is presumably deliberately ambiguous to preclude undue focus on events or circumstances that produce adverse effects on performance.

The remaining phases in the AS/NZ framework of 'analyse risks', 'evaluate risks', 'treat risks', 'monitor and review', correspond closely with the 'risk estimation', 'risk evaluation', 'risk treatment', and 'monitoring' phases in the AAIRM framework (Table 7.1). The risk-reporting phase in Table 7.1 does not appear as one of the sequential phases in Table 7.2. However the AS/NZ framework incorporates this activity as a parallel 'communicate and consult' activity that is on-going through all the RM process phases.

7.5   THE OGC PROCESS FRAMEWORK

A third generic RM process framework of interest is that published in *'Management of Risk: guidance for practitioners'* by the UK Office of Government Commerce (2002). This guidance is more extensive than that provided in the two standards just discussed. The RM process is broadly similar, but additional phases included in the OGC process are worth noting. The phases in the OGC process are shown in Table 7.3.

Table 7.3 The OGC(2002) Risk Management Process Framework

Phase	Purposes and tasks in outline
Define a framework	Define or validate the RM policy to be adopted.
Identify the risks	Identify risks and causes of risk at organisation, programme, project, or operational levels.
Identify probable risk owners	Preliminary identification of people who could be tasked to manage particular sources of risk (threats).
Evaluate the risks	Assess probability and impact of individual risks taking into account any interdependencies or other factors outside the immediate scope under investigation, and timing of occurrence. Where appropriate, sort risks based on their importance.
Set acceptable levels of risk	Determine the overall level of risk which the organisation can tolerate for the given situation.
Identify suitable responses to risk	Identify several potential responses for each major threat and opportunity. Investigate possible effects of responses on other areas of activity.
Implement responses	Select the most appropriate set of responses. Finalise associated plans and implement them.
Monitor effectiveness	Monitor risk responses and assess effectiveness. Check for changes in risks and revisit responses and plans as necessary.
Embed and review	Continuous improvement requires periodic review of how well risk management processes and frameworks are embedded into every day management activities.

The first phase is somewhat similar to the 'establish the (RM) context' phase of Table 7.2, although use of the term 'RM policy' in Table 7.3 implies more standardisation across different RM applications than envisaged with the AS/NZ process. In the OGC guidelines, 'defining a framework' involves (OGC, 2002: p18):

- identifying relevant standards, policies and legal requirements;

- identifying the context and perspective for the situation;

- agreeing objectives for the RM process, constraints and concerns;

- identifying tools and techniques to be adopted;

- identifying a scale for risk evaluation;

- documenting the above to reflect the current situation.

Following the 'define a framework' phase, the OGC process comprises a sequence of phases involving identifying, evaluating and managing risks in a similar manner to the AS/NZ standard and AAIRM processes, although terminology is a little different. 'Evaluate' in Table 7.3 corresponds to 'analyse' in Table 7.2, 'set acceptable levels of risk' in Table 7.3 corresponds to 'evaluate risks' in Table 7.2, 'identify and implement responses' in Table 7.3 corresponds to 'treat risk' in Table 7.2. Note that the OGC process alone includes a phase explicitly identifying probable risk owners, that is, allocation of responsibility for managing particular sources of risk. In the AS/NZ standard this allocation is part of developing risk treatment plans, in the AAIRM standard allocation of ownership of a risk is only briefly mentioned as part of the risk profile produced in the risk analysis phases (identification, description and estimation).

7.6   A PROJECT CONTEXT PROCESS FRAMEWORK

Some of the most developed RM process frameworks focus on RM applications in a project context. Examples include the UK Association for Project Management (APM), *'Project Risk Analysis and Management (PRAM) guide'* (Bartlett et al, 2004); the US Project Management Institute (PMI) *'Project Management Body of Knowledge (PMBOK) Guide'* (PMI, 2000, Chap. 11); *'Control of risk: a guide to systematic management of risk from construction'*, published by the Construction Industry Research and Information Association (CIRIA), (Godfrey, 1996); and the *'Risk Analysis and Management of Projects'* (RAMP) guide, (Lewin, 2002). The

RAMP guide is a joint publication of the UK Faculty and Institute of Actuaries and the Institute of Civil Engineers, written by a working party drawn from members of these institutions. At the time of writing, both the PRAM and PMBOK guides are in the process of being revised. Additionally, the RAMP working party has established a separate methodologies cooperation working party involving representatives from those responsible for the PRAM, PMBOK, CIRIA, and OGC guides. The aim of this working party is to collate information about RM process frameworks and develop a more coherent view of best practice in RM.

These project context frameworks are of interest here because RM process issues in projects are generally pertinent to any organisation context. The main reason for this is that most organisation activities could be thought of as a project, or part of a project. Depending on one's time horizon, projects can be short-lived, small-scale tasks; major organisational developments, perhaps involving component projects; or long-term projects such as the setting-up and continued operation of a whole organisation. The project context is also of interest here because formal project RM processes and associated techniques are already widely used, often highly developed, and capable of much wider application than is currently the case.

A useful discussion and synthesis of RM process frameworks developed in the project RM literature (PMI, 2000; Bartlett et al, 2004; Lewin, 2002), is provided by Chapman and Ward (2003: Chap. 4) in the form of a process framework they refer to as the SHAMPU (Shape, Harness, and Manage Project Uncertainty) process. This widely used process framework is summarised in Table 7.4.

Table 7.4 A Nine Phase Portrayal of the SHAMPU Process
(Chapman and Ward, 2003. Copyright John Wiley & Sons Ltd,
used with permission)

Phases	*Purposes and tasks in outline*
Define the project	Consolidate relevant existing information about the project at a strategic level in a holistic and integrated structure suitable for risk management. Fill in any gaps uncovered in the consolidation process, and resolve any inconsistencies.
Focus the process	Scope and provide a strategic plan for the RM process. Plan the RM process at an operational level.
Identify the issues	Identify sources of uncertainty at a strategic level in terms of opportunities and threats. Identify what might be done in terms of proactive and reactive responses. Identify secondary sources of uncertainty associated with responses.
Structure the issues	Complete the structuring of earlier phases. Test simplifying assumptions. Provide more complex or alternative structures when appropriate.
Clarify **ownership**	Allocate both financial and managerial responsibility for issues (separately if appropriate).
Estimate variability	Size uncertainty which is usefully quantified on a first pass. On later passes, refine earlier estimates of uncertainty where this is effective and efficient.
Evaluate implications	Assess statistical dependence (dependence not modeled in a causal structure). Synthesize the results of the estimate phase using dependence assumptions which are fit for purpose. Interpret the results in the context of all earlier phases. Make decisions about proactive and reactive responses, and about refining and redefining earlier analysis, managing the iterative nature of the process as a key aspect of these tasks.

Phases	Purposes and tasks in outline
Harness the plans	Obtain approval for strategic plans shaped by earlier phases. Prepare detailed action plans. These are base plans (incorporating preventative responses) and contingency plans (incorporating reactive responses with trigger points) ready for implementation within the action horizons defined by appropriate lead times. Commit to project plans which are fit for implementation.
Manage implementation	Manage the planned work. Develop action plans for implementation on a rolling basis. Monitor and control (make decisions to refine or redefine project plans as required). Deal with crises (unanticipated issues of significance) and be prepared to cope appropriately with disasters (crises which are not controlled).

The SHAMPU process framework incorporates nine phases, including specific reference to 'define', 'focus', 'structure' and 'ownership' phases. These four phases broaden the scope of the process in comparison to simpler frameworks (Chapman and Ward, 2003; Bartlett et al, 2004), and have an important bearing on the quality and scope of RM. The define phase highlights the importance of documentation which consolidates information about the context of the RM activity. The focus phase recognises that individual RM applications need to be planned to ensure an efficient and cost-effective approach. The structure phase highlights the importance of understanding assumptions made and the potential for interdependencies between different sources of risk and their effects. The ownership phase draws attention to a central issue in RM, the appropriate allocation of risk, and associated incentives to manage it (Chapman and Ward, 2003).

There are clear similarities between the SHAMPU process phases in Table 7.4 and those in Tables 7.1 to 7.3, but there are also some significant differences. In broad terms, the SHAMPU process addresses a wider set of process issues than the processes is summarised in Tables 7.1-7.3. These issues are associated with particular phases as follows:

- the SHAMPU process starts with a 'define' phase which involves consolidating information about the application context including the parties involved, their objectives, the status of plans, and resource requirements.

- the 'focus the process' phase involves deciding on the scope of the RM application and deciding how to carry out the analysis.

- the 'identify the issues' phase is concerned not only with all sources of significant uncertainty, but includes the identification of responses and secondary sources of uncertainty associated with responses.

- a 'structure the issues' phase considers the nature of simplifying assumptions and interactions between context factors and sources of uncertainty.

- a 'clarify ownership' phase addresses the allocation of both financial and managerial responsibilities for risk issues.

- the 'estimate variability' phase is about 'sizing uncertainty' rather than estimating activity narrowly defined in terms of assessing probability and impact for individual events or conditions. There is also explicit recognition that estimation should be an iterative process that involves refining initial rough estimates were appropriate.

- the 'evaluate implications' phase is explicitly concerned with statistical dependence, and includes assessing alternative responses, and selecting appropriate responses.

- the 'harness the plans' phase involves formulating detailed action plans.

- the 'manage implementation' phase incorporates monitoring and reviewing of RM issues and plans, but includes managing the planned (project) work, dealing with crises and being prepared for disasters.

For ease of reference, the approximate alignment and scope of phases between the IRM, AS/NZ, OGC, and SHAMPU frameworks is set out in Table 7.5 at the end of this chapter. Table 7.5 also shows the phases involved in a more recent process framework published by the Committee of Sponsoring Organisations of the Treadway Commission (PricewaterhouseCoopers, 2004), described later in this chapter. This framework partially acknowledges the need to address several of the above issues, in particular: prior definition of objectives, interdependencies between possible events, the relative costs and benefits of alternative responses, secondary sources of uncertainty associated with responses, and the consequent need for an iterative approach before finalising RM action plans.

7.7   ITERATIVE PROCESSES

Identifying the phases of the SHAMPU process in Table 7.4 provides only a partial description of the SHAMPU process. A key aspect, not captured in this table, is the iterative nature of the process. Iterations involve revisiting or looping back to earlier phases to develop, refine, or reconsider aspects of the analysis undertaken to date *in a single application*.

If a single pass, or simple sequential approach to all phases of an RM process is employed, the process is likely to be highly inefficient and seriously ineffective. Time and effort will be wasted on issues that turn out be unimportant, and not enough time will be spent on the important issues which were not anticipated when the RM process started. Iterations are not a feature of any of the frameworks in Tables 7.1-7.3, but can play an important role in ensuring an efficient and effective RM process. In the SHAMPU process, iterative loops back from the evaluate phase to the estimate phase can be expected in order to refine estimates for sources of uncertainty and responses that evaluation has identified as being important. This can be followed by an iterative loop back to the define phase to refine understanding of the context, reconsider the scope and approach for risk analysis, and refine or revise the identification and structuring of sources of uncertainty, prompted by insights from earlier evaluation.

The lack of recognition given to the desirability of an iterative process in the process frameworks of Table 7.1 – 7.3 is surprising. This may reflect:

- a focus on high level, low resolution depiction of RM processes;

- concern to keep RM processes simple;

- satisfaction with quick, simple (simplistic) methods of identifying key risks;

- lack of concern with second level analysis of the effects of sources of uncertainty and associated response selection;

- reluctance or difficulty in quantifying risks.

Even if true, such explanations are more defensible if the concern is with a strategic, low resolution, risk assessment of an organisation's position. However, such explanations are less defensible for the higher resolution assessments needed at sub-corporate level.

7.8 THE COSO ENTERPRISE RISK MANAGEMENT FRAMEWORK

The COSO Enterprise Risk Management (ERM) framework (PricewaterhouseCoopers, 2004), is an important recent addition to the set of published RM process frameworks. Originally formed in 1985, the Committee of Sponsoring Organisations of the Treadway Commission (COSO), is a voluntary private-sector organisation dedicated to improving the quality of financial reporting through business ethics, effective internal controls, and corporate governance. In May 2001 COSO engaged PricewaterhouseCoopers to lead the development of the ERM framework after concluding there was a need for a broadly recognised common structure for enterprise RM. In developing the ERM framework, the PricewaterhouseCoopers team sought input from many sources including the members of the five COSO organisations: the American Institute of Certified Public Accountants, the American Accounting Association, Financial Executives International, the Institute of Management Accountants and at the Institute of Internal Auditors.

The COSO framework, comprises a substantial document which is intended to provide practical, 'how to' guidance for all organisations regardless of size, on building effective programmes to identify, measure, prioritise, and respond to risk. The COSO framework document is broad in scope and includes discussion of :

- the benefits and limitations of enterprise RM;

- the components of enterprise RM;

- the roles and responsibilities of members of an organisation for undertaking RM.

The COSO framework defines enterprise RM in terms of eight inter-related components. Separate chapters in the COSO document outline the scope of each of these components. A summary of each component follows.

COSO Component 1: The Internal Environment

The rationale for including internal environment in the ERM framework is that this provides the foundation of discipline and structure which influences all other components. The COSO framework identifies the following elements of the internal environment:

- the organisation's risk management philosophy;

- the organisation's risk appetite and risk culture;

- oversight by the board of directors;

- integrity, ethical values and competence of the organisation's people;

- management's philosophy and operating style;

- the way management assigns authority and responsibility, and organises and develops its people.

ERM involves appreciating how these elements of the internal environment may affect the operation of the other ERM components.

COSO Component 2: Objective Setting

Since risks are only defined relative to objectives, setting objectives must precede RM. Such objectives need to be set first at a strategic level to establish a basis for operations, reporting, and compliance. Below the strategic level, objectives are linked via a hierarchy of more specific objectives established for various aspects of the organisation's operations. The strategic objectives should support the organisation's mission/vision and be consistent with the organisation's risk appetite.

COSO Component 3: Event Identification

Event identification involves considering the full scope of the organisation and potential events which could affect the organisation's ability to successfully implement strategy and achieve objectives. Events with a potentially positive impact (opportunities) are 'channelled back' into the strategy and objectives setting processes. Interdependencies between events are identified and 'similar potential events' are grouped together to assist subsequent assessment.

COSO Component 4: Risk Assessment

Risk assessment involves assessing the effect of all potential events that are likely to have a significant impact on the organisation. Management should assess events from two perspectives, likelihood and impact, both in the absence of responses to alter the likelihood or impact ('inherent risk'), and after appropriate risk responses have been developed ('residual risk'). Impacts should be in respect of the various relevant performance measures. Assessment may involve consideration of how events are correlated, and where a sequence of events may produce a combined effect.

COSO Component 5: Risk Response

In determining potential responses to assessed risks, management should consider the relative costs and benefits of responses, including opportunities to achieve organisation objectives by going beyond dealing with a particular risk. Some responses may usefully address several risks simultaneously. For example, insurance is one response of this kind.

Evaluation of alternative responses should take into account risks that might result from the response itself . This implies an iterative process involving further identification and assessment of risks resulting from the response before management finalises a decision about response.

COSO Component 6: Control Activities

Control activities are policies and procedures to help ensure that chosen RM responses are carried out properly and in a timely manner. Control activities occur at all levels and in all functions of the organisation. They include a diverse range of activities such as: approval, authorisation, verification, reconciliation, reviews of operating performance, security, and duty segregation. In selecting control activities, management should consider how they interrelate, for example, a single control activity could address multiple risk responses.

COSO Component 7: Information and Communication

Effective RM requires pertinent information to be identified, captured, processed, and communicated in an appropriate form and in appropriate time frames. This information may be generated internally from ongoing operations, previous RM activities, and by collating information about external events. Information for ERM is integrated with existing information used to manage the organisation. Effective communication is an important requirement to ensure all personnel are aware of their responsibilities (including for RM), and how individual activities relate to the work of others. There should be a means of communicating significant information rapidly upstream, and for effective communication with external partners.

COSO Component 8: Monitoring

The monitoring component of ERM is concerned with assessing the presence and functioning of its various components over time, either through ongoing monitoring or periodic separate evaluations. Deficiencies in ERM components are reported upstream, with serious matters reported to top management and the board.

The COSO framework views the above eight components as being integrated with an organisation's operating activities and infrastructure. The framework emphasises these components as distinct elements of activity that may be carried out at various organisational levels (entity, division, business unit, and subsidiary, are named in the framework), and related to four categories of objective (strategic, operations, reporting and compliance). The focus is not on an individual application of RM in a particular context involving a process which steps through components 2-7. Rather than a sequential process, where one component affects only the next, ERM is presented as a dynamic, *'multi-direction iterative process in which almost any component can and will influence another'* (PricewaterhouseCoopers, 2004: p13).

7.9 DISTINGUISHING PROCESS AND CAPABILITY

Each of the frameworks described above distinguishes between monitor and review of the output from a specific RM application and periodic monitoring/review of the overall effectiveness of RM. In respect of a particular RM application for a specific purpose in a particular context, monitoring/review activity can lead to revisiting of previous phases and revising analysis and plans if unfolding circumstances warrant this. Additionally, review after each RM application can capture lessons to be learnt from particular application contexts.

Additionally, periodic monitoring/review activity on a less frequent basis is desirable to assess the efficiency and effectiveness of RM procedures in general, and to consider ways in which improvements and enhancements can be made to existing procedures and associated administrative systems. This is more of an audit activity which assesses the extent to which RM applications have delivered net benefits, and the extent to which RM is applied where it could be useful, or is embedded in every day management activities (OGC, 2002: p31).

These two aspects of monitoring and review highlight the need to clearly distinguish between the quality of the process involved in individual applications, and an organisation's capability to carry out RM across a variety of applications. This distinction is important because very diffeent issues are involved in making the most of individual applications of RM and managing the organisation's RM capability. In individual applications attention is focused on how best to apply the phases of the RM process in a particular context. Creating a RM capability involves developing a corporate policy on RM that clarifies the organisation's understanding of what RM is for, and expectations of how and where sources of risk will be assessed and managed. Like any formal processes, RM processes require continuous support. This involves establishing and maintaining a supporting infrastructure including appropriate information systems and resources to facilitate effective applications of RM. Developing RM capability is discussed in more detail in Chapter 10.

The distinction between individual RM applications and organisational capability for RM could be much more clearly drawn in the AAIRM, AS/NZ, and OGC frameworks. Failure to adequately draw this distinction results in RM being presented and perceived as a monolithic, 'big bang', corporate process, in much the same way as ideas like total quality management were presented (and implemented). This is unfortunate because it encourages:

- a preoccupation with high level, low resolution overviews and simplified forms of analysis in order to avoid undue complexity;

- an assumption of a single context, whole organisation perspective, and a uniform approach to the RM process.

This effect is readily observed in the way many organisations have established formal RM as part of corporate governance compliance. Establishing a RM capability becomes synonymous with operating a particular RM process primarily concerned with identifying key risks to organisation performance and developing a 'corporate risk profile'. One result is that perceptions of how RM can be applied to improve organisation performance, and how RM practice can be developed, are inappropriately narrow. To fully appreciate the potential scope and potential contribution of RM, one needs to consider, as part of capability development, the range of potential applications of RM and the context for application as an important, initial aspect of any RM application. Consideration of context allows for a more detailed appreciation of issues that need to be addressed by RM and highlights requirements in terms of RM capability.

7.10 CONCLUSION

RM process frameworks developed and promoted by professional organisations (AAIRM Standard, 2002; Lewin, 2002; OGC, 2002; PMI, 2000; Bartlett et al, 2004; Australia/New Zealand Standard, 1999), have an important role to play in the development of RM best practice. Among other things, they can bring together experts with different experiences, synthesise their experience, and tailor general approaches to particular types of context or application. However, in the interests of developing RM practice, different process frameworks need to be subjected to constructive critique and useful features from different frameworks incorporated into a more common set of basic concepts.

In broad terms, there is a general convergence between different guidelines and standards in respect of generic RM process frameworks. Most incorporate the basic phases of identification, analysis, evaluation, and response selection, although the terminology used can vary, leading to sometimes subtle, and perhaps unintended, differences in emphasis and focus. Rather more detailed RM process frameworks can be found in guidance on project RM. In particular, the more detailed project RM process frameworks facilitate the recognition and management of a wider range of RM issues than simpler frameworks.

One such issue is the desirability of pursuing an iterative approach to individual applications of RM. Other important issues emerge from a closer consideration of what individual phases of the RM process involve. This is the subject of the next chapter.

Table 7.5 Comparison of different risk management process frameworks, showing the approximate alignment of phases.

COSO	AIRMIC, ALARM, IRM	AS/NZ	OGC	SHAMPU
Objective setting	Organisational strategic objectives	Establish the context	Define a framework	Define the context
				Focus the process
Event identification	Risk identification	Identify the risk	Identify the risks Identify probable risk owners	Identify the issues
				Structure the issues Clarify ownership
Risk assessment	Risk description and estimation	Analyse risk		Estimate variability
	Risk evaluation	Evaluate risks	Evaluate the risks Set acceptable level of risk	Evaluate implications
Risk response	Risk treatment	Treat risks	Identify suitable responses	
				Harness the plans
Control activities			Implement responses	Manage implementation
	Risk reporting and monitoring	Monitor and review 1	Monitor effectiveness	
	Monitoring 2	Monitor and review 2	Embed and review	

8

PHASES OF THE RISK MANAGEMENT PROCESS

8.1 INTRODUCTION

The previous chapter considered the nature and scope of generic risk management (RM) process frameworks. This chapter considers the scope of component tasks that make up the RM process. The chapter is structured around the component phases of the SHAMPU process framework in Table 7.4 (Chapman and Ward, 2003), because this provides a detailed characterisation of the RM process and facilitates comprehensive consideration of issues that need to be addressed to achieve efficient and effective RM. Readers more familiar with other process frameworks should be able to relate the topics discussed here to these other frameworks without much difficulty.

Much of the discussion here is summarised from Chapman and Ward (2003) where a more extensive discussion of each phase, including techniques, can be found. Discussion of particular tools and techniques applicable in different phases of the RM process, while important, is beyond the scope of this text.

8.2 DEFINE THE CONTEXT

Any application of RM takes place in a particular context to support a particular undertaking. The purpose of the 'define the context' phase is to consolidate relevant existing information about the context and its management in a suitable documented form. Without an adequate appreciation of context there is no basis on which to undertake RM.

The MoR guide (OGC, 2002) identifies four main contexts for RM: the *strategic* level, *programme* level, *project* level, and *operational* level. Usually these levels are thought of as relative to the whole organisation, so the strategic level might be equivalent to corporate level. However all of these levels could relate to different decision levels (all contexts) within a particular unit or part of a larger organisation.

At the *strategic* level management is concerned with setting strategic direction, and associated strategic objectives. At the strategic level the concerns are about where the organisation wants to go, how to get there, and how to ensure survival. Effective RM at this level is challenging because of the need to have a clear strategic overview and understanding of key aspects of context, avoiding excessive detail, while at the same time avoiding excessive simplification. This is a difficult task and one reason for the substantial attention given to strategic issue analysis and situation audit in the strategic management literature. Such strategic level context information is required for effective strategy formulation. Gaps or flaws in this information can seriously undermine an organisation's ability to formulate and adopt effective corporate strategies. RM at a corporate level needs the same information as a basis, and this alone is a compelling reason for RM to be fully integrated with strategic decision processes. RM which purports to take a corporate view, but which is carried out as a separate exercise from strategy formulation and planning will be at best inefficient, and at worst ineffective, or strategically irrelevant.

At the *programme* level managers are concerned with transforming high-level strategy into programmes for action. Context here includes the nature of corporate strategies and associated objectives as well as all aspects of the organisation and wider environment that interact with particular programmes, and a clear understanding of what stage the programme has reached.

At the *project* level managers are concerned with designing, planning, and executing particular projects within a given programme context. In terms of applying RM, there is a need to understand the position of the project to date, and what future stages of the project are expected to involve.

At the *operational* level managers are concerned with maintaining and improving existing day-to-day operations. Understanding context is easiest at this level since the repetitive nature of operations naturally facilitates the acquisition of a deep understanding of particular operations by the managers of those operations. However this understanding may not be particularly well-documented and available for those undertaking RM.

At any of the above levels, the RM context may involve a particular decision or even part of a decision process. This can reduce the extent of organisation or wider environmental context that needs to be understood, although great care is needed to avoid defining the relevant context too narrowly. Applying RM to a particular decision also highlights the need to understand how far the decision process has progressed, what analysis has so far been undertaken, what assumptions have been made, and whether there are aspects of the decision process that may need revisiting. (See Chapter 5.)

Whatever the context, a useful starting point to obtaining sufficient understanding of the context for RM purposes is to address six basic questions (Chapman and Ward 2003: p10):

1. Who   who are the parties involved?

2. Why   what do the parties want to achieve?

3. What   what is it the parties are interested in?

4. Whichway   how it is the strategy to be implemented?

5. Wherewithal what resources are involved/required?

6. When   what are the pertinent timescales?

All of these questions have a direct bearing on the level of uncertainty and risk associated with the particular context and therefore need to be clearly understood to begin with. Table 8.1 indicates what each question is concerned with.

Table 8.1 Six Aspects of Context (based on Chapman and Ward, 2003)

Context who
Any organisational context will involve two or more parties working together. Parties may be individuals, units of an organisation, or organisations as a whole. In any given context, the relationships between the various parties may be complex, often involving a hierarchy of contractual arrangements. Such relationships bring fundamental complications that have a profound influence on uncertainty and risk. It is important to identify all relevant interested parties, and to distinguish individual players (organisations) who may have significantly different agendas.

Context why

A key aspect of any risk analysis is appraising the implications of relevant performance criteria and related objectives. This is particularly important when taking a corporate perspective. For example, corporate concerns about strengthened market position, a more favourable position with regulating authorities, or a 'greener' public image, may be significant. Lack of clarity about objectives makes this concern more important, not less important.A clear idea of prevailing objectives is important in planning for risk analysis because the structure and form of objectives ought to drive the structure and form of the risk analysis. This assessment needs to consider the nature of the objectives, their relative importance, how they might be measured, and the extent to which tradeoffs can be made between them. For example, in a project context, project managers must generally consider the relative priorities to be placed on cost, time and quality, recognizing that tradeoffs are possible between these basic performance criteria, and may be different for different parties. If this is not done, different parts of the project team will make internally inconsistent decisions, and the project organisation as a whole will show confusion and lack of focus.

If quantification of uncertainty is sought, the need to be clear about priorities is intensified, because the RM process must exploit these priorities and the structure of the uncertainty involved. Quantification may be desirable because it forces organisations to clarify priorities.

Context what

Often, a highly valued feature of successful RM reports is a carefully crafted summary of key features of the application context. Usually the material is selected from reports prepared as part of the normal planning process. In such cases the added value of the risk analysis reports is simply pulling it together in an integrated form. Sometimes this integration process reveals missing detail, occasionally it reveals major flaws. In effect, it is an independent review, by a risk analyst who is by vocation someone prepared to ask lots of dumb questions, in order to write his or her simplified view of what the context and associated undertaking is all about, with a strong drive for internal consistency and clear definitions of relationships. Sometimes apparently dumb questions have no effective answers, revealing cracks which need serious attention.

Context whichway

For RM purposes there is a need for an overview description of how the context undertaking is to be implemented. A significant issue is how much detail to go into. Distinguishing too many component activities could induce an overly detailed risk analysis that tends not to see the wood for the trees. For example, in a project context, half-a-dozen activities may be sufficient detail to employ for RM of a modest project, and even very large projects might be adequately described for RM purposes by only 20 to 30 major activities. Keeping things as simple as possible, but not simplistic is a key requirement here.

Context wherewithal

A review of resource requirements implied by the context activity plans should be part of defining the context, because an obvious source of risk in any context is key resources not being available when needed. This is particularly important if different parties have been responsible for estimating and defining the needs for different kinds of resource, cost estimates, and planning schedules. For example, are cost estimates prepared by the accounting department, consistent with planning schedules drawn up by line management?

Context timing, the when

A further aspect of context description is the assumed timing and sequencing of key context activities. Clarifying these assumptions for RM purposes is important because this facilitates identifying and questioning key assumptions, and identifying possible useful alternative approaches to implementing the context strategy.

The define phase deliverable is a clear, unambiguous, shared understanding of all relevant key aspects of the RM context, appropriately documented, verified, assessed as 'fit for purpose' and reported. A comprehensive and complete define phase should clarify all relevant key parts of the context which the RM process addresses, in a manner accessible to all relevant personnel. A single document achieving these ends is often held to be a key benefit of a formal RM process, especially by senior managers.

Because some aspects of the context may not be clearly defined when the define phase begins, and they may take some time to be defined, the define phase may be ongoing. However, the initial concern should be to make as much progress as possible with the define phase before moving on. The greater the level of unfinished business from the define phase, the lower the efficiency and effectiveness of the following RM phases.

8.3   FOCUS THE RISK MANAGEMENT PROCESS

Any systematic efforts at RM must be carefully designed and managed if cost-effective use of resources is to be achieved. Generic process frameworks provide a phase structure for RM, but the precise scope and detail of analysis in each phase will depend on the context. There is no 'best approach' for all circumstances.

Much of the need to vary the approach taken hinges on why it is being undertaken. A requirement for effectiveness and efficiency demands that we design or select our models and processes according to our purposes. If more than one purpose is being pursued, we may need more than one model and process, running in a separate but linked manner.

The focus phase involves two specific tasks:

1. *Scope the process* – this task addresses issues such as who is doing the analysis for whom?, why is a formal RM process being undertaken (what benefits must be achieved)?, and what is the scope of the relevant uncertainty? It culminates in a 'strategic' plan for the RM process. This provides a framework for more detailed planning of the RM process. It also ensures that management is aware of any limitations of the proposed analysis that may warrant further attention outside the RM process context of immediate concern;

2. *Plan the process* – this task addresses issues such as the appropriate structure and level of detail in the analysis using what models and methods (techniques), what software, what other resources over what time-frame, and so on, and culminates in a 'tactical' plan for the RM process, to make the process operational.

A comprehensive and complete focus phase should clarify all the key aspects of the chosen approach in a manner accessible to all relevant personnel. The target deliverable is a clear, unambiguous shared understanding of the proposed approach.

The key players should be:

1. Senior managers, to empower the process, to ensure the risk analysis effort reflects the needs and concerns of senior managers, and to ensure it contains the relevant judgments and expertise of senior managers;

2. All other relevant managers, to ensure the risk analysis services the whole context management process;

3. All relevant technical experts, to ensure the risk analysis captures all relevant expertise for communication to all relevant users of that expertise in an appropriate manner;

4. A risk analyst or risk analysis team, to provide facilitation/ elicitation skills, modelling and method design skills, computation

skills, teaching skills which get the relevant messages to all other members of the organisation, and the management skills needed to allow the risk analysis function to develop and evolve in a way which suits the organisation.

In relation to all key players the RM process should be seen as immediately useful and valuable, in the sense that it more than justifies the demands made upon them.

8.4 PLAN THE RISK MANAGEMENT PROCESS

Even in an organisation with well-established formal RM processes, decisions need to be made, consciously and regularly, about which models to use in individual applications. A 'model' in this context is the deliberate simplification of reality we use as a basis for analysis. Most models of interest have a mathematical form, but of particular concern is their associated graphical form, which can clarify our understanding of their implications. If decisions about models are not made consciously, then decisions are being made by default which may prove very costly. On some occasions the models used may be too simple, obscuring important issues which should be addressed. On other occasions the models may be too complex, involving effort that is not cost effective. Using an inappropriate model to analyse uncertainty and related issues is a RM planning error directly comparable to undertaking a construction project with an inappropriate plan.

Failing to consider this issue is rather like operating a car hire firm that always offers a Rolls Royce, or a Mini, regardless of the potential customer's wallet or needs. It is difficult to overemphasize this point because the systematic, generic nature of some RM process frameworks can easily seduce those who ought to know better into the adoption of a single modelling approach for all purposes in all application contexts. 'If the only tool in your toolbox is a hammer, every problem looks like a nail', is a situation to be avoided.

Many corporate RM processes, particularly those addressing Turnbull compliance (ICAEW, 1999) follow a standard process on a periodic basis. In effect, the focus phase has been carried out once only, when formal RM was first established, and it is not reconsidered before every subsequent application of RM, because the corporate context is considered to be essentially unchanged. Such an approach is certainly efficient, but it may encourage rigidity in the RM process and thereby discourage the use of more detailed (ad hoc) risk analyses to explore particular key developments, or particular aspects of corporate strategy.

8.5   IDENTIFY THE ISSUES

Most RM process descriptions emphasize a need to identify sources of risk early in the process, typically restricting this to potential events, and sometimes to just threats. As discussed in Chapter 3, effective RM needs to address uncertainty in a broad sense, with early consideration of all sources of uncertainty and associated responses. As indicated in Table 7.4, the SHAMPU identify phase involves not only identifying sources of uncertainty, but also associated possible responses and secondary sources arising from these responses. For convenience, we refer to individual sources, their associated responses and secondary sources as 'issues'. It is these issues rather than sources of uncertainty that need to be identified and managed. Identifying issues involves two specific tasks:

1. *search* for sources of uncertainty and responses, employing a range of perspectives and techniques;

2. *classify sources* to provide a suitable structure for defining sources and responses, aggregating/disaggregating particular issues as appropriate.

In terms of documentation, the identify phase involves the production of a list or register of sources. However, it is important to coordinate 'source list' equivalents with lists generated earlier in the define phase and later lists involving responses and secondary issues. The key deliverable is a clear, common understanding of the sources of uncertainty associated with the application context, and what can be done about them. Opportunities need to be identified and managed with the same resolve as threats as part of the same process. Often a RM process is particularly successful because the process of generating and reviewing responses to threats leads to the identification of important opportunities, with implications well beyond the uncertainty which led to their identification.

In a given context, the identify phase is best treated as an iterative process in its own right, starting with a rough 'first cut' at the identification of sources of uncertainty, associated responses, and secondary sources of uncertainty. Subsequent iterations then refine this identification until it is 'fit for purpose'. Unfortunately, it can be very difficult to decide when this point has been reached. On a first pass it is appropriate to aim for a higher level overview than is likely to be necessary in later passes, to avoid detailed analysis which would later prove wasted. This principle should be followed on subsequent passes too, but there is always a risk that further iterations do not happen. Furthermore, inefficiencies associated with too many iterations to reach sufficient depth of analysis in a given area may add to the cost of analysis significantly, depending upon how iterations are managed. This reinforces the case for making the identify phase as complete as possible before proceeding to the next phase. If sources, and responses, and associated secondary issues (response chains) are not properly understood, any subsequent RM can be a complete waste of resources.

The identify phase should involve the identification of at least one assumed response for each identified source. A generic 'do nothing' response is one option, but this will not be appropriate in some cases. A preliminary list of obvious response options indicating preferences associated with all sources is a recommended output on a first pass. Detailed lists of response options may be deferred until later passes for those sources which prove significant, but early identification of response options can form the basis of a concerted opportunity identification process which goes beyond simple threat management.

Often the identification of a possible response to a particular source is a simple task. Once a source has been identified it is frequently obvious how one could respond. However, the most easily identified possible response may not be the most effective or the most risk-efficient response; other responses may be worth identifying and considering. Where an issue is particularly significant, a systematic examination of a range of possible responses, perhaps with a view to applying several responses in parallel, may be worthwhile.

The use of formal procedures to systematically capture personal experience can be very effective in identifying issues and possible responses. However, it is important that the experiences of a wide range of personnel are sought, particularly early on in the identify phase, to ensure a comprehensive set of issues are identified. Individual managers may not have sufficient breadth of experience to provide this comprehensive view. Identification of sources and responses can be an individual activity or involve other people in a variety of ways, including: interviewing individuals, interviewing groups, or various group processes such as brainstorming and decision conferencing. A key concern is to stimulate imaginative thinking and draw on the experiences of different individuals.

A detailed discussion of identification techniques is given by Chapman and Ward (2003: Chap. 7), and Dickson (2003).

8.6 STRUCTURE THE ISSUES

All the earlier RM phases necessarily involve some structuring of identified issues. The structure phase is concerned with reviewing and extending this earlier structuring. The objective is to improve understanding of the relative importance of different sources of uncertainty given identified responses, to explore the interactions between issues, and to test the assumptions implicit or explicit in all earlier steps. This can lead to refinement of existing responses and prompt the development of new, more effective responses. It can also lead to new models or analyses.

Structuring involves reviewing and exploring possible interdependencies or links between context activities, resources, involved parties, sources of uncertainty and responses, and seeking to understand the reasons for these interdependencies. The structure phase involves testing simplifying assumptions, and developing a more complex structure when necessary. Failure to do so can render RM extremely misleading. For example, assuming a large number of sources are independent will allow their individual effects to tend to cancel out with respect to the overall effect, on a 'swings-and-roundabouts' basis. If, in practice, they are positively correlated (things tend to go well or badly at the same time), this cancelling effect will be significantly reduced, and such circumstances need to be appreciated. Making inappropriate assumptions about dependence or avoiding quantification because of dependence are potentially dangerous cop-outs which may negate the whole RM process.

Failure to structure can also lead to lost opportunities. For example, some responses to particular sources of uncertainty can deal with whole sets of sources, including sources which have not been identified. It is important to recognize the opportunities provided by such general responses.

The most effective way to understand uncertainty dependence is to model it in causal terms. Two common approaches used in a system-failure analysis context are fault-tree analysis and event-tree analysis. Event-tree analysis involves identifying a sequence of events that could follow from the occurrence of particular source-response configurations, and then representing the possible scenarios in a tree diagram where each branch represents an alternative possibility. In fault-tree analysis the process is reversed, working backwards from a particular event known as the top event, in an attempt to identify all possible sequences of events giving rise to the top event. Ishikawa or fishbone diagrams (Ishikawa, 1986) adopt a similar approach, showing necessary inputs to a particular final position.

A more versatile representation of causes and effects can be achieved with influence diagrams, as used in 'systems dynamics' (Forrester, 1958, 1961; Richardson and Pugh, 1981; Senge, 1990) and 'cognitive mapping' (Eden, 1988). One advantage of influence diagrams over tree diagrams is that much more complex interactions can be shown, including feedback and feed forward loop effects. The process of construction and interpretation of influence diagrams goes beyond identification of direct source-response and cause-effect relationships. It also assists in identifying potentially important links, such as the nature of source-response chains associated with vicious circles, or particular sources which influence many other sources either directly or indirectly. Increased understanding of cause-effect relationships can also prompt the formulation of additional responses.

As with other phases of the RM process, the structure phase should be regarded as an iterative process. In particular, we cannot assess the importance of some sources of uncertainty until we have identified responses and considered possible interactions between sources and responses. However, some prior assessment of the importance of identified sources is necessary to guide the initial structuring, to avoid too many or too few source and response categories.

The structure phase is about transforming the information generated earlier into a qualitative model of context uncertainty, ideally summarized in diagrams, with underlying computer-based models to handle changes where appropriate and feasible. The richer the information generated in the identify phase, the greater the need for care in the structure phase, to provide a sound basis for inferences to follow.

8.7   CLARIFY OWNERSHIP

In principle, making sure that every source of uncertainty and all associated responses have a manager and an owner in financial terms is recognized as basic good practice. In practice, this worthy ambition is not often achieved.

Failures of RM associated with the allocation of ownership of issues tend to arise because this activity is not recognized explicitly, or not given sufficient attention. Issue allocation always occurs in any situation where more than one party is involved in an activity. Just as roles and responsibilities are allocated to parties concerned, so too are uncertainty management issues associated with an undertaking. However, allocation of issues and consequently risk, can take place by default and need not be explicit, intentional or clearly articulated. The consequences of an allocation, particularly a default allocation, may not be fully appreciated, and the manner in which allocated issues are to be managed may be unclear, if they are managed at all.

The fundamental reason for being concerned about who is responsible for what sources is that this will influence how uncertainty is managed and in whose best interests this will be. Usually ownership of an issue implies responsibility for the management of that issue as well as responsibility for bearing its consequences. However, it is often important to distinguish between responsibility for managing an issue and responsibility for bearing the consequences of the issue. In particular it may be desirable to allocate these responsibilities to different parties, recognizing that the party best able to manage an issue may not be the party best able to bear the consequences of that issue. Thus, while one party, perhaps a contractor, may be best placed to manage a source, it may not be appropriate or desirable for that party to bear all the associated financial consequences.

Part of the rationale for being clear about who owns issues before any estimation is to verify the feasibility of assumed responses and their effects. For example, in a project context, client-initiated redesign is a response which may invalidate all allocations of risk to a contractor, with knock-on cost implications which are orders of magnitude greater than the cost of the redesign itself.

8.8   ESTIMATE VARIABILITY

Efficient estimating involves a first pass to size uncertainty, followed by further iterations to refine estimates of uncertainty where this is effective and efficient.

A single pass approach is neither effective nor efficient. We want to minimize the time spent on relatively minor sources with simple response options, so as to spend more time on major issues that involve complex response options. To do this, a first pass with a focus on sizing uncertainty is needed.

The key deliverable of the estimate phase is the provision of a basis for understanding which sources and associated responses are important, based on numeric estimates of uncertainty associated with issues identified earlier in terms of cost, duration, or other performance criteria. Some approaches to RM suggest numeric probability distributions from the outset. Others suggest a non-numeric approach initially, using likelihood and criteria ranges associated with scenario labels such as 'high', 'medium' and 'low', commonly referred to as a 'qualitative assessment', with numeric measures later if appropriate. However, qualitative statements of beliefs about uncertainty in this sense are of limited use, and they are open to different interpretations by different people.

Some people argue that quantitative analysis is a waste of time if it has to be based on subjective estimates of probabilities. There are obvious concerns about the validity of subjective estimates. These concerns are reinforced by the recognition that no probability assessment (except 1 or 0) can be proven to be wrong. However, given that individuals are guided by their perceptions of uncertainty whether or not quantification is attempted, it makes sense to articulate these perceptions so that uncertainty can be dealt with as effectively as possible.

Targets, Expectations and Commitments

An important reason for quantifying uncertainty at some stage is that doing so helps to force all members of an organisation's management to appreciate the significance of differences between 'targets' which people can aspire to, 'expected values' used to provide an unbiased predictor of outcomes, and 'commitments' which provide some level of contingency allowance. *Targets, expected values* and *contingency allowances* need to be distinguished in terms of cost, time and all other relevant measures of performance.

In cost terms, *expected values* are our best estimate of what costs should be realized on average. Setting aside a contingency fund, to meet costs that may arise in excess of the expected cost, and making a commitment to deliver within the expected cost plus the *contingency*, involves a probability of being able to meet the commitment that an organisation may wish to standardize to clarify what commitments mean. If it is properly determined, a *contingency allowance* provides an uplift from the expected value which is not required on average. Setting commitment levels which have a 80% or 90% chance of not being exceeded is common. Determining this level of commitment ought to involve an assessment of perceived threats and the extent to which these may be covered by a contingency fund, together with an assessment of the opportunities, and the implications of both over- and under-achievement in relation to the commitment. Ownership of contingencies is a critical aspect of uncertainty and risk allocation between parties.

In cost terms, *targets* are set at a level below expected cost, with provisions accounting for the difference. Targets need to reflect the opportunity aspect of uncertainty and the need for goals which stretch people. Targets are sometimes referred to as 'stretch targets' to reflect this, and might be set at a level which has less than a 20% chance of being achieved. Targets need to be realistic to be credible, but they also need to be lean. If targets that are optimistic are not aimed for, expected costs will not be achieved on average, and contingency funds will be used more often than anticipated.

Organisations which do not quantify uncertainty have no real basis for distinguishing targets, expected values, and commitments. As a consequence, single value performance levels are employed to serve all three purposes, often with disastrous results, not to mention costly and unnecessary dysfunctional organisational behaviour. 'The cost estimate', 'the completion date', or 'the promised performance' become less and less plausible, there is a crisis of confidence when the goal posts are moved, and then the process starts all over again. Senior project managers involved when RM processes were introduced by BP in the 1970s stated that the avoidance of this cycle was the key benefit of RM processes for them. The ability to manage the gaps between targets, expected values and contingency levels, and the ability to set these values appropriately in the first place, is a central concern of RM. The recommended basis for refining estimates of targets, expected values and commitments is developed in more detail in Chapman and Ward (2002; 2003, Chap. 10).

8.9   EVALUATE IMPLICATIONS

The purpose of the evaluate phase is to combine the results of the estimate phase in the context of earlier phases and evaluate all associated decisions and judgments. The evaluate phase includes the synthesis of individual issue estimates, the presentation of results, the interpretation of results, process decisions like 'do we need to refine earlier analysis?', and management decisions such as 'is plan A better than plan B?'.

The deliverables will depend upon the depth of the preceding phases achieved to this point. Looping back to earlier phases before proceeding further is likely to be a key and frequent decision. For example, an important early deliverable might be a prioritised list of issues, while a later deliverable might be a diagnosed potential problem or opportunity associated with a specific contingency plan, and suggested revisions to this plan to resolve the problem or capture the opportunity. The key deliverable is diagnosis of any and all important opportunities or threats, and comparative evaluation of responses to these opportunities or threats.

Integrating or combining issues together so that their net effect can be portrayed is a central task of the evaluate phase. Typically this integration task is carried out with the aid of computer software based on Monte Carlo simulation (Hertz, 1964; Grey, 1995). This makes it relatively straightforward to add large numbers of probability distributions together in a single operation to assess the overall impact of a set of issues. Unfortunately, this convenience can seduce analysts into a naive approach that assumes independence between issues and overlooks the importance of dependency between issues. It also encourages analysts to set up the combination calculations to present just the end result and ignore intermediate stages. Also, the mechanics of how individual distributions are combined is not transparent to the user. Together these factors can lead to a failure to appreciate insights from considering intermediate stages of the combination process and dependencies between individual sources of uncertainty.

A central reason for employing formal RM should be to guide and inform the search for favourable alternative courses of action. Central to achieving this is the concept of 'risk efficiency', which is concerned with the trade-offs between expected performance and risk that must be made in selecting one course of action or investment strategy over another (Chapman and Ward, 2003). 'Risk efficiency' is a core concept in the literature of economics and finance, with a prominence underlined by the award of a Nobel prize for economics to Markowitz (1959) for his portrayal of it in terms of mean-variance portfolio selection models.

In relation to risk efficient plans and tradeoffs between risk and expected performance, risk analysis can help to:

- diagnose alternative risk efficient courses of action;
- demonstrate the implications of such alternatives;
- inform choices between alternative risk efficient responses.

(Chapman and Ward, 2003)

In this way risk management can produce very much more substantial improvements in performance than a limited focus on merely 'keeping things on track'.

8.10 HARNESS THE PLANS

The harness phase of the RM process is about taking the preceding analysis and converting this into action plans associated with the relevant context activities. In the 'define the context' phase, the nature of the undertaking of interest will have been defined and this will include the nature of plans for future action. These reference plans will be modified by the subsequent risk analysis to form what might be termed a 'base plan', incorporating proactive responses to uncertainty, but not reactive responses. In addition, the risk analysis should give rise to contingency plans which are an operational form of recommended reactive response to uncertainty and potential risks. Such contingency plans should include decision rules and define the trigger points which will initiate the selected reactive responses.

As part of the base plan documentation, an uncertainty analysis report at an overview level for the context of interest should include as a minimum, a comprehensive list of threats and opportunities assessed in terms of implications given recommended proactive and reactive responses, along with an assessment of alternative potential proactive and reactive responses. Uncertainty analysis needs to be documented to back up associated recommended modifications to reference plans, and to provide an explanation of the need for both proactive and reactive responses.

Chapman and Ward (2003: Chap. 12) argue that base plans and contingency plans should be developed in a two-tier process, first taking a strategic overview of modifications and additions to reference plans, and only then refining plans into more detailed tactical, operational plans. Deciding how far ahead it is worth planning in detail is an issue here. To some extent this depends on previously set objectives, but it may also be driven by the extent of uncertainty about the future. This two-tier approach makes for a more efficient use of planning and RM effort, particularly as more detailed tactical plans may warrant a second tier of RM processes at a more detailed and focused level.

This makes time that might otherwise be wasted on redundant detailed planning available for RM at both strategic and tactical levels. In terms of managing a RM process this is an important opportunity to discover and exploit uncertainty for organisations which currently base their confidence in plans on detailed deterministic planning. For organisations which use a RM process and currently see no need for this distinction, it may be useful to question the level that their RM process operates at. If it is *de facto* at a tactical level, because of the level of detail used from the outset, the opportunity to address strategic issues using RM processes is of considerable importance, and it should be pursued.

8.11 MANAGE IMPLEMENTATION

Most RM process frameworks have a final phase called something like 'monitor and review'. This refers to the desirability of monitoring the implementation of risk responses chosen after previous analysis and evaluation, reviewing their effectiveness and continuing relevance, and then revisiting earlier phases of the RM process if changes in risk responses appear to be warranted. However, this is a rather limited perspective which can reflect a view of RM as a 'bolt-on' rather than a 'built-in' part of planning and subsequent control of a particular undertaking. Once the results of risk analysis have been incorporated into plans for future action, management's concern is not merely with keeping things on track, but also with modifying plans if circumstances warrant this.

Managing implementation involves four different tasks which have to be managed in parallel: *manage planned actions, roll action plans forward, monitor and control, and manage crises.*

Translating plans into actions is seldom entirely straightforward. Excessive planning detail in a deterministic framework can be a serious handicap. A simply defined deterministic base plan embedded in even a simple understanding of the uncertainties involved, can be much more effective. The key is insight about what might happen, as distinct from what we hope will happen, with particular reference to the motivation of the parties involved, and a clear vision of what really matters and what does not.

Rolling action plans forward includes recognising changes in priority and urgency of risk issues. Each time plans are reviewed, eliminating the issues which have now been realized or avoided, confidence band assessments should contract, unless new issues are envisaged. Plotting how this process is progressing can be useful, especially if some serious set-backs have been experienced but the chance of achieving commitments is stable or improving. However, this is an example of a relatively complex portrayal of the monitoring process, best used infrequently at high levels. The lower the level, and the more frequent the monitoring activity, the simpler the devices have to be.

The distinction between target, expected value, and commitment estimates is of substantial importance in relation to the *monitor and control* task. Managing the process of reconciling what actually happens to these three types of estimates is essential if the monitoring process is to facilitate an understanding of the implications of departures from base plans.

It is worth remembering that people directly involved in an undertaking are usually all too well aware when things are going wrong. Usually the concern is not a need for devices to detect when things are going wrong; it is having ways of explaining what is going wrong in order to persuade appropriate people to take appropriate action. More generally, the concern is to ensure that processes are in place which encourage this level of communication to take place in an effective manner.

Managing planned actions can embrace the variations from base plans which do not warrant contingency plans and the management of variations via contingency plans. A major concern of formal RM is to avoid nasty surprises which give rise to crises, which then require *crisis management*. However, it is very unwise to be unprepared for crisis. 'Crisis' might be defined as 'a time of acute danger or difficulty', or 'a major turning point'. The best responses in general terms are based on insight, effective and efficient information systems, being prepared, being able to respond rapidly, and being decisive. Viewing crisis management as contingency management for significant unspecified and unanticipated events, a more effective crisis management strategy will make it effective and efficient to devote less time to contingency planning for specified and anticipated events.

8.12   CONCLUSION

Undertaking any RM process is not without costs, and a key concern is ensuring an appropriate trade-off between these costs and the effectiveness of the RM process. In practice, stepping through the phases of the RM process will often need simplification to meet the needs of a particular context, to provide *efficient* risk management. Efficient in this context means *doing things right* with respect to the RM process so that the process is efficient as well as effective. Simplification merely to economize on resources and the amount of time spent on RM is never appropriate. What is *always* appropriate is ensuring that the available resources are used to operate a RM process that is as effective and efficient as possible within the time available. What is *always* *desirable* is adjusting the time and resources available to an appropriate level, but sometimes this is not feasible.

The effectiveness and the efficiency of the RM process as a whole depends upon how well the process is used in an iterative way to obtain an initial understanding of which areas need the most attention, and which can receive less. Extensive probabilistic analysis based on carefully researched data can be very useful, but often such analysis is not appropriate. What is usually essential is an initial rough sizing of uncertainty from all the key sources that require management, followed by refinement in some areas where that refinement pays sufficient dividends. This assessment is itself prone to risk that must be managed. But treating all aspects of project uncertainty as equally important in a single pass process substantially reduces the effectiveness of RM.

The degree of formality sought in using a given RM process framework can be a key influence in achieving an effective and efficient approach. At one extreme a purely informal, intuitive approach could be adopted. At the other, a very high level of formality could be adopted, involving more cost but more benefits. Making the RM process less formal involves less explicit structure, less formal documentation, less explicit articulation of objectives and deliverables, and fewer explicit phases. Part of the role of formality is clarifying the need for a richer set of motives, as well as helping the pursuit of that richer set of motives.

Restricting the focus of a RM process involves limiting the objectives that are sought. An obvious way of doing this is to consider only significant threats to project performance, rather than all significant sources of certainty and their implications. Reducing the scope of analysis in a given context can be achieved in several ways, including:

- utilizing standard, pro-forma documentation such as check-lists;

- pre-specifying the form of qualitative and quantitative analysis to be undertaken;

- limiting the depth of analysis undertaken;

- adopting single pass processes which preclude revisiting earlier phases of the process;

- limiting the time and resources available for undertaking risk management.

In general all the above simplifications reduce the effectiveness of risk management and the benefits that can be obtained. A common reason for RM processes which are neither effective nor efficient is lack of appreciation of the benefits obtainable from comprehensive approaches which is usually linked to a lack of organisational capability or investment in RM.

Determining what can be simplified in a RM process, and what it is appropriate to simplify, is not a simple matter. To address this problem, organisations might adopt generic simplifications to RM process applications by using common guiding principles, or by making policy decisions which constrain the nature and scope of formal RM processes. Such generic simplifications are most likely to be made when a RM process is first established in an organisation, but they ought to be informed by knowledge of what is involved in a comprehensive RM process. Simply adopting a very specific, rigidly designed 'off-the-shelf' RM process touted by a consultancy, or 'borrowed' from another organisation, is not advisable. Such RM processes often involve quite specific (and simplistic) 'tools' or prescribed methods of analysis which encourage a mechanistic 'paint by numbers' approach to RM. The very well defined, 'tried-and-tested' nature of these processes can make them very attractive and amenable to rapid implementation. However, they represent a serious risk to the ongoing development of an organisation's RM capability. In particular, they can prematurely constrain employees' perceptions of what RM is all about, and what can be achieved with it. They can be comparable to patent medicines sold at a fair to cure all ills without the need for any kind of professional diagnosis of the patient.

9

ROLES OF THE CORPORATE RISK MANAGER

9.1   INTRODUCTION

Effective deployment and operation of risk management (RM) throughout an organisation requires top-down systematic development, co-ordination, monitoring, and support of RM activities. The board or its equivalent, has ultimate responsibility for RM and for creating and maintaining the infrastructure for RM to operate efficiently and effectively. Either directly, or by delegation to a sub-committee, the board needs to:

- support and facilitate organisation-wide application of RM;

- carry out RM at corporate level;

- review the effectiveness of RM activity.

The scope of these responsibilities was outlined in Chapter 2. As noted in Chapter 2, the increasing need for more visible, formal RM has resulted in most large organisations establishing a specific corporate RM function to assist top-down management with the above responsibilities.

The task of such a RM function and its chief officer, the corporate risk manager (CRM) is a difficult one, largely because of the enormous potential scope of the work, and the limited resources typically available. There is no well-defined set of tasks that a RM function should carry out, nor a single best way for a CRM to operate. The problem of supporting and facilitating organisation-wide RM is rather like deciding what a corporate communications manager should do to support and facilitate communication throughout the organisation. The scope is massive, and the work calls for selectivity and creativity to maximise effectiveness of the role. One way to deal with this scope problem is to pre-emptively restrict the scope of the CRM's role. While perhaps expedient, this may result in a failure to pursue valuable lines of development in RM capability.

This chapter considers the potential scope of the CRM's role beginning with a strategic perspective which draws on experience of similar issues with the role of corporate planners. Some empirical observations about CRMs in the UK are discussed to illustrate the variety of roles CRMs undertake. A final section considers the factors that influence selection of roles undertaken from the wider set of possible roles.

9.2   A STRATEGIC PERSPECTIVE

The problem of defining the role of the CRM is somewhat analogous to deliberations about the role of corporate planners in corporate strategic planning. For example, in respect of strategy making, Mintzberg (1994) suggests that corporate planners should make their contribution by supporting and facilitating strategic thinking by line managers, rather than driving strategy formulation in a way that reduces management's involvement in the process. Thus Mintzberg (1994) argues that planners could usefully contribute to strategy development by acting as 'finders of strategies', as 'analysts', and as 'catalysts'.

Following this line of argument, CRMs should not be *managers* of risk at all. They should make their contribution *'around'* the RM process rather than *'inside'* it, to use more of Mintzberg's terminology. Thus, titles like CRM, 'risk controller', and even 'risk co-ordinator' may be positively unhelpful, insofar as they imply responsibility for RM activity throughout the organisation, as well as responsibility for risk thinking. Yet both of these tasks ought to remain firmly with management. Instead, CRMs can contribute to RM development by acting as 'finders of strategies', as analysts and as catalysts, in much the same way as Mintzberg's (1994) planners can contribute to strategy development.

The Finder of strategy role

Paralleling Mintzberg's description of the finder's role, CRMs can track patterns of action in the organisation in order to identify approaches to RM which might warrant wider application, and effect corporate control by identifying realised RM strategies. CRMs can also track emerging possibilities and draw management's attention to associated threats and opportunities. They may also track RM experience in other organisations to develop bench-marking for RM processes, and exploit "isomorphic learning" from comparable risky situations elsewhere (Toft and Reynolds, 1997).

The Analyst role

CRMs could support RM processes via *ad hoc* analyses to stimulate risk thinking and creativity in risk-response development. Such analyses can help managers to question key assumptions and reconsider their perception of important issues. Analysis may also help to clarify the effects of uncertainty and present decision choices in a way that makes risk-return trade-offs more transparent.

The Catalyst role

In a strategy context, Mintzberg (1994: p381) argues that planners should be promoting future thinking in its broadest sense, not necessarily formalised procedures to produce articulated results. CRMs can play a similar role to encourage creative use of RM principles. The role of catalyst can also involve building awareness about potentially important developments in risk or opportunities, by facilitating discussions about important emerging issues.

The above three roles are reflected in more specific guidance on the responsibilities of the CRM from the UK based Association of Insurance and Risk Managers in Commerce (AIRMIC). The AIRMIC guidance suggests that the CRM should act as a coordinator and advisor with responsibilities to:

- design and .. establish an integrated RM strategy, ...philosophy, and policy statement for communication throughout the organisation;

- establish and maintain a detailed RM methodology appropriate to the company's needs; to include formalised risk identification techniques, quantitative and qualitative risk assessment and cost effective methods for risk reduction and transfer;

- advise business areas on the use of RM techniques;

- seek best working methods that acknowledge, understand and control risks;

- monitor the application and effectiveness of RM;

- co-ordinate the reporting on RM activities to the Board;

- act as a conduit for the inter-change of information on risk(s) and RM.

(Butterworth, Reddaway and Benson, 1996)

This is a fairly ambitious list of responsibilities, which envisages a comprehensive facilitatory role in developing an organisation's RM capability. This list also prompts three basic questions about the work of practising CRMs:

- what kinds of responsibilities do CRMs actually have?

- what approaches do CRMs employ to carry out these responsibilities?

- what factors influence the scope and focus of this work?

9.3   SOME EMPIRICAL OBSERVATIONS

Answers to the above questions were sought in a study by Ward (2001) of CRMs in 30 UK based organisations. A primary concern in this study was to identify the range of activities undertaken by CRMs, and the variety of factors influencing their work. This had two purposes. First, to guide and inform future research into RM development and the work of CRMs by clarifying the variety of activities and factors that warrant attention. Second, to inform and guide directly further development of RM.

Over two thirds of the thirty CRMs interviewed report directly to the finance director (or equivalent corporate officer). Two CRMs interviewed report to the company secretary, other cases included reporting to the personnel, technical or chemicals director. Health and safety was typically a separate function reporting through the director of human resources to the chief executive.

Table 9.1 Job Titles for Corporate Risk Managers

Group Risk and Insurance Manager (2)	Director of RM (3)
Group Insurance and CRM (2)	CRM (3)
Risk and Insurance Manager (2)	Head of RM
Insurance and CRM	Group CRM (3)
Director of Insurance and RM	General Manager, RM
	Head of Group RM
Director of Group RM and Group Audit	Director, Global RM
Head of Group Audit and RM	Director Group RM
Head of Group Control	Group RM Director
Head of RM Services	

Note: Numbers in brackets denote more than one interviewee with the same title.

The job titles of the CRMs interviewed carried a variety of designations, as indicated in Table 9.1. Fifteen of the CRMs interviewed had job titles incorporating the term 'risk management' with variations like 'head of', 'director of' or reference to 'group' or 'global' RM. A further eight had job titles incorporating the term 'insurance' either as 'risk and insurance', or 'insurance and risk (management)'. Two had titles incorporating both 'group audit' and 'group RM'.

The majority of interviewees had a background in insurance management or insurance broking. Three had a background in accounting or audit functions, one came from operations management, one from an IT background, and one from strategic planning. In all cases responsibilities included insurance, often substantially outsourced to brokers and captive insurance companies. In many cases an insurance management role underpinned any wider RM role. Interestingly, the presence or absence of the terms 'risk management' or 'insurance' in job titles, was no guide to the relative emphasis actually placed on insurance related work.

This prominence of insurance is perhaps not surprising, given that interviewees were all members of AIRMIC. In spite of this possible bias towards insurance management roles, Ward's study found that the CRMs interviewed operate in a variety of roles, and that the range of roles can vary significantly from one CRM to another. This seems to justify the view of AIRMIC that CRMs should have a wide ranging, corporate role involving the facilitation and coordination of RM activity.

Table 9.2 Roles of the Corporate Risk Manager

1. **Designing and establishing an integrated RM strategy, philosophy and policy statement**
   - raising awareness of RM
   - instill philosophy, potential benefits and general idea of RM
   - development of a "wide approach" to RM
   - developing company RM strategy
   - production of RM policy statements
   - development of a health and safety culture

2. **Establishment and maintenance of a detailed RM methodology**
   - coordination of different RM areas
   - preparation of manuals/guidelines
   - reviewing RM Standards/guidelines
   - formation and support of RM committee structures and processes
   - design of self assessment procedures for business units
   - setting up committees to look at the wording of contracts
   - developing corporate emergency procedures
   - developing corporate health and safety standards and performance improvement programmes

   Insurance management
   - identifying needs for insurance
   - negotiating insurance
   - provision of insurance programmes
   - rationalising insurance
   - streamlining administration of insurance
   - administrating insurance arrangements (eg brokers and captives)

3. **Advice to business units on RM techniques**
   - techniques for risk identification
   - investment proposals
   - contractual terms and conditions (warranties, indemnities, insurance aspects)
   - disaster recovery
   - insurance matters, reducing the cost of insurance
   - institute training courses (eg driver training)
   - site surveys/inspections
   - build awareness of continuity risks
   - encourage preparation of continuity plans
   - overseas travel arrangements

4. **Monitoring the application and effectiveness of RM processes**
   - approving risk financing strategies
   - ensuring particular risks are being managed (including site surveys/inspections)
   - audit of RM systems and practice
   - bench-marking studies

5. **Coordination of the delivery of information on risk and RM**
   – provision of (loss) statistics
   – provide Risk Profiles (to Board)
   – reviewing the appropriateness of aggregate group risk profile

6. **Acting as a conduit for the interchange of information on risk and RM**
   – identification of (under managed) risks
   – identify examples of good practice
   – production of in-house publications
   – advise on sources of good practice and (outside) expertise

Table 9.2 lists the various roles identified in Ward's (2001) study, grouped under the six broad areas of responsibility envisaged by AIRMIC. As might be expected, insurance related roles feature prominently. Nevertheless, the range of roles identified is very much wider than insurance or risk financing. Table 9.2 shows a lengthy list of different roles, yet each one of these roles can constitute a substantial agenda of work in itself. Typically individual CRMs and their departments appeared to be concentrating on a subset of these roles, often within to a subset of the six areas of responsibility.

Role 1. Designing an Integrated Risk Management Strategy

Several CRMs interviewed in Ward's study had a clear, long-term strategy which involved encouraging the development of RM thinking throughout the organisation. These CRMs employ widely targeted, ongoing campaigns to raise awareness of risk and introduce the concept of RM and its benefits. This can involve visits and presentations to business units, divisions, individual sites, or departments, depending on the size of organisation and level of the CRM. Subsequent visits then help to build relationships and allow the CRM to obtain an impression of local management's attitude to RM. For CRMs newly appointed in an organisation, this is an obvious initial strategy, although potentially quite time-consuming.

Some CRMs instigate broadly targeted risk-communication programmes involving a variety of devices such as in-house magazines, education packages, videos, pamphlets, key points cards, posters, key fobs, and specially designed computer mouse mats. The benefits of such programmes are difficult to assess, given that they are aimed at changing people's thinking and attitudes to risk and RM. Clearly such programmes have a greater chance of success when supported over time by visible activity of the RM departments, and by local management example. However, even with top management backing, developing RM thinking throughout the organisation is a slow, trickle-down process which can take a long time.

Activities like the above help to prepare the organisation for more formal approaches to RM which might be delineated in a RM policy statement and the development of a wide approach to RM. Generally CRMs and their departments are focussed primarily, if not exclusively, on the management of 'pure' risks, often with a strong risk financing and insurance emphasis.

Successfully contributing to the management of 'speculative' or 'business' risk can be difficult, as such risks are regarded by line managers as their 'bread and butter', and not part of the CRM's territory. This highlights the need for CRMs to emphasise their role as facilitators of RM processes, including risk identification, rather than as coordinators of strategies for managing risks.

Role 2. Establishing Risk Management Methodology

In general, CRMs are likely to use two devices to develop specific RM methodologies in their organisations: documented guidelines and standards on RM practice, and the formation of RM groups which meet on a regular basis.

Where documentation is issued, most CRMs would accept that it should facilitate effective RM in business units rather than introduce mandatory, bureaucratic processes and performance targets. Even where guidelines and standards issued by the corporate office are treated by business units or divisions as mandatory, CRMs may still wish to avoid appearing dictatorial in respect of RM processes.

The use of RM group meetings administered by the CRM is a widely used, but not universal, approach to introducing more formal approaches to RM. At its simplest it can take the form of a 'risk forum' or seminar held annually and attended by appropriate managers from across the organisation (see Chapter 2).

Role 3. Advice on Risk Management Techniques

Most CRMs will provide advice on RM as an important part of their work, but with varying degrees of formality. Ward (2001) found that advice is typically insurance related and motivated by concerns to reduce the 'cost of risk'. If the size of the organisation is not too large, this can involve site visits from the RM department to advise on risk control measures. In large organisations with many diversified business units, this advice is more likely to be in the form of guidelines and standards passed down to business unit management or business unit managers.

The potential scope of advice from CRMs is often not well appreciated by line management. A common scenario is of the CRM being approached initially for advice on insurance matters, this prompting the CRM to ask questions about the context, and consequently providing RM advice which goes beyond just insurance matters.

Role 4. Monitoring Risk Management Processes

In some larger organisations with a portfolio of business units, the corporate RM department may actively audit RM processes in the organisation's business units, seeking to understand the nature of processes in place and their scope. This role may be shared with an internal corporate audit function, or in some cases, may be entirely delegated to the internal audit function. In smaller, less diversified organisations, this audit function may be replaced by site surveys which consider how particular sources of risk are being managed, and whether any are under-managed.

In addition to bench-marking exercises and informal contacts, CRMs also make use of adverse experiences of other organisations which receive media attention. Learning from such experiences, which may not be in the same industry, serves to heighten perception of risks or raise awareness, but may also offer lessons for the development of RM processes.

Role 5. Coordination of Information on Risk Management

Given their responsibilities for insurance management, most CRMs undertake collation of data relating to losses and the financial performance of insurance arrangements, including performance of captive insurance companies. A key figure from this work is an estimate of the 'cost of risk', although it is widely recognised by CRMs that the true cost of risk is underestimated since it is difficult to capture costs and other impacts related to management time and disruption to operations.

A possible role for CRMs is in the development of a corporate risk profile, where the CRM is primarily a facilitator and administrator of a bottom-up process of collating, aggregating and prioritising a short list (perhaps a 'top ten') of risk areas for business units and corporate level management. Whether a single or multi-stage process, such exercises can engender substantial debate. For large organisations with many business units, developing risk profiles for business units in a consistent manner, and effective pooling of this information to portray aggregate effects, can be a major task.

Role 6. Acting as a Conduit for the Interchange of Information

The last set of roles listed in Table 9.2 concern the CRM acting as a conduit for the interchange of information on both sources of risk and the management of risk. This area of responsibility is closely associated with the other five areas listed in Table 9.2, but in principle could be pursued independently of the other areas of responsibility. For example, the role 'identification of (under -managed) risks' is likely to be undertaken by most CRMs, but most commonly as part of identifying the needs for insurance, establishing insurance programmes, and advising on associated risk control activities (Ward, 2001). However, this may also be carried out separately from insurance management, particularly where CRMs have a broad remit to improve RM throughout the organisation. One example is the development of links with other RM specialists in the organisation, such as internal audit, health and safety, security, business continuity, and strategic planning departments. Such links may be formalised via the establishment of a Risk Committee structure, but links may also be attempted by CRMs outside of, or in the absence of such a committee structure.

9.4   DRIVERS OF THE CORPORATE RISK MANAGER'S WORK

As noted earlier, individual CRMs in the UK appeared to be concentrating on a subset of the roles listed in Table 9.2. Given the substantial scope of work implied by all the roles in Table 9.2, this is not surprising. If simultaneous pursuit of all these roles is impractical, choices have to be made, and a variety of contextual factors are likely to influence both the choice of areas of work and the relative priorities given to them. The factors driving the direction and extent of CRM work appear to be associated with five aspects of context (Ward, 2001):

1   Top management influence;

2   External influences;

3   Nature of the business;

4   Corporate developments;

5   Characteristics of the RM department.

The factors associated with these aspects of context are summarised in Table 9.3.

Table 9.3 Factors influencing the extent of CRMs' roles

1 Top management influence
– direct instruction concerning primary tasks
– formal job descriptions
– location of RM department
– quality of support, both moral and resource, provided
– level of Directors' knowledge and enthusiasm for RM
2 External influences
– recommendations on corporate governance
– requirements for risk reporting
– published guidelines on RM processes
– learning from the experiences of other organisations
3 Nature of the business
– nature of products
– size of organisation
– diversity of business units
– degree of decentralisation
– organisation culture(s)
4 Corporate developments
– limitations of past RM efforts
– the pace of expansion (rate of acquisitions)
– experience of risk exposures
5 Characteristics of the RM department
– origins of the RM department
– management perceptions of expertise in the RM department
– quality of personnel (experience, track record, credibility, knowledge of the business)
– resources available

Factor 1. Top Management Influence

Top management can have a major influence on the roles undertaken by the CRM. Top management can scope responsibilities in greater or lesser detail at will, by direct instruction, or via job descriptions. Top management can also influence the scope of the

CRMs activities indirectly by location of the RM department, and by the quality of support provided, including resources.

Reporting to a particular function's director tends to define expectations of the scope of work that the CRM will undertake. Reporting to the finance director is a natural choice if RM is regarded as an extension of insurance management and risk financing, but then extending influence beyond the management of insurable risks can be difficult without top management support, and may not be easy even with this support.

Factor 2. External Influences

A major consideration for CRMs is the recommendations on corporate governance by the Cadbury, Hampel and Turnbull Committees (Cadbury, 1992; Hampel, 1998; ICAEW, 1999), which have obliged companies to give RM more explicit attention. The 'Combined Code' (Committee on Corporate Governance, 1998), requires companies to undertake a review of the system of internal control on, at least, an annual basis: *the review should cover all controls, including financial, operational and compliance controls and RM.* Subsequently, the Turnbull Committee confirmed earlier recommendations of the Hampel Committee that companies should have effective RM and internal control systems that consider all relevant risks, not just narrowly defined financial risks. Several CRMs in Ward's (2001) study reported that the Cadbury and Hampel reports had definitely increased willingness to develop RM in their organisations. Proposals by the ICAEW for reporting on risk by including a section on risks and their management in Company Annual Reports and Accounts, have also served to raise the profile of RM (ICAEW, 1998).

Factor 3. Nature of the Business

Basic characteristics of the organisation that might be expected to drive the direction of RM effort include the nature of products, the size of the organisation in terms of the number and diversity of business units, and the extent to which business units are decentralised.

In broad terms, the nature of many sources of risk confronting commercial organisations are very similar. However, attention to these sources and approaches to their management can vary in emphasis. Thus organisations in the passenger transport business may place high priority on safety, while a chemical manufacturer may be primarily concerned with Health and Safety and environmental impact. A strong quality bias in a large scale manufacturer might lead to an emphasis on accident prevention and minimising employee absences.

A key factor limiting the role of corporate RM departments is the number of business units in the organisation, and the extent to which these are decentralised. Developing good working relationships with business unit management becomes more difficult in large groups of decentralised business units, where local management wish to minimise what they regard as 'corporate interference'. Business units may agree that RM is useful, but in practice may only give lip service and limited resources to RM. One possible explanation for this is a management pre-occupation with improving performance in the short term, and activities with immediate tangible benefits.

Factor 4. Corporate Developments

The scope and priorities for CRMs are often influenced by what has happened in the past, and what is currently going on in the organisation.

For some CRMs the issue is what needs doing, given what has been done before. For example, changes in legislation, or in the insurance market can force attention towards reassessing insurance arrangements and the implications for RM action. Alternatively, recent experience of large, single source losses can provide a useful lever to encourage greater efforts in RM. Not surprisingly, major incidents can bring about sea-changes in risk perception, and heightened concern for safety over cost-cutting.

Factor 5. Characteristics of the Risk Management Department

Clearly, characteristics of the RM department itself must influence what the department is capable of doing and what roles it might take on, given the opportunity. Key factors include: the origins of the RM department, line management perceptions of the RM department, the quality of personnel, and the level of resources.

Where a RM department has been historically an insurance department, insurance management may persist as a core activity, with other work being derived from this insurance base. Thus queries from business units about insurance matters create a contact which CRMs can build on, as noted earlier. This suggests that expertise in and responsibility for insurance can be a useful way for the CRM to make a wider contribution to RM in their organisation. However, an 'insurance expert' label can make it difficult for some CRMs to broaden the scope of their work, assuming they wish to do so.

It is likely that the ability of CRMs to contribute to the assessment of 'speculative' risks may depend heavily on the perceived credibility and track record of CRMs, together with their knowledge of the business and awareness of key issues. An obvious question is what special skills, outside of insurance expertise, can CRMs bring to the management of both 'pure' and 'speculative' risks. One CRM in Ward's (2001) study suggested that a key skill was *an ability to think outside of the box*, facilitated by the position of the RM department in the organisation, and its perceived role. This recognises that an individual such as the CRM, with a wide remit to improve the quality of RM, can provide a useful oversight of risk. Unfortunately, a somewhat insubstantial 'ability to think outside the box' may not be enough to convince sceptical or complacent managers that CRMs in particular have something to offer.

Where CRMs have considerable opportunity to develop their role in whatever ways they see fit, it seems likely that individuals will select roles and approaches which play to their strengths, interests and expertise. This suggests that CRMs need to be selected with great care, and with a clear idea of the qualities needed. For example, important qualities might reasonably include: good knowledge and experience of the organisational context, a broad knowledge of RM, tenacity, initiative, drive, and good negotiating skills.

In addition to the influence of the quality of personnel in the RM department, the quantity and scope of work undertaken must also be constrained by the resources available to the RM department. In respect of human resources, the majority of CRMs interviewed in Ward's study headed up small departments of less than ten personnel including secretarial support. Larger departments were involved in insurance administration and/or internal audit.

There can be little doubt that in many, if not all, organisations, RM efforts are restricted because of a low level of resources. In such circumstance, there can be an ongoing problem for the CRM of managing a heavy workload, a major part of which is typically insurance management tasks. Prioritising work can be difficult, forcing a reactive, anticipatory approach to tasks. Under these circumstances, it can be very difficult for CRMs to contemplate taking on a wider scope of work, even if the potential for this exists. Faced with this situation, perhaps the CRM's role should be focused on recognising, managing and marshalling resources that can be called upon to further RM.

9.5   CONCLUSION

There is certainly room for substantial improvement in the quality and scope of RM in most organisations. One problem is the need for CRMs to ensure that their contribution is fully appreciated. Without this, it is difficult to argue for additional resources and commitment to improving RM capability. A second, related problem is that while RM departments make a significant contribution to organisational performance, they are not always best placed or equipped to progress the general development of RM throughout the organisation. A variety of contextual factors influence the activities undertaken by CRMs and the relative priorities given to them. Although the list of contextual factors in Table 9.3 may be incomplete, it does offer a list of areas that CRMs ought to address when formulating their department's strategy for RM development.

10

DEVELOPING RISK MANAGEMENT CAPABILITY

10.1 INTRODUCTION

Much of this book has been concerned with understanding the ways in which risk management (RM) ought to be developed. Previous chapters have considered what form RM can take, in what contexts it can be applied and for what purposes, what sources of risk need to be addressed, and how RM effort might be organised. This chapter is more concerned with understanding the nature of an organisation's current ability to undertake RM, and what may be needed to make organisations more capable in RM terms. As noted earlier, it is important not to treat establishing a RM capability as synonymous with operating a particular RM process, such as one focused on identifying a corporate risk profile. To be sure, such corporate processes cannot operate without appropriate administrative structures, but developing RM capability is about facilitating effective application of RM throughout the organisation and in a wide range of management contexts. It is not confined to establishing and maintaining a single monolithic corporate RM process. Ultimately it is about establishing RM that is fully integrated and embedded in all aspects of decision making at all levels in the organisation.

10.2 ASSESSING RISK MANAGEMENT CAPABILITY

A natural starting point for developing capability is to first assess the extent of existing capability. This can involve self-assessment of current levels of RM activity, comparisons with practice in other organisations through bench-marking, or comparisons with generic 'maturity' models of RM capability.

In terms of self-assessment, the six dimension framework described in Chapter 1 could be employed. Table 1.1 indicated six basic directions in which organisations might develop RM:

1. The what dimension — the focus of attention;

2. The when dimension — the application contexts;

3. The why dimension — the objectives adopted;

4. The whichway dimension — the nature and quality of RM processes employed;

5. The who dimension — the parties involved and the allocation of responsibilities for RM;

6. The wherewithal dimension — the resources applied to RM.

In Chapter 1, the primary motive for introducing this six dimension framework was to indicate the directions in which organisations might develop RM processes. However, a secondary use for the six dimension framework might be in guiding assessments of the current level of RM activity in an organisation. Such assessments, based on the six dimensions, might then be used to facilitate inter-organisation bench-marking exercises. Organisations seeking to compare their RM activity with that of other organisations could limit their attention to a subset of dimensions, for example just focussing on the nature of RM processes employed (the 'whichway' dimension). However, Table 1.1 illustrates how limited such a comparison would be. While bench-marking against all six dimensions might be difficult, the framework at least highlights areas where comparisons might be attempted, thereby offering some guidance in the design of bench-marking studies.

One approach to developing generic bench-marks involves the concept of a 'risk maturity model' (Hillson, 1997; DeLoach, 2000). Maturity models attempt to simplify the bench-marking process by defining a specific number of 'maturity levels' ranging from organisations with no formal RM processes to a state of fully integrated RM. Table 10.1 summarises two examples. The first, from De Loach(2000), is an adaptation of a capability maturity model for software engineering organisations developed by the Software Engineering Institute (SEI) of Carnegie-Mellon University (Paulk et al,

1993; 1995), and identifies five levels of maturity: initial, repeatable, defined, managed, and optimising. The second example is from Hillson (1997); this model is also influenced by the SEI maturity model. Hillson's model identifies just four levels of RM maturity: naive, novice, normalised, and natural. Hillson recognises that some organisations may not fit neatly into the specified categories of maturity, but argues that his four levels *are sufficiently different to*

Table 10.1 Example of Risk Management Maturity Models

Example 1 (DeLoach, 2000)

Maturity Level	1 Initial	2 Repeatable	3 Defined	4 Managed	5 Optimising
Capability	(Ad hoc/chaotic) No institutionalised processes. Reliance on competence of individual.	(Intuitive) Processes established and repeating. Reliance on individuals reduced.	(Qualitative/quantitative) Policies, processes and standards defined and uniformly applied across the organisation.	(Quantitative) Risks measured and managed quantitatively, and aggregated enterprise wide. Risk/reward tradeoffs considered.	(Continuous feedback) Emphasis on taking and exploiting risk. Knowledge accumulated and shared.

Example 2 (Hillson, 1997)

Maturity Level	1 Naive	2 Novice	3 Normalised	4 Natural
Definition	No structured approaches for dealing with uncertainty. Reactive crisis management. Reliance on competence of individuals.	Experimentation via nominated individuals and specific projects. No effectively implemented organisation wide process.	Generic risk policies and procedures formalised and widespread.	Proactive approach required to RM in all aspects of the organisation. Common organisation wide understanding of activities, roles and responsibilities for RM. Standard processes and tools tailored to specific applications. Formal assignment of responsibility for RM. Organisation wide training.

accommodate most organisations unambiguously. ... more than four levels would increase ambiguity without giving sufficient additional refinement to aid use of the model' (Hillson, 1997: p37).

In both maturity models, each level is described in terms of a set of characteristics, the main ones being summarised in Table 10.1. DeLoach (2000) provides a short, unstructured list of features for each maturity level. Hillson (1997) provides substantially more detailed characterisation of each maturity level, identifying features under four attributes: 'culture', 'process', 'experience', and 'application'. Hillson then goes on to list the problems facing an organisation that wishes to progress from one maturity level to the next, and he suggests lists of actions appropriate for increasing risk maturity.

More recently Hopkinson (2002) describes the use of a computerised risk maturity model (RMM) assessment tool developed by HVR-CSL which builds on the principles described in Hillson (1997). At the organisation or business unit level, this involves assessing six aspects of capability: management, risk identification, risk analysis, risk control, risk review, and culture. The RMM comprises a collection of questions, each one of which can yield information about the RM system of interest from one or more of the six aspects. Responses contribute to a weighted rating assessment of RM capability. A feature of this RMM is that the overall assessment is considered to be only as high as the lowest rating amongst the six aspects. The rationale for this is that an overall system for RM is only as strong as its weakest aspect. Given the inevitable weaknesses in methodology, any attempts to simply measure the level of RM maturity (or capability), must be of questionable value. However, prioritising improvements in capability by identifying the weakest links may be a more useful, operational concept.

Maturity models like those in Table 10.1 provide a simplified and pragmatic method for roughly assessing the level of RM in an organisation. The main purpose of this is to facilitate the recognition of ways in which improvements in RM practices can be made. For example, Hillson offers four sets of possible actions to move risk maturity from one level to the next (or maintain it), although these sets of actions are presented as unstructured lists so their rationale or completeness is unclear. Nevertheless, in the absence of any other frameworks, such advice is potentially very helpful. However, it does not facilitate appreciation or consideration of the full range of possible choices for RM development. Partly this is due to anchoring advice on a few specified scenarios (the maturity levels), which may not correspond particularly closely to prevailing RM practices in a particular organisation. It is also due to the limited way in which maturity levels are described. Even Hillson's use of four attributes to designate features of each maturity level falls short of including the scope of features captured with the six dimension framework of Table 1.1. Lest important aspects of RM development are overlooked, any risk maturity framework ought to explicitly incorporate descriptors relating to each of the six dimensions in Table 1.1.

Conversely, the limitations of the six dimension framework in describing RM 'maturity' should also be recognised. This framework describes directions for development of RM practice, but it does not identify all aspects of an organisation's RM capability. In particular, it does not capture management's knowledge and understanding of the nature of RM and its potential benefits, the motivation of individuals to manage risks, or cultural factors such as attitudes to risk, willingness to change, tolerance of mistakes, etc. Such aspects will influence the selection of RM strategies and the ability to implement them. Consequently, such aspects might be usefully included in any bench-marking exercises.

10.3   ASPECTS OF RISK MANAGEMENT CAPABILITY

Essentially there are two sets of factors that might be used to characterise an organisation's RM capability: descriptors and facilitators. The descriptors are factors that characterise the nature and quality of RM that is carried out. Facilitators are factors that either facilitate or hinder the organisation's ability to undertake RM. Table 10.2 suggests the range of factors that might be used to describe RM capability. This list draws on the six dimensions of development in Table 1.1, and expands on the risk maturity model attributes of culture, experience, and management. In doing so the list also draws in aspects of RM discussed in Chapters 2-9. Following sections discuss each of the factors in Table 10.2 in turn.

Table 10.2 Aspects of Risk Management Capability

<table>
<tr><td>

Descriptors

The focus of attention
Threats, opportunities and threats, or uncertainty

Application contexts
RM applied to operations, projects, programmes, or strategies

The nature and quality of risk management processes employed
To degree of formality, level of documentation, the scope of processes, the nature of steps involved, the tools and techniques employed, the extent and quality of quantification

Facilitators

Supporting risk management infrastructure
Guiding principles, objectives and scope of RM, policies (operating rules), allocation of responsibilities for RM, formal processes for administration of RM applications, information systems, resources applied to RM

Supporting organisational capabilities
Administrative structures, communication, information systems, knowledge management, organisation learning

Organisation culture
Attitude to risk and uncertainty, tolerance of mistakes, level of trust, openness, etc.

Human resource capability for risk management
Knowledge and experience of RM methodology and techniques, perceived roles and responsibilities, motivation to undertake RM, motivation to develop RM expertise

</td></tr>
</table>

10.4 THE FOCUS OF ATTENTION

The 'focus of attention' aspect of capability was introduced as dimension 1 of RM development in Chapter 1. Dimension 1 was presented in Table 1.1 as three levels of focus: addressing risks solely in threat terms, or in opportunity and threat terms, or as a wider concern about uncertainty. Chapter 3 considered the limitations of a threat management focus and arguments for combined attention to both opportunities and threats. However, an uncertainty management focus is more desirable because it facilitates consideration of a much wider set of uncertainty related issues that need to be managed.

It was argued in Chapter 3 that restrictive definitions of risk can obstruct the development of RM, and that a broad definition is appropriate, defining risk as the *implications of significant uncertainty about the level of performance achievable.* Defining risk in terms of events, conditions, or circumstances, does not facilitate consideration of potential variability in performance that is driven by underlying ambiguity. Sources of ambiguity related to the basis of estimates, gaps in plans, the nature of objectives, and working relationships between different parties, can have major implications for performance, and they require careful management. To achieve this, organisations need to adopt an explicit focus on understanding where and why uncertainty is important before seeking to manage it.

10.5   APPLICATION CONTEXTS

As noted in Chapter 1, fully integrated RM would imply among other things, that RM was applied in all organisational decisions large and small, strategic or tactical, complex or simple. The wider the application of RM in different decision contexts, and the more significant these decisions, the greater an organisation's RM capability.

The 'application contexts' aspect of capability was introduced as dimension 2 of RM development in Chapter 1. Dimension 2 was presented in Table 1.1 as four levels of decision context: operations, projects, programmes (coherent groups of projects), and strategies. This is a rather simplistic characterisation of decision areas, but it serves as an indication of the range of possible application contexts, characterising operations as largely about short-term tactical decisions, and strategy as about longer term, major investment decisions. A more detailed characterisation of decision contexts was given in Chapter 6. Here it was suggested that all decision contexts can be regarded as embedded in a parent strategy whose development can be described in terms of a strategy life cycle. The stages and steps of the strategy life cycle shown in Table 6.4 provide a more detailed characterisation of decision areas warranting RM. Still more resolution could be obtained by dividing the steps into more detail, or by breaking down programmes and projects into similar life cycle stages and steps (Chapman and Ward, 2003). The purpose of such frameworks is to highlight the range of potential application contexts for RM, the significance of each context, and its relationship to other decision contexts.

High RM capability in terms of application contexts involves not only use of RM to inform the full range of decisions, but also an appreciation of how and why the focus of attention should vary for different decision contexts. A common pattern is of RM applied largely in the maintenance of different aspects of operations, while the use of RM to guide and inform major investment decisions is relatively limited. This pattern suggests a rather low level of capability in terms of application contexts.

In respect of developing capability, decisions must be made about the range of contexts that will be subject to formal RM processes, and the extent to which RM will be required in such contexts or merely facilitated. The ultimate target may be 'all contexts and all significant decisions', but this would imply different levels of RM for different types of context. For example, a cost-effective approach to RM in projects implies different levels of detail and effort for different sizes and types of projects, and for RM applications at different stages in the project life cycle (Chapman Ward, 2003).

10.6   THE NATURE AND QUALITY OF RISK MANAGEMENT PROCESSES EMPLOYED

Ultimately, the efficiency and effectiveness of RM depends on the nature and quality of the RM processes employed, and consequently, much of the RM literature focuses on the nature and content of the generic RM process. Dimension 4 in Chapter 1, the 'whichway' dimension, characterised RM processes in terms of:

- the degree of formality;
- the scope of the process;
- tools and techniques employed;
- extent of quantification.

Developing capability in terms of RM process formality requires the introduction of formal, documented processes, the use of a generic process framework, and appropriate quantification. As noted in Chapter 8, part of the role of formality is clarifying the need for a rich set of motives for undertaking RM, as well as helping to pursue these motives. A high level of capability involves expert use of formal processes, adopting a flexible approach that intelligently varies the depth and complexity of analysis to suit the context. Low-level capability is evident in the use of highly bureaucratic documented processes, using simplistic forms of analysis in a rigid 'one size fits all' manner that encourages a mechanical 'paint by numbers' approach.

A full discussion of RM processes and techniques is beyond the scope of this text, and the issues relating to the quality of RM processes are numerous and often complex. However, Chapters 7 and 8 provided an overview of key issues. Chapter 7 focused on comparing a number of RM process frameworks. One conclusion was that project RM process frameworks are typically more detailed, and consequently facilitate the recognition and management of a wider set of RM issues than simpler frameworks defined in terms of basic phases such as: identification, analysis, evaluation, and response selection.

The second conclusion from Chapter 7 was that more capable processes involve an iterative approach to individual applications (as opposed to repeated applications over a period of time). This involves revisiting earlier phases of the process to develop, refine or reconsider aspects of analysis undertaken to date in a single application. Single pass processes which adopt a sequential, once only approach to the phases of the RM process are likely to be highly inefficient and seriously ineffective. This is because time and effort will be wasted on issues that turn out to be unimportant, and not enough time will be spent on important issues that emerge from the analysis.

Chapter 8 outlined key issues that should be addressed in a high quality RM process, particularly in relation to:

- defining the application context;

- scoping and planning the analysis;

- identifying assumptions and inter-dependencies between context factors and sources of uncertainty;

- explicitly considering risk allocation issues;

- evaluating the implications of dependence, and the choices presented by alternative responses.

Chapter 8 concluded with some comments about the need for cost-effective RM processes. However, simplification merely to economise on resources and the amount of time spent on RM, is never appropriate. Capable RM makes design choices about the scope of RM processes in the full knowledge of what is involved in a comprehensive RM process.

10.7   SUPPORTING RISK MANAGEMENT INFRASTRUCTURE

As noted in Chapter 2, it is important to distinguish between the RM infrastructure and the individual RM activities it facilitates and supports. The substance of any RM infrastructure should be driven top-down by strategic decisions about the possibilities for RM development described in Chapter 1. Development of RM infrastructure should not be led solely by the nature of one particular RM process as this may well obstruct consideration and development of wider RM applications.

The components of a RM infrastructure were outlined in Chapter 2:

- assignment of formal roles for the top-down, systematic development, co-ordination, and support of RM activities.

- guiding principles which relate to the fundamental nature of the organisation's business and associated risks.

- a strategy for RM use and development which sets out when and why RM is to be employed, and how it is to be developed and supported in terms of the six dimensions in Chapter 1.

- policies and guidelines for RM which indicate how RM can and should be undertaken in various contexts and applications.

- the nature of decision support and information systems.

This infrastructure needs to address all aspects of the organisation's RM capability. In particular, the strategy for RM development and infrastructure provision needs to specify the levels of capability the organisation will aspire to in terms of each of the dimensions in Table 1.1. This strategy also needs to address what will be needed to achieve this in terms of human resource capability and supporting organisational capabilities.

A key driver of RM strategy and infrastructure provision is the set of objectives to be pursued by RM activity. Chapter 6 discussed possible objectives in some detail. Table 6.3 described a multi-level structure of possible objectives for RM that relate to: quality of the RM process, purpose in a given application, RM performance criteria, and the development of RM capability. A key message was that organisations should identify and pursue objectives at all four levels, recognising that achievement of lower level objectives is a prerequisite for achievement of higher level objectives. Limited efforts focused solely on basic process and application objectives will signal a low level of RM capability whatever an organisation does in respect of other RM development dimensions. The danger is that objectives are inappropriately restricted by particular parties. What is needed is a RM champion who is aware of the potential benefits that can accrue from an effective RM capability, and who has the will and the influence to maintain an ambitious view of what can and should be achieved.

In setting priorities amongst possible objectives and applications for RM, management should be guided by a top-down, strategic view of context uncertainty. This can be informed by the different perspectives on uncertainty discussed in chapters 4 and 5. Priority should be given to deploying RM in areas where there is greatest need, where increased capability to manage uncertainty will produce the largest benefits for key stakeholders. Clearly this requires an appreciation of the full range of potential benefits obtainable from RM plus a well-informed appreciation of key areas of risk. For example, contracting organisations might choose to focus RM effort on improved competitive bidding processes aimed at:

- improving transparency in quality of cost estimates;
- devising procedures to address uncertainty about the probability of winning with different bids;
- establishing efficient computer-based risk analysis processes which can produce analyses in the short timescales required;
- being able to evaluate the implications of proposed contractual conditions;
- rapidly evaluating alternative ways of carrying out components of the proposed contract.

(Chapman and Ward, 2002)

For contractors facing an increasingly competitive environment and ever more demanding customers, the prospect of obtaining a new core competence in risk analysis should be a major incentive to adopt a more systematic RM.

10.8 SUPPORTING ORGANISATIONAL CAPABILITIES

As noted in Chapter 2, all RM activity takes place within the environment provided by an organisation's administrative infrastructure. This is a rather obvious but important observation. How the organisation operates will have a major impact on what can be achieved in terms of RM. Organisation structure, co-ordination and control systems, environmental scanning capability, communications and information systems, knowledge management, and support for organisation learning, are all key facilitators of RM. Such factors define the basic resources that RM must work with, and they set the tone for how RM will be able (or allowed) to operate. Such factors can enable RM to flourish, or can present barriers to its development no matter how capable and determined the champions of RM effort.

Organisations which have efficient and effective systems for co-ordination and control, environmental scanning, and organisation learning will be comparatively well placed to foster efficient and effective RM. Unfortunately, many organisations exhibit deficiencies in their approach to uncertainty and learning which can act as barriers to RM development. Sometimes shortcomings in organisational capabilities are not evident until systematic attempts to identify and manage uncertainty are made. For example, Chapman and Ward (2002) identify the following shortcomings:

Disconnected left and right hands – the left hand does not know what the right hand is doing, in organisational terms.

Tunnel vision – inability to see the big picture or the wood for the trees.

Lack of focus – inability to see the trees that matter in the wood. This can be viewed as a simple converse of tunnel vision. However, it is common to find both conditions together when there is detailed analysis of what people understand, but important issues are ignored because they seem too difficult.

Wasted experience – the same mistakes are made time after time.

Propensity to panic – high levels of uncontrolled crisis and unhelpful fear. Often this is driven top-down by senior management making bad situations worse.

Boredom – lack of constructive tension, excitement, and fun.

These conditions are not so much cultural, as unintended, emergent consequences of weaknesses in the organisation's capability for co-ordination, decision support, knowledge management, and organisation learning.

One aspect of this issue concerns the factors affecting the role of a corporate risk manager, discussed in Chapter 9 and listed in Table 9.3. Senior management's expectations of the scope of work, the nature of the business, corporate developments past and present, and the extent of decentralisation in the organisation, can all affect the scope and quality of the corporate risk manager's work. A particular problem is that RM departments are not always best placed or sufficiently resourced to progress the development of RM. Table 9.3 offers a list of contextual factors that ought to be addressed by corporate risk managers when formulating their strategy for RM development. This may involve seeking to build desirable, supporting organisational capabilities.

10.9   ORGANISATION CULTURE

In Chapter 4, it was suggested that culture could operate as an organisational control mechanism, and reflect employees' beliefs about how they are valued by the organisation. In Ward's (2001) study of corporate risk managers, some corporate risk managers observed that the quality of RM undertaken in business units can be driven by the organisation culture prevailing in business units. This culture can be manifest in a variety of ways, such as attitude to: planning, formal procedures, regulations, criticism, mistakes, uncertainty, and risk. These cultural characteristics can either facilitate or hinder the development of RM.

Attention to uncertainty may be limited for a variety of reasons. In many operational areas, uncertainty may not be regarded as sufficiently important or significant to warrant attention in systematic RM terms. Such uncertainty as exists may be considered manageable as part of day-to-day operations. More generally, events may be considered too unpredictable to prepare for, or too unpleasant to contemplate and therefore best ignored in the hope that 'it may never happen'. Such attitudes reflect a perception of uncertainty as something to be avoided, and may encourage decisions and actions that favour 'playing safe' or reducing uncertainty, whatever the cost.

These perceptions may not be defensible, but to the extent that they exist, they must be managed in any attempts to increase levels of RM.

Chapman and Ward (2002: Chap. 12) argue that some of the most significant barriers to effective RM are based on unfavourable features of organisational culture. Sometimes these barriers are induced from outside the organisation in the form of convictions, prejudices, biases, and routines of professional groups that can blinker thinking. These may arise from a wish to make decisions efficiently in a particular context according to recognised scientific or professional standards. Such professionally based convictions can strongly influence different groups within the same organisation, making it very difficult to adopt holistic, enterprise-wide RM processes. However, most organisations also exhibit a number of more generic culture based behaviours or conditions inimical to effective RM. As an illustration, Chapman and Ward (2002) list a number of often observed dysfunctional behaviours that relate to general attitude to uncertainty and behaviours. These include:

Po-faced pessimism – simplistic, unmitigated pessimism, normally limited to parts of the organisation concerned with hazard and safety management.

Eldorado optimism – simplistic unmitigated optimism which may be coupled to a lack of controls, inappropriate contracts, and a willingness to escalate commitment by taking massive gambles against the odds (see also Chapter 5).

Conspiracy of infallibility – the belief that crisis is unlikely, and disaster is not possible.

Conspiracy of optimism – strong corporate pressures to avoid revealing bad news. In many organisations this is associated with a 'can-do' corporate culture, an emphasis on team loyalty, and a Darwinian survival-of-the-fittest struggle between competing projects.

Macho management – a belief that 'real' managers are those who can cope in a crisis. Good 'fire-fighters', managers who face serious problems and sort them out, are recognised and rewarded over managers who appear to have had no problems (and therefore, it is assumed, must have had an easy job). This leads to a vicious circle where macho managers recruit 'in their own image'. Coupled with a 'can-do' corporate culture, this can lead to habitual overloading of managers, and inevitably, more problems to be wrestled with. (Repenning and Sterman, 2001)

A blame culture – a belief that there is no such thing as bad luck, that when something goes wrong or performance targets are not met, someone, or some group, must be at fault and appropriate sanctions should be applied. This can give rise to 'finger-pointing', 'passing the buck', and 'witch-hunts' with knock-on implications for future working relations between different individuals or groups.

Naked emperor phenomenon – no one is prepared to acknowledge a high level of uncertainty which clearly exists. This applies to the all-too-common insistence of senior management on minimal uncertainty in estimates for planning and other purposes. It may be driven by a pathological dislike of uncertainty at the top, encouraged by an authoritarian culture.

Management by mis-direction – constraint setting without appreciation of the consequences for other performance objectives.

Some of these conditions may seem mutually exclusive. For example, it might be assumed that an organisation cannot simultaneously exhibit both 'po faced pessimism' and 'El Dorado optimism'. In practice different parts of an organisation can exhibit conflicting conditions like these two. However, half a dozen or so complementary cultural conditions seems to be the norm, in terms of a characterisation of conditions significant enough to warrant attention and treatment.

Essentially these behaviours seem to evidence the difficulty management has in coping with complexity and uncertainty in decision making. In particular, they can reflect an inability or unwillingness on the part of managers or groups to recognise the difference between (a) bad management and things that are not under a manager's control; and (b) good managers who apply proactive RM to reduce problems and enhance performance, and managers who are just lucky. As noted in Chapter 6, addressing such conditions can be one of the most significant benefits of formal RM processes.

10.10 THE HUMAN RESOURCE CAPABILITY FOR RISK MANAGEMENT

The effectiveness of RM is clearly dependent to a substantial degree on the capability and experience of the people undertaking RM. The parties involved in developing and maintaining an organisation's RM capability include those who might champion the initiative, the individuals or teams responsible for making things happen, those who use the associated RM systems and procedures, and those who subsequently support and maintain the RM capability. Outside parties may also be influential, such as banks or major customers. The experience, seniority and role of the RM capability project manager is obviously of critical importance. That such a manager is appointed with these responsibilities is a basic tenet of effective project management.

Skills and experience

For effective RM in a given context, a clear idea of the skills and experience required is a necessary precursor to the selection of the party who can best undertake the RM.

For individuals, long personal experience of technical problems in a particular area of operations may not be as useful as a wide experience of both technical and commercial problems in several areas of operations over a shorter period, especially if the organisation concerned makes use of new and rapidly developing technology, or is otherwise undergoing rapid change. Training is always an option to improve skills in risk identification and analysis, but it is not a panacea, and training can be deficient or outdated in important respects. A limited perception of the nature and scope of RM might be one reason for this deficiency.

Where the party responsible for undertaking RM is a team, department or organisation, the forgoing comments obviously apply to the individual members of these groups. However, these comments also apply to the group as a whole, since we can talk of organisational capability and experience that transcends reliance on the skills of particular individuals.

The skills required for a strong corporate capability in RM are similar to the skills required for a good internal operational research/information systems consultancy group. Some of the most successful groups of this kind are used as an elite training ground for future senior executive recruiting and development, as well as a core competitive weapon in the immediate RM support role. The idea is to attract very bright younger staff as junior consultants who will develop skills that remain very valuable when most of them move on to line management roles. Some will stay on in management consultant roles, and some will become the custodians of RM processes, training, and staff development. However, the spin-off of very effective line managers and future executives is a central feature. Leadership is the key issue for such groups. This is a classic potential problem that needs to be managed as an opportunity. Organisations which move everyone on to different jobs every two or three years have particular problems with this issue, although some have dealt with it very successfully by modifying their usual rules to some extent.

Motivation

Motivation is a key factor in the conduct of any organisation participant, and a key management concern is to ensure that all organisation participants are motivated to work towards appropriate organisation performance objectives.

In respect of RM, organisation participants need to be convinced that RM activity will help them meet their own objectives in a cost effective manner, both directly and indirectly through enhanced organisation performance. If not, then participants will be motivated to ignore risk or manage it in their own interests, and they will be less concerned about the impact on organisation performance or other participants' objectives. Such considerations apply in all principal-agent relationships whether internal or external to an organisation.

Consider for example, the relationship between a client and contractor. For powerful clients putting work out to competitive tender, a requirement that all tenders include a RM plan is sufficient inducement for offering contractors to comply at some level. However, enlightened client organisations expecting contractors to manage uncertainty in the client's interests will take pains to demonstrate how contractors themselves can benefit directly by improved cost estimation, greater efficiency, improved project control, and, ultimately, higher profitability. Such clients will be only too aware of the moral hazard of claims seeking behaviour by contractors who think they are going to lose money on an onerous fixed-price contract.

Similar motivation issues arise in persuading different units in the same organisation to undertake RM. Motivation is a particularly pertinent consideration if organisations wish to encourage 'whistleblowing'. Unfortunately employees often hold a belief, sometimes well founded, that 'blowing the whistle' on poor practices or shortcomings in management systems and decision making is unlikely to do them much good personally, indeed quite the opposite.

Incentives for individuals to own up to their own failings or 'near misses' are even more unclear. Moreover, employees or other agents working under aggressive, difficult to achieve performance targets may be motivated to hide problems from others. For example, Repenning and Sterman (2001) cite the motto of hard-pressed development engineers in one firm which was *'never reveal you have a problem until you also have the solution'*. In another firm *'engineers called the weekly progress review meetings the Liars Club – each participant overstated the progress of his subsystem and hid known defects from others in the hope that others would be discovered first, giving them time to catch up'* (Repenning and Sterman, 2001).

An obvious effect of staff reluctance to speak out about problems must be that when problems do become obvious, they are bigger than they would otherwise have been. Fear of personal repercussions may be accompanied by self-censoring of doubts as 'defensive avoidance' behaviour. This can happen if the concern is about a single event, and its likelihood of being repeated is uncertain ('the problem might just go away anyway'). It can also arise where the organisational culture encourages team building, camaraderie, and makes strong assumptions of a shared common cause/professional integrity. This can cause real 'show-stopper' problems to build up. In any given organisation unit, there is a danger that a culture develops which tolerates or condones 'low-level alarms going off'. A potential whistleblower may well have gone along with, or have been part of this culture, until things escalate beyond the individual's threshold of acceptability. Self-preservation will motivate them to be concerned about how much they have been part of the situation and increase the threshold at which they feel impelled to speak out.

Effective RM should provide a process that has visible, direct benefits to the parties involved. This may be difficult to achieve with conventional 'whistleblowing' processes. Instead organisations concerned about potential failings in their operations probably need to adopt much more proactive systems-focused RM processes.

10.11 MANAGING DEVELOPMENT

In terms of building RM capability, a common approach is to begin with a simplified RM process, perhaps limited to probability impact diagrams and checklists, introduced fairly rapidly with a minimum of piloting. Following rapid introduction, the intention is to continue operating the simplified process in a well-defined administrative framework, without major changes in format. However, to achieve effective RM it is essential to understand the nature of a comprehensive RM process. Ideally this understanding needs to be developed in a methodical fashion on a widespread basis, not confined to one or two individuals charged with the rapid introduction of a limited new corporate RM process. Chapman and Ward (2003) advocate a pilot study approach, applying a comprehensive RM process to a particular context to learn on, such as a selected project, which has three characteristics:

1. The context has been very well managed to date;

2. Despite its successful management to date, important sources of uncertainty raise concerns which need to be addressed;

3. There is sufficient time to undertake a comprehensive RM process.

A pilot study approach of this kind should ultimately lead to relatively effective RM procedures, but it may be relatively slow as a learning process.

The process of instituting formal RM procedures as a standard corporate policy is not without risk. The essential threat is that the policy fails to bring sufficient benefits, perhaps because procedures are inappropriate, not properly implemented or only partially adopted. Once difficulties are encountered the credibility of the initiative may suffer, making it very difficult to revive a RM initiative at a later date. Such threats and their underlying causes need to be recognized and managed in much the same way as any significant organisational change.

Walsham (1992) has suggested a management framework which views organisational change as a jointly analytical, educational and political process where important interacting dimensions are the context, content, and process of the change. Significant aspects of context include: stakeholders' perspectives and relationships between those affected by a particular change initiative, the history of existing procedures and systems, informal networks and procedures, and infrastructure needs (for example, skills and resources required). The process of change involves the dynamics of interaction between participants and others who are affected by the change or who can affect it. Significant aspects of process include power-politics and organisational culture. Implementing a significant change like the introduction of RM processes and associated infrastructure needs to take these dimensions into account.

Other writers on the management of change have related the implementation process to Lewin's (1947) model of planned change that involves three phases: unfreezing-changing-refreezing. Each phase is concerned with changes in the balance of (psychological) forces in the organisation and the degree to which they restrain or drive change. Unfreezing involves disturbing the equilibrium of the status quo by increasing the balance of driving forces over restraining forces, decreasing restraining forces, or a combination of these. Effective unfreezing generally involves increasing driving forces while managing a reduction in restraining forces to reduce resistance to change. Refreezing involves the systematic replacement of the temporary change-inducing forces with more permanent forces that can maintain the new status quo.

Forces for change in terms of building RM capability are likely to be derived from a senior management recognition of the potential benefits as noted earlier. Resistance to change coming from other parties may be due to some or all of the following:

1   Parochial self-interest in maintaining the status quo;

2. Inability to perceive a need for change;

3. Pressure of other work;

4. Concern about the costs of introducing new procedures;

5. Individuals concerned that they will be unable to carry out the new procedures;

6. Uncertainty and suspicion about the nature of the change.

Suggested strategies for reducing resistance to change often include education, communication, participation and involvement, facilitation and support, and offering incentives. This implies a change process that first clarifies the need for and relevance of formal RM, seeks to improve stakeholders' understanding of what is involved, and provides motivation for individuals to use the new formal processes. Additionally, there is a need to ensure that RM skills are developed, and that individuals have sufficient time and resources to apply RM in individual contexts. Subsequently, administrative systems for coordinating and monitoring the application and effectiveness of RM applications can be introduced.

Operating RM systems in a multi-national organisation presents additional challenges. The range of risks and uncertainties is greater due to: the diversity in operating environments, the greater difficulties of achieving a common RM culture, greater communication difficulties, and greater difficulties in coordinating and controlling RM activities. Of course the opportunities and choices for action, including strategic flexibility are also greater. All these aspects have a bearing not just on the nature of sources of uncertainty requiring management, but also on the operability of RM processes in organisation units which are widely dispersed with often significantly different attitudes to risk and perceptions of risk.

10.12 THE WAY FORWARD

At a basic level, organisations must have some capability for RM to continue to survive. Much, if not all, management practice is implicitly about managing risk and uncertainty. The basic management tasks of planning, setting objectives, co-ordination, and control procedures are all about clarifying what is to be done, by whom, with what resources, and trying to make sure the right things actually happen. So why separate out RM for special attention? The answer lies in the fact that uncertainty and risk are so pervasive in all organised activity. Any methodologies, tools, or techniques for analysing and treating risk and uncertainty in one area of management are likely to be transferable to a wide variety of other areas and contexts. Accordingly, the pay-offs in terms of improved organisation performance, of adopting an organisation-wide systematic focus on RM, are potentially enormous. Organisations that have not yet bolstered traditional management concerns of planning, co-ordination and control with systematic efforts to develop RM capability, are missing a major opportunity. Most organisations are a long way from fully exploiting this opportunity. Consequently, those organisations who seek to develop their RM capability are likely to gain significant competitive advantage.

A starting point is to assess the extent of existing RM capability. This needs to consider the level of attainment in respect of all six dimensions of RM development shown in Table 1.1, not just the nature of RM processes employed. This assessment also needs to recognise the importance of facilitating factors such as supporting organisational capabilities, organisation culture and the capability of employees (Table 10.2). Current efforts to facilitate this assessment via bench-marking against levels of maturity are in the early stages of development.

Building RM capability needs a strategy, if only because the possible courses of action are so numerous. As noted in Chapter 1, plausible strategies for developing RM capability need to consider the suitability, feasibility, and acceptability of initiatives. Large-scale imposition of formal, 'stand alone' processes may offer the promise of rapid progress (at least initially), but require substantial investment of time, money and effort. Such initiatives often involve the use of proprietary software, simplified processes, and simple forms of analysis on grounds of efficiency and ease of use. However, such approaches can stifle subsequent development of more sophisticated and more effective RM processes. Also such initiatives can fail to address significant underlying shortcomings in capability associated with organisational culture, and the capability of employees in respect of RM.

More efficient, cost-effective approaches to developing RM capability may involve more focused, incremental development that is incorporated into existing decision support systems. Such approaches involve carefully targeting key pulse points in an organisation's activities where uncertainty and risk matter most, and where improvements in the quality of decision making will have the greatest impact. However, the success of this approach depends heavily on the knowledge and expertise of RM possessed by key influencers. For example, if top management believes that RM is merely a formal process for identifying things that might go wrong and ranking these events in a rough order of priority for future attention, then most of the reasons for building RM capability will not be recognised, let alone pursued.

The real pay-offs from RM come from taking a broad perspective of risk and uncertainty, and from appreciating the ways in which RM can be employed to improve the quality of decision making and organisation performance. This book does not provide all the answers, but hopefully it will help to point most managers in the right direction.

REFERENCES

AIRMIC Integrated Risk Management Special Interest Group (1999) *A guide to integrated risk management.* London: The Association of Insurance and Risk Managers in Commerce.

AIRMIC, ALARM, IRM Standard (2002) *A risk management standard.* London: AIRMIC, ALARM, IRM.

Ansoff, H.I. (1984) *Implanting strategic management.* Englewood Cliffs, New Jersey, Prentice/Hall International.

Ansoff, H. I. (1987) *Corporate strategy.* Revised edition, Penguin.

Australia/New Zealand Standard (1999) AS/NZS 4360-1999 *Risk Management.* Strathfield, NSW: Standards Association of Australia.

Bartlett J., Chapman C., Close P., Davey K., Desai P., Grppm H., Hillson D., Hopkinson M., Gerdes R., Major E., Newland K., Simister S., Greenwood M., Campbell P., Wiuliams T. (2004) *Risk Analysis and Management Guide.* Second Edition, High Wycombe, APM Publishing Ltd.

Bazerman, M. (1998) *Judgement in managerial decision making.* 4th edition. New York: John Wiley and Sons Ltd.

Bazerman, M.H., Giuliano, T. and Appleman, A. (1984) Escalation of commitment in individual and group decision making. *Organisational behavior and human performance,* 33 (2), 141-152.

Belbin, R. M. (1981) *Management teams: why they succeed or fail.* London: Heinemann.

Bourgeois, L.J. III (1981) On the measurement of organizational slack. *Academy of Management Review,* 6(1), 29-39.

Brockner, J. (1992) The escalation of commitment to a failing course of action: towards a theoretical progress. *Academy of Management Review,* 17 (1), 39-61.

213

Butterworth M., Reddaway R., and Benson T., 1996, *Corporate Governance- a guide for insurance and risk managers.* London: Association of Insurance and Risk Managers.

Cadbury A. (Chair), The Committee on the Financial Aspects of Corporate Governance, 1992, *The financial aspects of corporate governance,* London, Gee Publishing Ltd.

CFO Research Services (2002) *Strategic risk management- new disciplines, new opportunities.* Boston, Mass. CFO Publishing Corp.

Challenger, J. (1996) Risk of corporate Alzheimer's. *Bank Personnel News,* April.

Chapman, Chris B. and Ward, Stephen C. (2000). Estimation and evaluation of uncertainty: a minimalist first pass approach. *International Journal of Project Management.* 18, 369-383.

Chapman, Chris and Ward, Stephen (2002). *Managing project risk and uncertainty: a constructively simple approach to decision making.* Chichester, UK: John Wiley & Sons Ltd.

Chapman, Chris B. & Ward, Stephen C. (2003). *Project risk management: processes, techniques and insights.* Second edition, Chichester, UK: John Wiley & Sons Ltd.

Committee on Corporate Governance, the London stock exchange (1998). *The combined code.* London, Gee Publishing Ltd.

Connell, T. (2003) *What are the risks faced by high-street rate retailers that fail to offer their customers good levels of customer service and customer satisfaction?* MSc dissertation, University of Southampton.

Cook, S. (2002) *Customer-care excellence.* 4th edition, London: Kogan Page.

Cooper, K. G. (1980) Naval ship production: a claim settled and a framework built. *Interfaces,* 10(6), 20-36.

Courtis, J. (1986) *Managing by mistake.* London: Institute of Chartered Accountants.

Deal, T. and Kennedy, A. (2000) *The new corporate cultures – revitalising the workplace after downsizing, mergers and re-engineering.* London: TEXERE Publishing.

DeLoach J.W. (2000) *Enterprise wide risk management: strategies for linking risk with opportunity.* London: Financial Times/Prentice Hall.

Dickson, G. (2003) *Risk analysis.* 3rd edition, London, Witherby.

Dowie, J. (1999) Against risk. *Risk Decision and Policy.* 4(1): 57-73.

Eden, C. (1988). Cognitive mapping: a review. *European Journal of Operational Research,* 36, 1-13.

Eden, C. and Radford, J. (1990) *Tackling strategic problems: the role of group decision support.* Sage Publications.

Forrester, J. (1958) Industrial dynamics: a major breakthrough for decision making. *Harvard Business Review,* 36(4), 37-66.

Forrester, J. (1961) *Industrial Dynamics.* Cambridge, MA: MIT Press.

Fortune, J. and Peters, G. (1995) *Learning from failure – the systems approach.* Chichester: John Wiley and Sons Ltd.

French, S., Kelly, N., and Morrey, M. (1992) Towards a shared understanding – how decision conferencing helped structure decision problems in the international Chernobyl project. *OR Insight,* 5(4), 23-27.

Frost, C., Allen, D., Porter, J. and Bloodworth, P. (2001) *Operational risk and resilience- understanding and minimizing operational risk to secure shareholder value.* Oxford, Butterworth-Heinemann.

Furnham, A. (2003) *The incompetent manager: the causes, consequences and cures of managerial failure.* London and Philadelphia: Whurr publishers.

Georgopolous, B. S. (1973) An open system theory model for organisational research. In Negandhi, A. R. (Ed.) *Modern organisation theory.* Kent, Ohio: Kent State University Press, 102-131.

Gilovich, T., Griffin, D., Kahneman, D. (Eds) (2002) *Heuristics and Biases: the psychology of intuitive judgment.* Cambridge: Cambridge University Press.

Godfrey, P. (1996) *Control of risk: a guide to the systematic management of risk from construction.* London: Construction Industry Research and Information Association.

Goodwin, P. and Wright G. (2003) *Decision analysis for management judgment*. 3rd edition, Chichester, John Wiley & Sons Ltd.

Green, SD. (2001) Towards an integrated script for risk and value management. *Project management*. 7(1), 52-58.

Grey, S. (1995) *Practical Risk Assessment for Project Management*. Chichester, John Wiley & Sons Ltd.

HM Treasury (2001) *Management of risk: a strategic overview with supplementary guidance for smaller bodies*. London: HM Treasury.

Halpern, J. J. (1989) Cognitive factors influencing decision making in highly reliable organisations. *Industrial Crisis Quarterly*, 3(2), 143-158.

Hampel R. (Chair), The Committee on Corporate Governance, (1998), *Final report*, Gee Publishing Ltd, London.

Hartman F, Snelgrove P. (1996) Risk allocation in lump sum contracts – concept of latent dispute. *Journal of construction engineering and management*. September, 291-296.

Hartman F, Snelgrove P, Ashrafi R. (1997) Effective wording to improve risk allocation in lump sum contracts. *Journal of construction engineering and management*. December, 379-387.

Hertz, D. B. (1964) Risk analysis in capital investment. *Harvard Business Review*, 42(1), 95-106.

Hill, T. and Westbrook, R. (1997) SWOT analysis: its time for a product recall. *Long Range Planning*, 30(1), 46-52.

Hillson, David A. (1997). Towards a risk maturity model. *The international journal of project and business risk management*. Spring 1(1), 35-45.

Hodgkinson, R. (2001) Enterprise-wide risk management. Chapter 3 in Hunt, B. (editor) *Risk management guide 2001*. London: White Page.

Hoffman, L.R. and Maier, N.R.F. (1964) Valence in the adoption of solutions by problem solving groups: concepts, methods, and results. *Journal of Abnormal and Social Psychology*, 69, 264-271.

Hopkin, P. (2002) *Holistic risk management in practice*, London: Witherby & Co. Ltd. ISBN 1 85609 207 5

Hopkinson, M. (2002) Maturity models in practice. *Risk Management Bulletin,* 5(4).

Hunt, B. (ed) (2001) *Risk management guide 2001,* London: White Page.

Hunt, B. (2003) *The timid corporation – why business is terrified of taking risk.* Chichester, John Wiley & Sons Ltd.

ICAEW Internal Control Working Party (Chair: Nigel Turnbull), (1999) *Internal control – guidance for directors on the Combined Code.* London, The Institute of Charters Accountants in England and Wales.

ICAEW, 1998, "Financial reporting of risk – proposals for a statement of business risk", London: The Institute of Chartered Accountants in England and Wales.

Institute of Internal Auditors (1998a) *Standards and Guidelines- for the professional practice of internal auditing.* London: The Institute of Internal Auditors, UK.

Institute of Internal Auditors (1998b) *Managing risk.* Professional Briefing Note 13, London: Institute of Internal Auditors, UK.

Isenberg, D. J. (1984) How senior managers think. *Harvard Business Review,* November – December, 81-90.

Ishikawa, K. (1986). *Guide to Quality Control,* Second Edition. White Plains, NY: Asia Productivity Organization/Quality Resources.

Janis, I. L. (1973) *Victims of group think: a psychological study of foreign policy decisions and fiascos.* Boston: Houghton Mifflin.

Janis, I. L. (1982) *Groupthink.* Second Edition, revised. Boston: Houghton Mifflin.

Janis, I. L. and Mann, L. (1977) *Decision making: a psychological analysis of conflict, choice and commitment.* New York: The Free Press.

Johnson, G. (1992) Managing Strategic change: strategy, culture and action. *Long Range Planning,* 25 (1), 28-36.

Johnson, G. and Scholes, K. (2002) *Exploring corporate strategy.* Sixth edition. Harlow: Pearson Education Ltd.

Kahneman, D. and Tversky, A. (1979) *Prospect theory: an analysis of decisions under risk.* Econometrica, 47, 263-291.

Kahneman, D. and Tversky, A. (1981) *The framing of decisions and the psychology of choice.* Science, 211, 453-458.

Kahneman, D. and Tversky, A. (1984) *Choices, values and frames.* American psychologist, 39, 341-350.

Kaplan, R. S. and Norton, D. P. (1992) The balanced scorecard – measures that drive performance. *Harvard Business Review,* 70(1), 71-79.

Kaplan, R. S. and Norton, D. P. (1993) Putting the balanced scorecard to work. *Harvard Business Review,* 71(5), 134-147.

Kaplan, R. S. and Norton, D. P. (1996) Using the balanced scorecard as a strategic management system. *Harvard Business Review,* 74(1), 75-85.

Kelly J. and Male S. *Value management in design and construction: the economic management of projects.* UK: E&FN Spon, 1993.

Lewin, C. (ed) (2002) *RAMP Risk analysis and management for projects,* Second Edition. London: Institute of Civil Engineers and faculty and Institute of Actuaries, Thomas Telford.

Lewin, K. (1947) *Frontiers in group dynamics.* Human relations, 1(1), 5-41.

Lyles, Marjorie A. (1981) Formulating strategic problems: empirical analysis and model development, *Strategic management journal,* 2, 66-75.

Maier, N.R.F. (1967) *Assets and liabilities in group problem-solving.* Psychological Review, 74, 239-249.

Markowitz, H. (1959) *Portfolio selection: efficient diversification of investments.* New York: John Wiley & Sons Ltd.

Marples, C. and Riddle, D. (1992) Formulating strategy in the pod. *OR insight,* 5 (2), 12-15.

Martin, J. and Siehl, C. (1990) Organisational culture and counter-culture: an uneasy symbiosis, in Sypher, B. D. (Ed.) *Case-studies in organisational communication.* New York: the Guilford Press.

Miller, K.D. and Waller, H.G. (2003) Scenarios, real options and integrated risk management. *Long Range Planning* 36, 93-107.

Mintzberg, Henry (1994) *The rise and fall of strategic planning.* Hemel Hempstead, Herts: Prentice Hall International (UK) Ltd. [See also a short summary of the ideas from this text in Mintzberg, Henry (1994) The fall and rise of strategic planning, *Harvard Business Review,* Jan-Feb, 107-114.]

Moorhead, G., Ference, R., and Neck, C.P. (1991) Group decision fiascos continue: space shuttle Challenger and a revised groups think framework. *Human relations,* 44 (6), 539-550.

Morgan, M. G. and Herion, M. (1990) *Uncertainty – a guide to dealing with uncertainty in quantitative risk and policy analysis.* New York: Cambridge University Press.

Morris PWG, and Hough GH. (1987) *The anatomy of major projects.* Chichester: John Wiley, & Sons Ltd.

Mottershead, N. and Godfrey, A. (2001) From theory to practice: evolving your organisation's risk management. Chapter 2 in Hunt, B. (editor) *Risk management guide 2001.* London: White Page.

Myers, D. G. and Lamm, H. (1976) The group polarisation phenomenon. *Psychological Bulletin,* 83, 602-627.

Nash, S. and Nash, N. (2001) *Delighting your customers.* Oxford: How To Books.

National Audit Office (2000) *Supporting innovation: managing risk in government departments.* London, The Stationery Office.

Office of Government Commerce (2002) *Management of risk: guidance for practitioners.* London, The Stationery Office.

Paulk, M.C., Curtis, W., Chrissis, M. and Weber, C.B. (1993) Capability maturity model, Version 1.1, *IEEE Software,* 10(4), 18-27. Also, Paulk, M.C., Weber, C.B., Curtis, W. & Chrissis, M. (editors) (1995) *Capability maturity model: guidelines for improving the software process,* Addison-Wesley.

Peter, L. (1985) *Why things go wrong.* London: Unwin.

Porter, M.E. (1985) *Competitive advantage: creating and sustaining superior performance.* New York: Free Press.

Preble, John F. (1997) Integrating the crisis management perspective into the strategic management process, *Journal of Management Studies,* 34(5) September 769-791.

PricewaterhouseCoopers (2004) *Enterprise Risk Management Framework.* London: The Committee of Sponsoring Organisations of the Treadway Commission. www.coso.org.

Project Management Institute (2000) *A Guide to the Project Management Body of Knowledge,* 2000 edition. Newtown Square, PA, USA, Project Management Institute.

Quinn, J. (1989) Strategic change: logical incrementalism, *Sloan Management Review,* Summer, 45-60.

Quinn, J.B. (1982) Managing strategies incrementally, *Omega, The International Journal of Management Science,* 10(6), 613-627.

Rayner, J. (2003) *Managing reputational risk – curbing threats, and leverage opportunities.* The Institute of Internal Auditors UK and Ireland Risk Management Series. Chichester: John Wiley & Sons Ltd.

Reason, J. (1990) *Human Error.* Cambridge: Cambridge University Press.

Repenning, J. D. and Sterman, J.D. (2001) Nobody ever gets credit for fixing problems that never happened. *California Management Review,* 43(4), 64-88.

Richardson, G. P. and Pugh, A. L. (1981). *Introduction to Systems Dynamics Modeling with DYNAMO.* Portland, OR: Productivity Press.

Roberts, K H. and Gargano, G. (1989) Managing a high reliability organisation: a case for interdependence, in Glinow, M.A. and Mohrman, S. (eds) *Managing complexity in high technology organisations: systems and people.* New York: Oxford University Press.

Rochlin, G.I. (1989) Informal organisational networking as a crisis avoidance strategy: US naval flight operations as a case study. *Industrial Crisis Quarterly,* 3 (2), 159-176.

Senge, P. M. (1990). *The Fifth Discipline: The Art and Practice of the Learning Organization.* New York: Doubleday.

Shimmell, P. (2002) *The universe of risk- how top business leaders control risk and achieve success.* Harlow: Pearson Education Ltd.

Singh, J. V. (1986) Performance, slack, and risk taking in organisational decision making. *Academy of Management Journal,* 29, 562-585.

Starbuck, W.H. and Milliken, F.J. (1988) Challenger: fine-tuning the odds until something breaks. *Journal of Management Studies,* 25(4), 319-340.

Staw, B. M. (1981) The escalation of commitment to a course of action. *Academy of Management Review,* 6 (4), 577-587.

Staw, B. M. and Ross, J. (1987) Knowing when to pull the plug. *Harvard Business Review,* March – April, 68-74.

Swalm, R.O. (1966) Utility theory – insights into risk taking. *Harvard Business Review,* Nov-Dec., 123-136.

Toft B. and Reynolds S. 1997, *Learning from disasters – a management approach,* Second edition. Leicester: Perpetuity Press Ltd.

Tuckman, B. (1965) Development sequences in small groups. *Psychological Journal,* 63, 384-399.

Turner, B. A. (1994) Causes of disaster: sloppy management. *British Journal of Management,* 5(3), 215-219.

Turner JR. (1992) *The handbook of project based management: improving processes for achieving your strategic objectives.* New York: McGraw-Hill.

Turner JR, Cochrane RA. (1993) Goals and methods matrix: coping with projects with ill-defined goals and/or methods of achieving them. *International journal of project management,* 11, 93-102.

UK MoD (2002) *Ministry of Defence Acquisition Management System, Risk Management Guidance* (updated September 2002) www.ams. mod.uk/ams/content/risk/docs/INDEX.HTM.

US DoD DSMC (2002) *Risk management guide for DoD acquisition* 3rd Ed. US Department of Defense, Defense Acquisition University, Defense Systems Management College. Fort Belvoir, VA 220 60-55 65, US: DSMC Press.

Vroom, V. H. and Jago, A. G. (1988) *The new leadership: managing participation in organisations.* Englewood Cliffs, N.J.: Prentice Hall.

Vroom, V. H. and Yetton, P. W. (1973) *Leadership and decision making.* Pittsburgh: University of Pittsburgh Press.

Walsham, G. (1992) Management science and organisational change: a framework for analysis. *Omega – the International Journal of Management Science,* 20 (1), 1-9.

Ward, S.C. (1999) Requirements for an effective project risk management process. *Project Management Journal,* (USA Project Management Institute), 30(3), 37-43.

Ward, S. (2001). Exploring the role of the corporate risk manager. *Risk Management: an international journal.* 3(1) 7-25.

Ward, S. (2003) Approaches to integrated risk management: a multi-dimensional framework. *Risk Management: an international journal,* 5(4), 7-23.

Ward, S. (2004) Developing project risk management. *Proceedings of the Project Management Institute Research Conference, London.* Newtown Square, Pennsylvania: Project Management Institute.

Ward, S. and Chapman, C (2003) Transforming project risk management into project uncertainty management. *International Journal of Project Management,* 21, 97-105.

Waring, A. and Glendon, A.I. (1998) *Managing risk – critical issues for survival and success into the 21st century.* London: Thomson Learning.

Weick, K. (1976) Educational organisations as loosely coupled systems. *Administrative Science Quarterly,* 21, March, 1-19.

Whyte, G. (1989) Groupthink reconsidered. *Academy of Management Review,* 14 (1), 40-56.

Wilkinson, S. (2003) *Risk control.* London: Witherby.

Williams, T., Eden, C., Ackerman, F., and Tait, A. (1995a) The effects of design changes and delays on project costs. *Journal of the Operational Research Society,* 46, 809-818.

Williams, T., Eden, C., Ackerman, F., and Tait, A. (1995b) Vicious circles of parallelism. *International Journal of Project Management,* 13, 151-155.